THE GWR STARS, CASTLES & KINGS

David & Charles Locomotive Monographs

General Editor:
O. S. NOCK, B.Sc., C.Eng., F.I.C.E., F.I.Mech.E.

Published titles

The Caledonian Dunalastairs, by O. S. Nock

The GWR Stars, Castles & Kings, Parts 1 and 2, by O. S. Nock

The LNWR Precursor Family, by O. S. Nock

The Midland Compounds, by O. S. Nock

The Stirling Singles of the Great Northern Railway, by Kenneth H. Leech and Maurice

In preparation

The Gresley Pacifics, by O. S. Nock

The Standard Gauge 4—4—0s of the GWR, by O. S. Nock

*The restored and preserved 'King George V' in steam at H. P. Bulmer & Company's
track, Hereford
(from a painting by Terence Cuneo)*

DAVID & CHARLES LOCOMOTIVE MONOGRAPHS

THE GWR STARS, CASTLES & KINGS

PART 2 : 1930-1965

O. S. NOCK, B.Sc., C.Eng., F.I.C.E., F.I.Mech.E.

DAVID & CHARLES : NEWTON ABBOT : DEVON

0 7153 4743 8

First published 1970
Second impression 1973

© O. S. NOCK, 1970, 1973

Printed in Great Britain
by W J Holman Limited Dawlish
for David & Charles (Holdings) Limited
South Devon House Newton Abbot Devon

CONTENTS

PREFACE TO PART 2

THE second half of the fascinating saga of Great Western four-cylinder 4—6—0 locomotive history has many difficulties, and not a few pitfalls for its author. The span of few British locomotive families has extended over so long a period, and rarely under the same continuing influence all the time. In this respect the 'Stars', 'Castles' and 'Kings' differed profoundly from other dynasties of equal, or near-equal longevity. The Great Western itself may have ceased to exist at the end of 1947, but the British Railways management, while drafting new standard designs to the Western Region never presumed to dictate alterations to purely Great Western designs, as for example the Midland had done to the North Western after grouping. Swindon retained complete autonomy so far as ex-GWR classes were concerned. In this respect the story from 1930, and especially

that from 1948, is straightforward. Inevitably, however, over so long a period there were many changes of detail, on individual engines, and faced with a vast amount of factual data, one has to be careful to distinguish between those changes which were significant, and those which were purely matters of convenience or expediency in the course of repair work at Swindon. I am indebted to many enthusiasts for a plethora of notes of this kind, some of which have been included in the footnotes to the case histories of the three classes.

As regards the main line of development, which occupies most of the space in this book, I had the privilege, from Mr Hawksworth and his successors at Swindon, of seeing much of it at first hand, with frequent opportunities of seeing tests in progress on the stationary plant, and from the dynamometer car;

The Churchward memorial headstone in Stoke Gabriel churchyard

9

The Churchward window in Stoke Gabriel parish church, South Devon

and Paddington, and from the end of the second world war until the end of steam haulage on these services I compiled detailed logs of well over 1,000 journeys behind 'Stars', 'Castles' and 'Kings'. These engines and their performance were not only of great interest to me as a railway enthusiast, but their reliability in service was an important factor in my business life. The background to this book is thus a very extensive experience of the daily work of these engines. Studying it in retrospect, the record of reliability is positively massive. Apart from one or two instances during the glacial winter of 1946-7 when owing to disruption of services, unprepared, or inadequately serviced engines were called upon in emergency, my records in regular business travelling over twelve years do not include one single engine failure, and the occasions on which any time could be booked against engines amount to less than one per cent of all journeys made. Curiously enough the only two occasions over the whole period when an engine had to be given up en route took place when I was riding on the footplate, on the West of England road, and were both due to a combination of quite exceptional circumstances.

Taken all in all, this volume is a record of stirring achievement in locomotive design, construction and operation. The indebtedness of the Great Western Railway, and of the Western Region afterwards, to Churchward, is something that his successors never forgot, and in the highly modernised dynamometer car of 1955 there was room for a handsome portrait of 'The Old Man'. To add my own modest tribute I have included in this preface two of my photographs taken in the village of his birth, Stoke Gabriel, beside the River Dart.

O. S. NOCK

Silver Cedars
High Bannerdown
Batheaston
Bath
August 1969

of studying drawing office and test records, and of riding many thousands of miles on 'Stars', 'Castles' and 'Kings'. The Running Superintendents, first W. N. Pellow and then H. E. A. White, frequently made special allocations of engines to trains, so that I could observe workings on particular duties. These included 'Stars' on such important trains as the 9 am Bristol to Paddington, and the down night Postal Special. Quite apart from special occasions of this kind, I was travelling in the ordinary course of business regularly and frequently between Bath

CHAPTER 1

THE BRILLIANT PRELUDE

AT the opening of the third decade of the twentieth century the Great Western Railway still had an impressively long lead over the other British railway companies in locomotive practice and achievement. It is true that important changes in detail design had greatly improved the Gresley Pacifics of the LNER, but on the LMS the 'Royal Scots', although potentially good engines, were unduly prone to casualties, and the much publicised 'Lord Nelsons' of the Southern fell a long way short of the high hopes expected of them. Against these the 'Stars', 'Castles' and 'Kings' were in superb form. Well designed, immaculately maintained, supplied with good coal and both driven and fired by men who were enthusiasts as well as experts, each class was incomparable in its particular category of loading.

It was this very supremacy that led to each one of them being outclassed before that momentous decade was out. In 1930 the Great Western Railway had locomotives that were supremely master of all tasks envisaged for some time. The year was one of mounting depression on a world-wide scale, and by the summer of 1931 the economic whirlwind had struck Great Britain. With such tools at its disposal there was no need for the Great Western Railway to incur expense in designing new express passenger locomotives. Even Sir Felix Pole, with all his enthusiasm, had been rather shocked at the capital cost of the new patterns and tooling incurred in the production of the 'Kings'. From 1930 to the outbreak of war in 1939 it was not a case of Swindon resting on its laurels, and, in a spirit of complacency,

Up two-hour Bristol - Paddington express near Stoke Gifford : engine No 4016 'Knight of the Golden Fleece', rebuilt as 'Castle'

splendid isolation, or whatever other derogatory term one likes to apply, allowing others to go ahead; there was then no economic nor engineering justification for doing otherwise.

And yet that decade was extremely fruitful and significant, in more subtle if less spectacular ways. I am referring to the science and practice of locomotive engineering, rather than of achievement on the road. There was certainly no subtlety about Great Western locomotive performance in those early years of the decade, when the 'Castles' established their reputation as world beaters. Before passing on to the developments in practice that were eventually to have effects influencing the very last years of steam on main lines far distant from the confines of the Great Western itself, it is pleasant to recall the brilliant saga of the 'Cheltenham Flyer' in those otherwise depressing years 1931 and 1932. The critics may well argue that the 'Cheltenham Flyer' was not representative of everyday Great Western passenger train service; that it was a 'stunt'

train, having little commercial value. These criticisms may be justified; but as a means of displaying the capacity of Great Western locomotives it was ideal, and the results achieved over the years are of great importance in the history of the 'Castle' class locomotives.

In the winter of 1929 I had my first experience of running on the 70-min schedule that then prevailed. It was a remarkable trip with engine No 5003 *Lulworth Castle,* and that most expert of drivers, Wasley of Old Oak Common. With a load of 275 tons we made an average speed of 84·5 mph over the 20·5 miles from Steventon to Reading, after which the engine had necessarily to be eased down. But the very fast running on level track, up to a maximum of 86·5 mph, was something of an eye-opener to us all. In September 1931 a modest 3 min was cut from the schedule, and despite the prevailing industrial depression the Great Western Railway made the inauguration of this accelerated timing a positively gala occasion. On the first three

'Holiday Haunts' special excursion near Reading West : engine No 6025
'King Henry III'

Up two-hour Bristol express topping Filton bank : engine No 4033 'Queen Victoria'

days, 14, 15 and 16 September, the engine crews were encouraged to 'have a go'. *Launceston Castle* was the engine on each run, with different crews, and on the three successive days the overall start-to-stop times over the 77·3 miles from Swindon to Paddington were 59 min 36 sec, 58½ min by the guard's journal, and a fully authenticated world record of 58 min 20 sec. After this astonishing inception of the new schedule, drivers were instructed to avoid further running ahead of time. Nevertheless the 'Cheltenham Flyer', with its booked average

speed of 69·2 mph, was then indisputably the 'world's fastest train', and for some time it carried a special headboard advertising the fact.

The Great Western authorities were nevertheless not content with the record achievements of September 1931. The run made on 16 September, with its average speed of 79·5 mph, surpassed by too slender a margin the previous world record made in the USA on the Reading Railroad, when the 55½ miles from Camden, Philadelphia, to Atlantic City were covered in 42 min 33 sec, an average

Engine No 5016 'Restormel Castle' showing the modified style of painting on tender

speed of 78·3 mph. So, in June 1932 a deliberate attempt to make a 'record of records' was organised. In doing this the Great Western people were mindful of the assertion that the route of the 'Cheltenham Flyer' was 'all downhill'—which of course it is far from being!—and a very fast run was projected by the corresponding down express on the same day. Arrangements were made to have the two runs logged in the most minute detail, and Mr Cecil J. Allen and Mr Humphrey Baker of Bath were invited to collaborate in this task. To emphasise the special nature of the day's proceedings the 5 pm down Cheltenham Spa Express, which normally made its first stop at Kemble, was stopped specially at Swindon to set the recorders down. More than this, the 5.15 pm up 2-hour Bristol express, normally non-stop from Temple Meads to Paddington, was stopped at Swindon to take up Messrs Allen and Baker and get them back to London in quick time.

The record of 16 September 1931 was certainly beaten, reducing the overall time from 58 min 20 sec

to 56 min 47 sec and yielding an average speed of 81·7 mph start to stop, but it is most important to appreciate that this was not an absolutely all-out effort, in which everything was to such a degree at concert pitch that it would be unlikely to be repeated again, and certainly not in ordinary conditions. It is true that the engine was a picked one, and all the running circumstances were favourable, including the limitation of the load to six coaches; but to remove any suggestion of abnormality about the run of 6 June 1932 I must take the story briefly forward five years, to 30 June 1937. Then the blaze of railway publicity had shifted to the northern lines. On the previous day the LMSR 'Coronation Scot' had made her somewhat hectic Press Trip, with its maximum of 114 mph a little too near Crewe to be comfortable; and on 30 June itself the LNER 'Coronation' made its *début*, with a fast run from Kings Cross to the Barkston triangle and back. On that day one of the most celebrated Old Oak drivers was on the 'Cheltenham Flyer' and quite unofficially he set out to show that the northern

THE 'CHELTENHAM FLYER'							
Three Record Runs							
Date		16/9/31		6/6/32		30/6/37	
Engine No		5000		5006		5039	
Engine name		*Launceston*		*Tregenna*		*Rhuddlan*	
		Castle		*Castle*		*Castle*	
Load: cars		6		6		7	
tons E/F		184/195		186/195		223/235	
Dist miles		Actual m s	Speeds mph	Actual m s	Speeds mph	Actual m s	Speeds mph
0·0	SWINDON	0 00	—	0 00	—	0 00	—
2·3	*Milepost 75*	—	—	3 28½	64	3 43	59
5·7	Shrivenham	6 15	80	6 15	81	6 35	80·5
10·8	Uffington	9 55	85	9 51	85·5	10 10	90
13·4	Challow	11 45	85	11 42	87	11 57	90
16·9	Wantage Road	14 10	87	14 05	89	14 12	94
20·8	Steventon	16 50	90	16 40	90	16 45	95
24·2	DIDCOT	19 05	88	18 55	91	18 57	90·5
28·8	Cholsey	22 15	87	21 59	91	21 58	91
32·6	Goring	24 55	82	24 25	92	24 25	88
35·8	Pangbourne	27 10	85	26 33	90	26 40	86·5
38·7	Tilehurst	29 15	84	28 28	92	28 40	90
41·3	READING	31 05	85	30 12	91	30 27	86·5
46·3	Twyford	34 35	86	33 31	89	33 50	90
53·1	Maidenhead	39 15	88	38 08	87	38 17	93
58·8	SLOUGH	43 15	85	42 10	87	42 08	90·5
64·1	West Drayton	46 55	85	45 51	84	45 47	84
68·2	Southall	49 55	84	48 51	81·5	48 46	82
71·6	Ealing Broadway	52 20	84·5	51 17	84·5	51 40	eased
76·0	Westbourne Park	56 00	—	54 40	—	57 40	—
77·3	PADDINGTON	58 20		56 47		61 07	
Average speeds: mph							
Uffington - Cholsey		87·8		89·0		91·6	
Cholsey - Reading		85·2		91·4		88·5	
Twyford - Slough		86·5		86·7		90·5	

Royal Train (LNWR stock) on the Westbury avoiding line : engine No 4082
'Windsor Castle'

companies should not have it all their own way. Fortunately a very experienced recorder in the person of the Rev J. E. T. Phillips was a passenger, and his log shows that the time of the 'record of records' was beaten by 5 sec to passing Southall; more important still is the fact that over the 62·5 miles from Shrivenham to Southall the time on 30 June 1937 was 42 min 11 sec, against 42 min 36 sec on 6 June 1932. Still greater significance is attached to the later run in that the gross load behind the tender was 235 tons, against 195 tons in 1932.

The detailed logs of the fastest of the September 1931 trilogy, the 'record of records', and the run of 1937 deserve the closest study. It shows that *Tregenna Castle* did not begin to draw seriously away from *Launceston Castle* until after Didcot, and then that the improvement was due to some exceptionally fast running on the winding stretch of line beside the Thames from Goring to Reading. By this time the 1932 record-breaker was roughly a minute ahead. After that the times between Twyford and Ealing were almost identical. Then *Tregenna Castle* gained considerably by an exceptionally rapid approach to Paddington. But her rather sensational 2 min 7 sec over the final 1·3 miles in from Westbourne Park was mild compared with the 1 min 45 sec of the record-breaking 'Ocean Mail' of 9 May 1904, with the 4—2—2 engine No 3065 *Duke of Connaught*. As a locomotive performance, however, as distinct from a display of enginemanship the improvement of *Tregenna Castle* over *Launceston Castle* can be considered as little more than marginal, seeing how much pre-preparation was made for the 1932 run. Details of the engine working with *Tregenna Castle* were subsequently published, and showed that the

regulator was gradually opened to the fullest extent by Shrivenham, and that the cut-offs were:

    17 per cent Shrivenham to Goring
    18 per cent Goring to Maidenhead
    17 per cent Maidenhead to Southall
    18 per cent Southall to Milepost 2

No details were given of any fluctuations in boiler pressure, but east of Reading it would seem there must have been some fall, or easing of the regulator, because the speed fell slightly on what is normally one of the fastest stretches of all, between Twyford and Maidenhead. It will be seen that *Launceston Castle* was accelerating here from 86 to 88 mph whereas *Tregenna Castle* fell from 89 to 87 mph even though continuing with the 18 per cent cut-off which had produced 92 mph on the level at Tilehurst. The easing of the cut-off at Maidenhead from 18 to 17 per cent may well have been to help rally the boiler.

We then come to the astounding performance of *Rhuddlan Castle* on 30 June 1937. With the extra coach the start was understandably slower, but then some magnificent speed was developed, rising to a maximum of 95 mph at Steventon. Somewhat easier running was made along the riverside section, though I certainly use the word 'easier' in no more than a relative sense. Then after Reading there came another display of tremendous speed, with a maximum of 93 mph at Maidenhead. By this, despite the heavier load, slower start, and easier running between Goring and Reading, *Rhuddlan Castle* took the lead from *Tregenna* from Slough onwards to Southall. The importance of this run is that it was a quite unrehearsed and unofficial effort: the combination of an expert driver and fireman, and a superb engine. It so happens that there *was* a representative of the Chief Mechanical Engineer's

Bristol - Paddington express near Sonning : engine No 4080 'Powderham Castle'

department on the footplate, a young engineer whose duty it was to check the working of the speedometers then being fitted as a standard item of equipment to all the 'Castle' class engines. The driver did not have any instruction to run specially fast for the purpose of this test. The engineer who was riding was Geoffrey Tee, now Carriage Works Manager at Wolverton, and he confessed to me many years later that he was taken completely by surprise at the speeds developed. This run shows clearly, however, that the 'record of records' could have been appreciably lowered, if necessary. The summary of fastest times in the table on page 14 gives an overall of 56 min 1 sec, by taking the times of *Tregenna Castle* from Swindon to Shrivenham, Cholsey to Twyford, and Ealing to Paddington; *Rhuddlan Castle* from Shrivenham to Cholsey, and Twyford to Southall; and *Launceston Castle* from Southall to Ealing. Collectively, this average of 82·8 mph is a resounding tribute to the high-speed prowess of the 'Castle' class engines.

Reverting to the events of 6 June 1932, the honour must certainly be shared between *Tregenna Castle* and No 5005 *Manorbier Castle*, which made the running on the 5 pm down express shown in the accompanying log. As Cecil J. Allen expressed it at the time, it was a pity about the odd second—60 min 1 sec start-to-stop from Paddington to Swindon—but in the interests of pure accuracy it had to be! The actual logs of Messrs Allen and

Baker gave this remarkable summary on that memorable afternoon:

Swindon	dep	3.48 pm
Paddington	arr	4.44¾ pm
„	dep	5 pm
Swindon	arr	6 pm
„	dep	6.6 pm
Paddington	arr	7.12½ pm

Between Southall and Shrivenham, by which points

	5 pm PADDINGTON—SWINDON		
	Load: 6 cars, 199 tons tare, 210 tons full		
	Engine: 5005 *Manorbier Castle*		

Dist miles		Actual m s	Speeds mph
0·0	PADDINGTON	0 00	—
1·3	Westbourne Park	2 34	—
5·7	Ealing	6 52	74·5
9·1	Southall	9 25	81
13·2	West Drayton	12 26	85·5
18·5	SLOUGH	16 03	86·5
24·2	Maidenhead	20 14	82·5
31·0	Twyford	25 17	79
36·0	READING	29 01	81·5
41·5	Pangbourne	33 03	83
48·5	Cholsey	38 03	84
53·1	DIDCOT	41 23	85·5
56·5	Steventon	43 47	83·5
60·4	Wantage Road	46 35	81·5
63·9	Challow	49 13	80
66·5	Uffington	51 13	78·5
71·6	Shrivenham	53 05	81·5
76·0	*Milepost 76*	58 15	83·5
77·3	SWINDON	60 01	

practically full speed had been attained on both down and up runs, the difference in altitude is approximately 200 ft, representing an average inclination of 1 in 1650. On 6 June 1932, the average speeds over this 62·5 miles were 88 mph up and 82·5 mph down. Taking modern figures for train resistance, which one could reasonably expect to apply to coaching stock in first-class condition used on the 'Cheltenham Flyer', the resistance in lbs per ton can be taken at 14·2 and 12·7 respectively. Using these values the average equivalent drawbar horsepower work out at 550 by *Tregenna Castle* and 675 by *Manorbier Castle*. On the latter engine the cut-offs used were:

20 per cent Southall to Slough
19 per cent Slough to Reading
20 per cent Reading to Goring
19 per cent Goring to Didcot
20 per cent Didcot to Uffington
21 per cent Uffington to Highworth Jc

So far as engine performance is concerned the honours rest with *Manorbier Castle,* and the continuous working at 19 to 21 per cent cut-off with full regulator at 82·5 mph must be regarded as something very near the maximum steaming capacity at such speeds. Using the same basis of calcula-

tions, the running of *Rhuddlan Castle* at 93 mph on the falling gradient of 1 in 1320 between Twyford and Maidenhead indicates an equivalent drawbar horsepower of about 650. This output, which probably represents about the optimum with a standard 'Castle' of pre-war vintage, should be borne in mind for reference to achievements of the modified engines from 1951 onwards. It is perhaps not without significance that *Rhuddlan Castle* belongs to one of the later pre-war batches when constructional methods at Swindon had improved the accuracy of erection, with probable improvements in the free-running qualities of the engines concerned. This point is dealt with in Chapter 2 of this book.

So far as the achievements of 6 June 1932 are concerned, sentiments that were felt by all of us at the time were aptly summed up by Cecil J. Allen in *The Railway Magazine*. He wrote:

> The remembrances of the day still leave me breathless, but at the same time happy to have been a personal witness of all that transpired, and proud of the fact that British railways, and locomotives, and men were exclusively responsible. For a record of this character is not merely the private possession of one single railway and its staff; it is a national triumph, and a national asset.

Down West of England express leaving Bristol : engine No 6025 'King Henry III'

CHAPTER 2

THE 'CASTLES' : PHASE TWO

THE express passenger locomotive situation on the Great Western Railway at the end of 1930 could have been interpreted by an outsider in various ways. Apart from the rebuilding of the original four-cylinder simple engine *North Star* in 1929, no additions to the 'Castle' class had been made since July 1927 and the relative strengths of the three classes of four-cylinder 4—6—0 were: 'Stars' 67, 'Castles' 46, and 'Kings' 30. The last ten 'Kings' were built just three years after the then-last batch of 'Castles' numbered 5003 to 5012. It was representatives of this latter batch that were chosen for the record-breaking runs of June 1932. When a new batch of 'Castles' was turned out in that same year there were certain outside observers who jumped to the conclusion that because a reversion had been made to the older and smaller design of four-cylinder 4—6—0 that the 'Kings' were unsatisfac-

tory. In the restless times of the early 1930s, when signs of development and modernisation were looked for on all hands as a means of climbing out of the depression, to fall back upon a locomotive design of 1923, however well it had served its purpose, seemed to the neophytes a little retrograde.

From a traffic-working point of view the 'Castle' was an ideal engine. It had a high route availability, and could be used on many services where the 'Kings' were precluded on account of weight. Furthermore, quite a high proportion of the fast express trains were lightly loaded, and even if their route availability had permitted it, use of 'Kings' would not have been economical. Those engines, in their original form with low-degree superheat, were at their most efficient when being heavily worked, as on the West of England and Wolverhampton trains. The 'Castles' of the 1932, 1934 and 1935

Engine No 4082 'Windsor Castle', draped and decorated for the funeral journey of King George V, in January 1936

Up South Wales express climbing to Patchway : engine No 4089 'Donnington Castle'

batches were built as replacements for older 4—6—0 express locomotives that were withdrawn at roughly the same time. In the prevailing conditions of financial stringency it might be questioned as to whether it was really necessary to make such replacements when the duties that were subsequently worked by 'Castles' were being quite satisfactorily handled by 'Saints' and 'Stars'. The construction of those 30 'Castles', ten in each of the years 1932, 1934 and 1935, was to a large extent a matter of accountancy, and was justified in the following manner.

Each year a sum of money had been set aside to cover the depreciation of locomotives, and to allow for their renewal after an appropriate working life; and in the years of which I am now writing most new Great Western locomotives were built out of the Renewals Fund. As a *quid pro quo* the account expected the annual programme of new construction to be balanced by the withdrawal of at least an equal tonnage of old locomotives. In the ordinary way 'Saint' and 'Star' class 4—6—0s were first-class assets, good for any number of further years of service; but the times were far from 'ordinary', and in the stringent financial circumstances economies in running the railway had been made, as in war-

time, by making certain groups of locomotives work longer mileages between repairs. The top-line engines like the 'Castles' and 'Kings' were always maintained at concert pitch, but the lesser lights suffered, and it is always the older members of a class that suffer most in such circumstances. Thus the situation developed that a number of 'Saints' and 'Stars' began to need very extensive repairs. The fund was low, but on the other hand the Renewals Fund was in a healthy state; so it was a logical accounting step to scrap the older engines needing heavy repairs, and build new engines to replace them. 'Castles' were the only and obvious replacements. In consequence, between the years 1931 and 1935 twenty 'Saints' and ten 'Stars' were scrapped. The 'Stars' concerned were:

4001	*Dog Star*	Jan	1934
4002	*Evening Star*	June	1933
4005	*Polar Star*	Nov	1934
4006	*Red Star*	Nov	1932
4008	*Royal Star*	June	1935
4010	*Western Star*	Nov	1934
4011	*Knight of the Garter*	Nov	1932
4024	*The Dutch Monarch*	Feb	1935
4027	*The Norwegian Monarch*	Oct	1934
4029	*The Spanish Monarch*	Nov	1934

THE GWR STARS, CASTLES & KINGS

The new 'Castles' built from 1932 onwards had sufficient differences from the originals as to be given a new designation, and they were known as the '5013' class. Their names were all pleasing and euphonious, and for the most part well known. *Wigmore Castle* revived memories of the old 7 ft 8 in single that ran off the road on Box Tunnel, and two were 'poached' from the territory of other railways, namely, *Corfe Castle* and *Rhuddlan Castle*. These thirty new engines replacing scrapped 'Saints' and 'Stars' were:

5013	*Abergavenny Castle*
5014	*Goodrich Castle*
5015	*Kingswear Castle*
5016	*Montgomery Castle*
5017	*St Donats Castle*
5018	*St Mawes Castle*
5019	*Treago Castle*
5020	*Trematon Castle*
5021	*Whittington Castle*
5022	*Wigmore Castle*
5023	*Brecon Castle*
5024	*Carew Castle*
5025	*Chirk Castle*
5026	*Criccieth Castle*
5027	*Farleigh Castle*
5028	*Llantilio Castle*
5029	*Nunney Castle*
5030	*Shirburn Castle*
5031	*Totnes Castle*
5032	*Usk Castle*
5033	*Broughton Castle*
5034	*Corfe Castle*
5035	*Coity Castle*
5036	*Lyonshall Castle*
5037	*Monmouth Castle*
5038	*Morlais Castle*
5039	*Rhuddlan Castle*
5040	*Stokesay Castle*
5041	*Tiverton Castle*
5042	*Winchester Castle*

There were one or two superficial details by which the '5013' class could be distinguished from the '4073' class, such as the shaping of the front casing over the inside cylinder valve chests, and the introduction of a compartment above the centre and trailing coupled wheel splashers on the left-hand side, to accommodate the fireirons. This latter had first been fitted on No 4085 *Berkeley Castle*, as a trial, and it became standard from No 5013 onwards. There was also an alteration to the springing, omitting the compensating beams between the springs. The most important design change, which was the reason for a new class designation, was in the boiler and firebox. In the '4073' class, to get the maximum possible firebox heating surface and grate area the water spaces between the inner and outer fireboxes had been made narrower than standard, and complaints had been made about the difficulty of cleaning this narrow space. In the '5013' class the water space was increased to normal; the number of small tubes was reduced from 201 to 197, and the grate area was reduced to 29·4 sq ft from the original 30·3 sq ft. On locomotives worked as were the Great Western four-cylinder 4—6—0s this reduction in grate area was of no consequence. The normal practice was to run with a deep fire built up 'hay-cock' fashion, and it was an ability to burn coal economically in such conditions, rather than mere grate area that governed the capacity of Great Western locomotives.

It was on the 1934 batch of 'Castles', commencing with No 5023 *Brecon Castle*, that a very important improvement in constructional methods was introduced. The performance of a locomotive, and its general reliability in service, depend to a large extent upon the accuracy with which the engine is built, and particularly the alignment of the frames, axle-box guides and cylinders. At Swindon, as nearly everywhere else, the traditional method of alignment with wires, centre-pop and trammels had hitherto been used. In the 1930s the German State Railways were making use of Zeiss precision optical gear for lining up locomotive frames, and the experience of that administration was that the time of lining up was cut to between one-quarter and one-third of that previously taken. Furthermore, a locomotive so treated would run a greater mileage between repairs than previously. This method was studied by the engineers of the Great Western Railway, and after modification of the Zeiss apparatus to suit production methods at Swindon it was adopted as standard practice for all new and repaired locomotives.

The basis of the apparatus was a telescope mounted within a tube, arranged so that it could be pivoted in vertical or horizontal planes by two dials. When these two dials were both set at zero, the telescope was in exact central alignment with its external tube—which was set with a self-centring spider—in the front bellmouth of one cylinder, and by an adaptor in the stuffing box at the back of the cylinder. A spirit-level ensured that the vertical and horizontal axes were correct, and a measuring surface set level with the front cylinder face by a straight edge provided zero for distance. The overall width across each pair of horns was measured by

Down two-hour Birmingham express : engine No 5081 'Penrice Castle', later renamed 'Lockheed Hudson'

a vernier, after which a sighting scale was clamped to each horn in turn and the scale read through the telescope. The sighting scale was similar to a surveyor's staff and the reading gave the distance of the cylinder axis to the outside edge of the horn. The distance plus half the width over that pair of horns gave the distance to the theoretical centre line of the engine. If that sum did not amount to the same total at each horn, the cylinder axis was not parallel with the centre line of the line. A certain tolerance could be allowed there and the telescope pivoted horizontally until its centre was parallel with the engine centre line; but if the correction would have been beyond the allowed limit it would have been necessary to cut down some stiffeners or cross stays and reset the frames.

Assuming that the telescope was set parallel with the theoretical centre line of the engine, the sighting scale was removed and a collimator, clamped to a tube in such a way that it was dead at right-angles to the axis of the tube, was supported at the driving horn, the tube being right across the frame between both driving horns. The tube was held in a stand, the top of which could be moved vertically or horizontally to or from the cylinder, and through an angle horizontally. The collimator was an optical apparatus carrying two sets of cross scales illuminated by an electric lamp, and had the property of accepting at zero on its infinite scale only rays parallel with the telescope. If on sighting from the telescope the telescope cross lines cut the horizontal and vertical lines of the infinite scale of the collimator at zero, then the telescope and collimator were truly parallel, though not necessarily at the same place. How much they were out of plane could be read by focussing the telescope on the infinite scale of the collimator and reading the graduations. The horizontal, vertical and angular adjustments provided for in the collimator stand allowed the latter to be brought easily into alignment with the telescope. As the collimator was then parallel with the telescope and was fixed accurately at right-angles to the collimator cross-tube, it followed that the cross-tube was then between the driving horns at right-angles to the cylinder axis.

A dial indicator was used to obtain the distance of each horn cheek from the collimator cross-tube, and the latter was traversed longitudinally until it was central between the driving horns. A length gauge with dial indicator from locating points on the telescope tubes and the collimator tube gave a direct reading of the distance from the cylinder face

Up Swansea and West Wales express approaching Patchway : engine No 5046 'Clifford Castle', later renamed 'Earl Cawdor'

to the centre of the driving horn, and from the collimator cross-tube a locating stud on each frame was set at a definite distance from the horn centre. Length gauges enabled further locating studs to be set at each of the other horns, ie, 'leading', 'intermediate', and 'trailing', and from those similar measurements could be made to each of the corresponding horn cheeks. By means of the accurate rods and the dial indicator, all those measurements could be easily read to within a thousandth of an inch, although the total length between the leading and trailing horn centres might have been as much as 20 ft.

Thus a very accurate survey of the salient points of a locomotive frame could be made expeditiously, and from this decisions taken as to the amount of corrections to be made. I have dwelt on the process at some length because it proved the very cornerstone of Swindon constructional practice. It enabled valve gear parts to be made with precision, with an absolute minimum of clearance when new, so that newly out-shopped locomotives ran with the quietness of sewing machines. Such was the tightening up of clearances possible as a result that the situation became one that was vividly described by one

ex-Great Western man, after nationalisation when the differing practices of other famous locomotive manufactories came under review. This engineer said: 'We scrap at the amount of clearance they start with'. Dimensions previously maintained to within an accuracy of plus or minus 0·010 in were henceforth made to within an accuracy of plus or minus 0·002 in. This apparatus was used on older engines as they went through the works, and it is not without significance that the twenty engines of the 'Castle' class numbered between 5023 and 5042 quickly gained the reputation of being the best yet, of the whole class. No 5030 *Shirburn Castle* achieved the remarkable record of running 420,000 miles before the removal of the boiler from the frames. This engine had, of course, received intermediate repairs.

The policy of maintaining older engines as far as possible in a first-class state of repair, and the standardisation of methods at Swindon led to a number of 'Castle' features being incorporated in 'Stars' from time to time. There did not seem to be any overall policy with regard to these changes, and something like the putting of 'new wine into old bottles', as it were, resulted in improvisation at times of general overhaul. All the 'Stars' had new cylinders in the course of their lives, many of them more than once. To extend their lives, some engines had liners in their cylinders; but the maximum to which 'Star' cylinders could be bored out was $15\frac{5}{8}$ in diameter, and if the cylinder diameter was not to be reduced below 15 in the maximum thickness of liner was only $\frac{5}{16}$ in. This thickness permitted of only one rebore, at overhaul, and this particular expedient was quickly judged to be not worth the candle.

From 1929 onwards thirteen of the 'Stars' received new outside cylinders with outside steampipes, similar to those of the 'Castles'. The original outside cylinders were fed by steam pipes which emerged from the rear of the smokebox saddle between the frames. To accommodate the outside steampipes the piping in the smokebox had to be altered, and a hole cut in each side of the smokebox. This was all very well if one could be certain that a modified boiler was available for fitting to an engine with new cylinders and outside steam pipes. But this cut right across the principle of having standard boilers that could be fitted to any engine. Furthermore, the 'Star' boiler was normally interchangeable with those of the 'Saints' and the '28XX' 2—8—0s. The smokeboxes were not interchangeable, and until worn out stayed with their boilers. Inevitably

there were times when in the course of ordinary repair work a modified boiler had to be fitted to a non-modified engine, and then in the case of the 'Stars' a sharply-curved steampipe was fitted to connect the smokebox aperture with the flange on the cylinder casting between the frames. In retrospect it is a little difficult to see the justification for fitting 'Castle' type cylinders to 'Stars', if for nothing else than the lack of standardisation it introduced. Only the most comprehensive individual costing records would show if any economies were effected. Certainly there is no record of any improved performance on the road. By the beginning of the 1930s the 'Stars' were past their prime in any case. All their finest work, as recorded in Part I of this book, was done with the original layout of cylinders and piping.

The drawing which is reproduced on the following page has been prepared from a Swindon drawing dated March 1929. The first engine to be so treated was No 4024, in February of that year, so that the arrangement drawing, as was not infrequently the case, was a record of what had been done rather than an instruction to the shops. The alterations to the smokebox were such as could quite readily have been made without a drawing. The other twelve engines that received 'Castle' type

West to North express near Patchway : engine No 4043 'Prince Henry',
with outside steampipes

Smokebox layout of 'Star' class engine fitted with 'Castle' type cylinders and outside steampipes

cylinders were:

4040	*Queen Boadicea*	Feb	1930
4057	*Princess Elizabeth*	Apr	1930
4001	*Dog Star*	Oct	1930
4035	*Queen Charlotte*	Jan	1931
4043	*Prince Henry*	Oct	1931
4053	*Princess Alexandra*	Oct	1933
4049	*Princess Maud*	Feb	1935
4048	*Princess Victoria*	Oct	1938
4052	*Princess Beatrice*	Apr	1939
4060	*Princess Eugenie*	Aug	1944
4051	*Princess Helena*	Dec	1944
4055	*Princess Sophia*	May	1945

Two of the engines so equipped, namely the first one No 4024, and No 4001 *Dog Star,* were among the earliest engines of the 'Star' class to be scrapped. The case history at the end of this book refers to those engines which at one time or another received modified boilers, while retaining their old cylinders, and therefore had the so-called 'elbow' pipes. Engine No 4002 *Evening Star* had this arrangement as early as December 1929, when there was only one engine running with 'Castle' type cylinders, rather suggesting that at first boilers were being modified more quickly than new cylinders were being manufactured. But when a complicated procedure like this is set in motion the subsequent peregrinations of individual boilers provide a field for endless research for those who are so minded. It was seemingly a case of improvisation and expediency rather than a definite development in locomotive design, and as such it can be left without further comment. It can be added, however, that I had an excellent run behind the modified 4002 *Evening Star,* in June 1930, on the 7.50 pm from Birmingham to Paddington with a heavy train of 445 tons. While the work was not up to the most brilliant standards of the 'Stars' it was certainly very good. Curiously enough the train was worked down from Chester by No 4040 *Queen Boadicea,* which had been fitted with 'Castle' cylinders only four months earlier. The latter engine was stationed at Wolverhampton, and was much in demand on the sharply timed trains on the north road. I had several other good runs behind her that summer.

Reverting to the 'Castles' proper, an important accessory introduced as standard on the 1935 batch was the speedometer. Many times my motoring friends have expressed astonishment that for so many years speedometers were unheard of on British locomotives, and although speed restrictions were laid down for many parts of the line, their observance was left to the driver's judgment.

Furthermore, there were few trackside indications to show what the speed limits were. With the older and lighter engines considerable liberties were often taken, and it must be confessed that some of the most spectacular achievements of the 'Stars' included violations of speed orders, as when the driver of No 4055 *Princess Sophia* on the 12 noon up from Birmingham took Banbury station at a completely unchecked 80 mph instead of the stipulated 60 mph! With engines of the size and weight of the 'Kings' more rigid control was necessary, and following some experiments made on 'Castle' class engines Nos 5003 and 5008 in 1933-4, a very simple device was standardised, and in a short time fitted to all engines of the 'Castle' and 'King' classes.

The arrangement adopted as standard consisted of an alternating current generator driven direct from the driving wheel, and a voltmeter in the cab, which had a scale graduated to read in miles per hour. The dial was of 5 in diameter and was fixed on a corner of the firebox just below the driver's look-out window. It was mounted on Sorbo rubber blocks to absorb vibration, and insulated from the effects of heat by fibre washers. The drive to the ac generator was from a small return crank incorporated in the crank-pin washer of the right-hand trailing coupled wheel. A block on that crank engaged in a slotted link, mounted on a spindle carried on the same centre line as the coupled-wheel axle by a bracket suspended from the footplate. The slot was long enough to allow for the greatest possible displacements of the coupled wheel relative to the footplate bracket. The drive was transmitted through bevel gears to the generator, the armature of which ran on a vertical axis at $2\frac{1}{2}$ times the driving axle speed. An armoured cable conveyed the alternating current to the voltmeter in the cab, first passing through a rectifier, so that the voltmeter gave a unidirectional reading for both directions of running. Like most forms of speedometers they were not always accurate; but in many thousands of miles riding on the footplate of Great Western locomotives I did not come across one that was seriously out. If there was an error it was usually that they read high; although it was a fault on the safe side, it sometimes led to slight losses of time, from drivers assuming that they were travelling faster than was actually the case.

An amusing interlude in the history of both 'Castle' and 'King' classes began in the early months of 1935. Certain German and American locomotives intended for high-speed running had been streamlined, to lessen the air resistance, and the first of the Gresley 'P2' class, the *Cock o' the North* had an

Engine No 5005 'Manorbier Castle', with original layout of streamlined fairings

exterior form that could be so described, although the front-end included a considerable air-pocket. In 1935 Great Western Railway would be celebrating its centenary, and certain members of the Locomotive Committee of the Board were anxious that the company should be obviously 'with it' in this latest trend of locomotive engineering practice. Collett thought otherwise, but orders being orders something had to be done about it. He had a paperweight model of a 'King' on his desk. An office boy was sent out to buy some plasticine from a toy shop, and then Collett in a few minutes determined the shape the new streamlining should take by rubbing plasticine across the front and down the sides of the running plates, round the cylinders, and filling the spaces behind chimney and safety valve covers

where eddies occur. A hemispherical 'blob' was stuck on the front of the smokebox. Then the model thus decorated was sent to the drawing office, and a draughtsman was given the job of producing the necessary working drawings, for both a 'King' and a 'Castle'. I regret to add that the whole exercise was regarded as something of a joke, and the seal was set upon it when a popular music hall and radio comedian visited Swindon Works and in a BBC broadcast referred to the 'engine that looks as if it had Teddy Brown welded on the front' (Teddy Brown was the leading fat-man comedian of the day).

The engines thus decorated were Nos 6014 *King Henry VII* and 5005 *Manorbier Castle*. Lightheartedness apart, they were the very first British

The up Bristolian near Ashley Hill hauled by the semi-streamlined No 6014 'King Henry VII', shrouding over cylinders removed

Paddington - South Wales excursion near Patchway : engine No 5005 'Manorbier Castle',
with shrouding over cylinders removed

locomotives to have definite streamlined fairings added to them. They preceded the 'A4' Pacifics of the LNER by about six months. It was perhaps typical of Collett that in shunning the limelight he missed a priceless opportunity of stealing the thunder of the LNER. A fully streamlined 'King' or 'Castle', accompanied by some appropriately faster running, would have gone far to keep the Great Western Railway in the forefront, when there was every sign of ground being lost to the northern lines. Had Collett seized his opportunity, when *Silver Link* appeared in September 1935 it would inevitably have been a case of 'another streamlined locomotive'. The illustrations of engines 5005 and 6014 show what a half-hearted attempt was made. The casings round the cylinders were soon found to be an encumbrance and a liability. The inside motion on the Great Western 4-cylinder 4—6—0s was difficult enough to get at anyway without a shrouding round the outside! On occasions there was overheating of the motion. The shrouding round the cylinders was removed in the autumn of 1935, and one by one the incongruous fairings were removed, and the whole episode quietly forgotten.

Authority was given for the construction of ten new 'Castles' in 1936, and for fifteen in 1937. These were to the standard '5013' class, but twenty-one of these engines achieved a modicum of distinction by being renamed *en bloc*, in 1937. In fact some of the engines of the 1937 batch bore their original names for no more than a few weeks. It was a complete break with tradition, in that none of the new names were those of 'Castles'. Oddly enough, this chain of events was set in motion by a change in the premiership of Great Britain. Shortly after the Coronation of King George VI, Stanley Baldwin retired, and duly created an Earl went to the House of Lords. Naming locomotives after political characters has its pitfalls, as the Great Central found to its cost; but Baldwin was in a different case altogether. Before he entered politics he had been a director of the GWR; his father was chairman of the company from 1905 to 1908, and there had been a 'Bulldog' class 4—4—0 named *Stanley Baldwin* for many years. On his elevation to the peerage the Great Western sought to honour him, and engine No 5063 which had gone into traffic in June 1937 as *Thornbury Castle* was renamed *Earl Baldwin* only a month later.

This gesture had immediate repercussions, because the GWR already had a class of 4—4—0s named after Earls, some of whom were directors of the company, and with the naming of a 'Castle' after Earl Baldwin it was felt inappropriate that

Engine No 5069 'Isambard Kingdom Brunel'

famous hereditary titles should exist on the useful, but definitely hybrid 4—4—0s of the '32XX' class. These latter were built, or rather rebuilt for the Cambrian section, using the 'Duke' type of boiler on a 'Bulldog' frame. More recently they have been familiarly known as the 'Dukedogs'. The names of these twenty engines 3200 to 3219 were transferred one by one to the 'Castles' Nos 5043 to 5062, and the original nameplates of these latter went into store at Swindon. All the 1936 batch was renamed, together with thirteen of the 1937 batch, though why it should have been necessary to rename 5064 *Tretower Castle* and 5065 *Upton Castle* as *Bishops Castle* and *Newport Castle*, ex Nos 5053 and 5058 respectively, is difficult to understand. The only engines of the 1937 batch that were not renamed at the time were 5066 *Wardour Castle* and 5067 *St Fagans Castle*.

The year 1937 was also notable for the decision to replace certain of the 'Abbey' series of 'Stars' by 'Castles'. Certain of the former engines needed new cylinders, and so a lot number was issued authorising the construction of ten new 'Castles' in replacement. The frames of the original engines were, however, in good condition so to some extent they were rebuilds. A batch of numbers in the general 'Castle' series was set aside for these replacements, namely 5083 to 5092, and using the old names the numbers were allocated to correspond with the original numbers—4063 becoming 5083, 4066 becoming 5086, and so on. The rebuilding was spread over $3\frac{1}{2}$ years. The first to be treated was *Reading Abbey* in April 1937 and the last was *Tintern Abbey* as late as 1940. It was curious that the two earliest engines of the 'Abbey' series were left out

of this procedure. Nos 4061 *Glastonbury Abbey* and 4062 *Malmesbury Abbey* survived to be among the very last 'Stars' withdrawn. The two engines were only outlasted by that great veteran 4056 *Princess Margaret*.

Ten 'Castles', Nos 5068 to 5077, were built in 1938, and another ten, 5078 to 5082 and 5093 to 5097, in 1939; and twelve out of these twenty engines were subjected to renaming in 1940-1, but for a very different reason to that concerning the 5043-62 series. In the wave of intense pride and patriotism that accompanied the achievements of the Royal Air Force during the Battle of Britain the Great Western interpreted popular sentiment by renaming twelve engines of the 'Castle' after aircraft, the names of which were household words by the end of 1940. The engines chosen were 5071 to 5082, and it was remarkable that all the 'Castle' names displaced were with one exception being displaced for the second time. It was only *Drysllwyn*, used for the first time on No 5076, that did not have that curious distinction. All those displaced names went into storage for the duration of the war, but all were eventually used on post-war 'Castles'. While on the subject of names, mention must be made of the happy choice of *Isambard Kingdom Brunel*, and *Sir Daniel Gooch* for engines 5069 and 5070, built in 1938. Full details of the naming and renaming of these engines is contained in the appendix. A final point to be mentioned before concluding Phase Two of the 'Castle' saga is that with engine No 5044, in March 1936, a chimney 3 in shorter than previously was fitted. This gave a greatly improved appearance, and this change was gradually extended to the whole class.

CHAPTER 3

PERFORMANCE : 1930-1939

DURING the late 1930s the standards of day-to-day locomotive performance on the Great Western Railway remained very high. In general, there were perhaps not those dazzling feats of individual enginemen that highlighted the golden age of the 'Stars', as recorded in Part I of this work; but all-round achievement was highly satisfactory. I was not travelling on the line myself quite so frequently in this period. My home was then in Hertfordshire, and although I had business interests in Chippenham my visits were occasional rather than regular. On the other hand train running was very comprehensively documented by the logs of a number of experienced recorders: by A. V. Goodyear and G. P. Antrobus on the Birmingham line; by R. E. Charlewood; by Sir James Colyer-Ferguson, who

was then at Oxford; and of course by Cecil J. Allen, who was travelling frequently to Chippenham and Bristol. Added to these were my own holiday journeys to Cornwall, and later some travelling on the West to North route via the Severn Tunnel. During all this period the 'Stars' continued to play an important part. With the building of more 'Castles' they had certainly been displaced from their earlier crack duties, but transferred to more distant depots, such as Worcester, Landore and Shrewsbury, they took over workings previously entrusted almost entirely to 'Saints'. The story of performance during the ten-year span of this chapter is therefore of all three classes of four-cylinder 4—6—0.

First then, to the 'Stars'. The inauguration of

Engine No 6005 'King George II', with indicator shelter

Up two-hour Bristol express near Stoke Gifford : engine No 4015 'Knight of St John'

the 'Bristolian' express in the centenary year of the GWR with its 1¾-hour schedule rather stole the thunder of the once-celebrated two-hour Bristol expresses; but there were drivers at Bath Road shed prepared to show that even with 'Stars', rather than 'Castles' or 'Kings', they could equal the speed achievements of their Old Oak counterparts on the 'Bristolian' itself. One such worthy got his chance when the 11.45 am up got a late start of 8½ min from Bristol. The brilliant result is tabulated herewith. Indeed No 4007 *Rising Star*, with a load well above the usual 'Bristolian' rake was driven at 'Bristolian' speed until all the lost time had been recovered. The schedule of the 'Bristolian' was then 78 min to passing Reading. After that there was no need for further hurry, and the 31·7 miles from Reading to Acton took 27 min 50 sec. Despite a final signal check the train reached Paddington 2¾ min early. There would have been not the slightest difficulty in running from Bristol to Paddington in 105 min or less, on such form as this, with an engine then thirty years old.

The insertion of stops at Bath, in place of the previous slip portions in the working of the two down two-hour Bristol expresses increased their difficulty of operation, with non-stop running between Paddington and Bath, 106·9 miles, booked in 102 min. Furthermore, the 11.15 am down included a heavy slip portion for Oxford, detached at Didcot. The engine workings were varied, so that occasion-

ally one had a 'Castle' or a 'King', but just as frequently a 'Star'. One could well imagine Churchward's heart glowing at the thought that his successors had sufficient confidence in the older engines to put 'Stars' on to the job, when the gross load well exceeded 400 tons for the first half of the journey. Two really splendid runs are tabulated,

GWR 11.45 am BRISTOL—PADDINGTON
Load: 267 tons tare, 280 tons full
Engine: 4007 *Rising Star*

Dist miles		Sch min	Actual m s	Speeds mph
0·0	TEMPLE MEADS .	0	0 00†	—
1·6	Stapleton Road . .		5 02	—
9·1	Coalpit Heath .		14 40	56
13·0	Chipping Sodbury .		18 49	60
17·6	Badminton . .	24½	23 27	60
27·9	Little Somerford .		31 40	82
34·7	Wootton Bassett .	41	37 26	54★
40·3	SWINDON . .	47	43 01	66
51·1	Uffington . . .		52 36	78
61·1	Steventon . .	65	58 58	81
64·5	DIDCOT . .	68	61 28	83
72·9	Goring . . .		67 38	76
81·6	READING . .	83½	74 32	65
93·4	Maidenhead . .	94½	85 18	70
99·1	SLOUGH . .	100	89 59	easy
108·5	Southall . .	109	98 05	
113·3	Acton . . .		102 22	
116·3	Westbourne Park .	116	104 30	
—			sigs	
117·6	PADDINGTON .	120	108 43	

★ Speed restriction
† Departure from Bristol 8½ min late

			GWR 11.15 am PADDINGTON—BATH					
Engine No .					4035		4072	
Engine Name .					*Queen Charlotte*		*Tresco Abbey*	
Load to Didcot tons E/F					394/420		436/460	
Load to Bath tons E/F					263/280		298/310	
Dist miles			Sch min	Actual m s	Speeds mph		Actual m s	Speeds mph
0·0	PADDINGTON	. .	0	0 00	—		0 00	—
1·3	Westbourne Park	. .		3 07	—		3 07	—
—				—	—	pws		
9·1	Southall .	. .	11	12 59	—		13 39	—
18·5	SLOUGH .	. .	20	21 58	68		22 45	67
24·2	Maidenhead .	. .		27 13	67		28 05	65·5
31·0	Twyford .	. .		33 20	67		34 06	—
36·0	READING .	. .	36	37 52	68		38 26	70
44·8	Goring .	. .		45 37	70·5		46 14	—
53·1	DIDCOT (slip)	. .	51½	52 50	—		53 54	65
60·4	Wantage Road .	. .		59 15	69		60 30	—
66·5	Uffington .	. .		64 39	—		66 00	—
71·6	Shrivenham .	. .		69 17	66		70 22	70
77·3	SWINDON .	. .	75	74 23	—		75 21	—
82·9	Wootton Bassett	. .		79 17	—		79 54	77
87·7	Dauntsey .	. .		83 11	82		83 31	85·5
94·0	CHIPPENHAM .	. .	90	88 06	—		88 24	—
98·3	Corsham .	. .		92 08	60		92 29	62
101·9	Box . .	. .		95 17	78		95 36	76·5
104·6	Bathampton .	. .		97 34	—		97 50	—
106·9	BATH .	. .	102	99 53			100 37	

with engines 4035 *Queen Charlotte* and 4072 *Tresco Abbey*. The schedule, in its point-to-point times, was somewhat uneven in its demands, booking 66 mph from Slough to Didcot after a very sharp initial 20 min from Paddington to Slough. Thereafter the slightly uphill length from Didcot to Swindon was booked at only 61·7 mph after the load had been reduced by about 140 tons. With such heavy trains as 420 and 460 tons the drivers of these two engines were justified in not attempt-

Bristol - Paddington express in Sonning cutting : engine No 4007 'Rising Star'

| | | | Run No . . . . | 1 | 2 | 3 | 4 |

GWR: OXFORD—PADDINGTON

Run No			1	2	3	4
Engine No			4038	4018	4049	4017
Engine Name . . .			Queen Berengaria	Knight of the Grand Cross	Princess Maud	Knight of Liege
Load, tons E/F			314/330	330/350	337/360	387/415

Dist miles		Sch min	Actual m s	Actual m s	Actual m s	Actual m s
0·0	OXFORD . .	0	0 00	0 00	0 00	0 00
5·1	Radley . . .		7 25	7 15	7 25	7 34
10·6	Didcot East Junc .	12	12 57	12 26	12 34	13 07
14·9	Cholsey . . .		17 47	17 25	17 10	17 48
18·7	Goring . . .		21 00	20 30	20 27	21 07
—			—	sigs	—	pws
21·9	Pangbourne . .		23 45	23 59	23 15	25 18
27·4	READING . .	27½	28 25	29 52	27 52	31 01
32·4	Twyford . .		32 35	34 01	32 01	35 11
39·2	Maidenhead . .		38 05	39 30	37 23	40 35
44·9	SLOUGH . .	42	42 50	44 00	41 57	45 09
50·2	West Drayton .		47 05	48 02	46 11	49 31
54·3	Southall . .	49½	50 30	51 32	49 38	53 17
—			—	sigs	sigs	—
57·7	Ealing . . .		53 10	sigs	53 08	56 26
—			—	—	—	sigs
62·1	Westbourne Park .	56	57 00	—	58 07	60 37
63·4	PADDINGTON .	60	59 45	61 19	60 20	63 21

ing to maintain strict time in the early stages even though it meant detaching their slip portions a little behind time at Didcot. Both engines attained maximum speeds of 70 mph on level track with their full loads, while *Tresco Abbey,* passing Didcot at 65 mph, gradually recovered to a full 70 mph on the rise to Shrivenham. Both engines were practically on time at Swindon, and ran fast onwards to Chippenham with maximum speeds of 82 and 85·5 mph on Dauntsey bank. After that the finish could be relatively easy.

The acceleration of the important 8.55 am express from Worcester to Paddington to make a 60-min non-stop run over the final 63·4 miles from Oxford, gave further opportunities for the 'Stars' to distinguish themselves. This was a much heavier train than the 'flyers' from the Bristol direction, and the working was made more difficult by the slack necessary round the Didcot avoiding line. Taking account of this the point-to-point times were only 1½ min more than those of the 'Cheltenham Flyer' between Reading and Paddington. It will thus be appreciated that with 'Stars' instead of 'Castles', and loads varying between 330 and 415 tons there was little time in hand. Among the four runs I have selected for tabulation it was only *Queen Berengaria* that actually got through from Oxford to Paddington in under the hour, though the other three engines would have been punctual but for delays. On the second run *Knight of the Grand Cross* was

checked at Pangbourne, losing 2 min in running; but then some splendid running was made east of Reading with a maximum of 77 mph at Slough. The arrears of time would certainly have been made up but for the concluding checks. *Princess Maud*, with 350 tons, also did very well, with some even faster running east of Reading and a top speed of 79 mph at Twyford. but the signal check at Ealing was a bad one, and prevented strict timekeeping.

The remarkable performance of *Knight of Liege* in the last column requires special mention and analysis. The start out of Oxford, with 415 tons, was practically indistinguishable from the previous runs, with considerably lighter loads, and after negotiation of Didcot east curve speed was worked up to 72 mph before the Pangbourne re-laying check. After Reading the average speeds make impressive reading: to Twyford 72 mph, on to Maidenhead 75·6 mph, and over the next 5·7 miles to Slough 77·7 with a maximum of 79 mph—with a 'Star' hauling 415 tons! The permanent way slack had however cost at least 2½ min, and even though the speed continued to rule high, with an average of 68·2 mph right on to Ealing Broadway, time could not have been kept. As far as I can calculate, however, the net time was exactly 60 min. The principal feature of the run was of course the attained maximum on level track of 79 mph at Slough in the course of a long-sustained spell of high speed, averaging 74·5 mph from Twyford to West Drayton.

Down Cornish Riviera Express (15-car train) near Aldermaston :
engine No 6000 'King George V'

This indicates a drawbar pull of about 2¼ tons at 77 to 79 mph—well above Churchward's famous target of a drawbar pull of 2 tons at 70 mph.

Turning now to the 'Castles', the 'Cheltenham Flyer' schedule is so often quoted as a yardstick in referring to Great Western performance over the Bristol route that one naturally turns to it first. I am quite aware that enthusiasts whose sympathies lie elsewhere tend to write off what was once 'The World's Fastest Train' as a mere stunt in high-speed scheduling: a lightly loaded train, run by picked engines, on an easy downhill course with no intermediate speed restrictions. The impeachment, over 'an easy course', has been dismissed in Chapter 1 of this book, and there is no doubt that picked engines were used; but the main thing to remember

Up Torbay express near Burlescombe : engine No 6018 'King Henry VI'

C

about the 'Cheltenham Flyer' was that unlike the later high-speed trains in other parts of Great Britain, there was no strict limitation of load. The minimum was certainly no more than seven coaches; but neither traffic nor locomotive departments had any compunction about putting on a few extras, and loads of eight or nine coaches were of quite common occurrence. Furthermore, unlike every other high-speed train in the country the 'Flyer' ran six days a week. There was no easing of the schedule on Saturdays even in the height of the summer; indeed, some of my own fastest runs on the train were made on Saturdays.

The question of additional load on trains timed at such speeds raises to my mind a matter of principle. The attitude of the Great Western Railway was beyond praise in this respect. If traffic was accepted that involved extra coaches—and this applied also to the pre-war 'Bristolian'—then an all-out attempt was made to keep the time publicly advertised. Far otherwise was the policy adopted in more recent times, for on occasions when the going was likely to be difficult extra time was given in special working notices, not communicated to the public. Thus a train could, for example, be 10 min late by the published times, but driver and

guard could book 'right time'. This, of course, was nothing short of dishonesty. It had its repercussions sometimes. On one post-war occasion the traffic department wanted to attach two extra coaches to the down 'Bristolian'. The running authorities said they could only accept such a load if 10 min extra time was allowed. Covertly this was agreed. A 'King' class engine instead of the usual 'Castle' was put on to the job and a locomotive inspector instructed to ride on the footplate. Having got an excellent engine the driver and inspector scorned the extra allowance and without any difficulty ran the train to the normal time, to receive a severe reprimand for their pains!

This chapter is, however, about times when the old spirit of the Great Western Railway still flourished, and the accompanying table gives details of some cases of overload on the 'Cheltenham Flyer' leading up to one on which the driver came very near to keeping time with a load of 435 tons—*four hundred and thirty-five tons*! These conditions of heavy loading involve some of the finest high-speed running I have ever seen with the 'Castles', and they are deserving of close study. The table includes runs with seven, eight, ten, and finally thirteen-coach trains. Some very spectacular run-

GWR: THE CHELTENHAM FLYER									
Run No					1		2	3	4
Engine No . . .					5055		5025	5018	5023
Engine Name . . .					*Lydford Castle*		*Chirk Castle*	*St Mawes Castle*	*Brecon Castle*
Load, coaches . . .					7		8	10	13
Load, tons E/F . . .					218/230		248/270	317/340	401/435
Dist miles			Sch min		Actual m s		Actual m s	Actual m s	Actual m s
0·0	SWINDON .	.	0		0 00		0 00	0 00	0 00
5·7	Shrivenham .	.			6 43		7 02	7 16	8 00
10·8	Uffington .	.			10 22		11 01	11 19	12 17
16·9	Wantage Road	.			14 25		15 31	15 58	17 07
24·2	DIDCOT .	.	21		19 13		20 44	21 22	26 15
32·6	Goring .	.			25 02		26 48	27 36	31 44
35·8	Pangbourne .	.			27 32		29 11	29 59	34 01
41·3	READING .	.	34		31 47		33 17	34 08	36 06
46·3	Twyford .	.			35 38		37 00	37 56	40 03
53·1	Maidenhead .	.			40 33		41 50	43 04	45 20
									sigs
58·8	SLOUGH .	.	47½		44 39		45 50	47 22	52 20
64·1	West Drayton .	.			48 26		49 41	51 24	57 19
68·2	Southall .	.	54¼		51 33		52 43	54 39	60 58
71·6	Ealing .	.			54 10		55 13	57 12	63 48
									sigs
76·0	Westbourne Park	.	61		59 00		59 19	60 41	68 35
77·3	PADDINGTON .	.	65		61 49		62 15	63 04	71 41
	Max speed mph .	.	.		93·5		86·5	82	79
	Location	.	.		Wantage Road		Maidenhead	Wantage Road Reading Ealing	Didcot

The up Bristolian, near Filton Junction : engine No 6027 'King Richa.d I'

ning could be expected if a driver decided to 'have a go' with a seven-coach train, and the first run in the table, made on the very stormy New Year's Day of 1937 includes some very fast times. There was a strong south-west wind, with heavy rain, and while this might have been of some assistance in the early stages it was certainly not so when the line turns south at Didcot. Thus engine No 5055, then named *Lydford Castle*, made a very rapid start and worked quickly up to a maximum of 93·5 mph by Wantage Road. Then from 90 mph through Didcot the speed came down to 76·5 mph at Pangbourne. After the line had turned eastwards again, and there was some shelter in the cuttings, the speed rose again into the middle eighties and Southall was passed 3 min early.

The eight-coach train was again a rough winter occasion, when I was travelling through from Gloucester to Paddington, and the train was late in arriving from Cheltenham. The driver did his best to recover some time, but with an east wind and driving sleet for most of the way it was not possible to do much. To get through in 62¼ min in such conditions was splendid work. Apart from a brief drop to 79·5 mph after Goring water troughs the speed never fell below 80 mph at any point between Uffington and Hanwell, and the average speed over this 59·1 miles was 82·6 mph. Then comes a splendid run with a ten-coach train weighing 340 tons behind the tender, logged by Mr H. F. Maybank. The driver of *St Mawes Castle* on this occasion was Burgess, who did so well with *Manorbier Castle* on the record run with the down 5 pm from Paddington

on 6 June 1932. Shrivenham was passed at 71 mph, and a maximum of 82 was attained by Wantage Road. After that the speed fluctuated no more than slightly between further maxima of 82 mph at Reading and Ealing, and minima of 76·5 mph at Twyford and 76 at Hayes. An ability to attain and sustain 81-82 mph on level track with 340 tons load was demonstrated on this journey.

Lastly there is the astounding run of *Brecon Castle* with the 13-coach train of 435 trailing tons, also logged by Mr H. F. Maybank. Speed never quite reached 80 mph. The maximum was 79 mph, sustained on the faint descent between Steventon and Didcot; but a speed of 77·5 mph on the dead level approaching Reading indicated the remarkable drawbar horsepower of 1,070, and the fact that speed had averaged 76·8 mph from Uffington to Maidenhead shows clearly that this was no mere flash in the pan, achieved by mortgaging the boiler. It was a most splendid example of sustained steaming at a very high rate of evaporation. It was very unfortunate that so magnificent an effort, the product solely of a keen and resolute engine crew, and a first-class engine, should have been marred by signal checks. From a careful examination of all the figures I am doubtful if strict time would have been kept. I think they would have been a minute out on arrival; but what is a mere minute against such a display as this! Of course there was a pair of real sportsmen on the footplate. The driver, F. W. Street, had as fireman C. E. Brown, who in Western Region days was a top link driver of rare calibre, too, and gave me some fine runs.

Besides such running all other contemporary work of the 'Castles' naturally pales; but mention must be made of their work on the Cornish main line. At that time the load limit was fixed at the extraordinary figure of 420 tons tare. It must be admitted that this was expecting a little too much over such gradients, where it was quite impossible to balance the long uphill slogging by some really free running downhill. With loads of around 350 tons they managed the Cornish Riviera Express quite comfortably; but an engine designed for work like that just described on the 'Cheltenham Flyer' did not have an ideal valve setting for the Cornish banks. A two-cylinder engine with Churchward's setting of the Stephenson link motion would have been much better.

In the first volume of this book some examples of outstanding work by 'King' class locomotives on the West of England main line were quoted. In the 1930s interest tended to shift to the Paddington—Birmingham service. For one thing, the introduction of the 1¾-hour trains between Paddington and Bristol in 1935 raised the natural question as to why Birmingham could not have an equally fast service. The distance was 7 miles shorter, and the

'King' class engines stationed at Wolverhampton included some of the finest units of the whole stud. These sentiments never got beyond a rather loud whispering campaign; but it was taken sufficiently seriously at Paddington and Swindon for some running diagrams to be prepared in the drawing office at Swindon to show how difficult it would be to operate a 105-min schedule, with a good paying load. Why the operating department insisted that nothing less than 300 tons tare would do, when the new Bristol express conveyed only 215 tons, was not explained. But it was all fairly obvious that the management did not want to do it.

The running diagrams which were published in *The Railway Gazette*, and which had been worked out in the fullest detail, were naturally based on the capacity of the 'King' class engines in continuous steaming. It is not possible to reduce to theoretical calculations that priceless attribute of the steam locomotive that enables a skilful driver and fireman to exact that extra effort on a bank, above the theoretical maximum, by mortgaging the boiler, possibly running down both pressure and water level, knowing that both can be recovered on the next downhill stretch. The Birmingham line in-

Birmingham and the North express topping Hatton bank : engine No 6017 'King Edward IV'

cluded a number of places where this could be done: Gerrards Cross bank, and the subsequent descent and slack through Wycombe; Saunderton bank, with Princes Risborough, and Ashendon to follow; Aynho slack following the ascent from Bicester to Ardley, and the Leamington stop before the attack on Hatton bank. The stretches where the engine was steaming hard continuously were relatively short; nothing to compare, for example, with the long, very slight, but absolutely continuous grind from Paddington up to Swindon, or the 20-mile pull from Exeter up to Whiteball Tunnel. The Wolverhampton drivers became experts to the last degree in running their own road to London, and although the pundits of the Swindon drawing office demonstrated that 400 tons was the optimum load for the Birmingham two-hour trains, these outstanding enginemen thought nothing of taking 500 tons out of Paddington, or, as Part I of this work showed, keeping time with a load of 475 tons throughout to Leamington—with a 'Castle'!

The runs I have chosen for inclusion here come mainly from the collection of G. P. Antrobus, who except at weekends and holiday times travelled on

the 6.10 pm down from Paddington every day, for several years. I have chosen six truly superlative runs for discussion. On all of them circumstances demanded something above the average if time was to be kept, and it was entirely in the spirit of the No 1 link at Stafford Road shed, Wolverhampton, that a whole-hearted attempt to produce that extra would be made as a matter of course. First of all it will be seen that against a schedule time that was at first 91 min, and was later cut fractionally to $90\frac{1}{2}$ min, the net times varied between 83 and 87 min; furthermore, on the first and second runs with no more than moderate loads, by 6.10 pm standards, still faster times could clearly have been made had not the effects of the earlier delays been wiped out by Bicester. In view of my earlier comments about extracting the additional efforts from the locomotives, however, we must look to the uphill work. The Gerrards Cross and Saunderton inclines provide ideal data for horsepower calculations, because in the former case the hard initial section from Denham frequently results in the minimum speed occurring near Gerrards Cross station, and a slight acceleration afterwards, while from West Wycombe

Up West of England express on Fairwood troughs : engine No 6002
'King William IV'

GWR: PADDINGTON—LEAMINGTON

Run No	1	2	3	4	5	6
Engine No	6005	6017	6017	6008	6008	6008
Engine Name	King George II	King Edward IV	King Edward IV	King James II	King James II	King James II
Load, tons E/F to B'cester	357/380	403/425	415/445	472/505	476/505	474/510
to B'bury	327/347	367/388	380/407	436/465	445/470	437/470
to L'ton	293/315	298/315	314/335	366/390	374/400	369/400

Dist miles		Sch min	Actual m s	Actual m s	Actual m s	Actual m s	Actual m s	Actual m s
0·0	PADDINGTON	0	0 00	0 00	0 00	0 00	0 00	0 00
1·3	Westbourne Park		—	3 13	3 06	3 49	sigs	—
3·3	Old Oak West Jc	7	5 41	6 54	7 31 sigs	7 40 sigs	6 43 sigs	6 35 sigs
7·8	Greenford	13	13 46 pws	13 42 pws	16 02 pws	14 16 pws	12 01	11 50
10·3	Northolt Jc	15½	17 31	16 15	20 40 pws	17 35	14 36	14 30
14·8	Denham		21 45	20 21	27 57 pws	22 15	19 04	19 00
17·4	Gerrards Cross		24 06	22 46	30 55	24 53	21 46	21 47
21·7	Beaconsfield		27 56	26 43 pws	35 36	29 21	26 22	26 44 pws
26·5	HIGH WYCOMBE	32	32 24	31 12	40 64	34 04	30 44	32 07
31·5	Saunderton		38 05	36 56	45 56	39 53	37 04	38 08
34·7	PRINCES RISBOROUGH	42	41 02	39 56	49 10	43 18	40 28	41 29
40·1	Haddenham		45 09	44 11	53 00	47 25	44 30	45 34
44·0	Ashendon Jc	49½	48 33	47 49	55 57	50 53	47 35	48 49
50·4	Blackthorn		54 33	54 13	61 34	56 31	53 30	54 49
53·4	BICESTER	58½	56 56	56 57	63 59	58 59	55 58	57 25
57·2	Ardley		60 27	60 51	67 32	62 45	59 37	61 15
62·4	Aynho Jc	67	65 18 sigs	65 43	72 00	67 33	64 19	65 59
67·5	BANBURY	72	70 40	70 40	76 44	72 11	69 12 pws	71 22 pws
71·1	Cropredy		74 22	74 14	79 52	75 24	73 31	76 21
76·2	Fenny Compton		78 54	78 58	84 15	79 53	79 01	81 40
81·2	Southam Road		82 45	83 16	87 47	83 40	83 02	85 35
83·6	Fosse Road		84 35	85 12 pws	89 23	85 59 sigs	84 59 sigs	87 24
87·3	LEAMINGTON	90½	88 26	89 27	92 59	90 45	89 23	91 08

Net time	min	84	87	83	86	86¾	86½

Principal speed mph:						
Denham	70	72	56	65	65	64
Gerrards Cross	65·5	64·5	52	58·5	57·5	55
Beaconsfield	68	66	56	58·5	56·5	54·5
Saunderton	61	61	54·5	53·5	52	51·5
Haddenham	83	82	91·5	87·5	90	85
Blackthorn	79	74	80	78	76	74·5
Ardley	62·5	59	63·5	60	62	59
Cropredy	64·5	63	69	66	52	54
Fosse Road	82	80	91	87	80	83

Calculated equivalent dhp:						
(a) Gerrards Cross bank	1,501	1,583	1,440	1,525	1,447	1,410
(b) Saunderton	1,642	1,815	1,785	1,761	1,694	1,676

the speed, on a good run, is usually rising slightly up the subsequent 1 in 164 grade to Saunderton.

Examination of the theoretical curves produced in the Swindon drawing office indicate that the uphill speeds were based on the maximum continuous steaming capacity of the 'King' class engine with a single fireman: a perfectly reasonable assumption in an exercise of this kind. With the 400-ton train the speeds shown on the graph are 57 mph at the upper part of Gerrards Cross bank and 50 mph at Saunderton. The gross load of such a train can be assumed as 420 tons behind the tender. The equivalent drawbar horsepowers involved are 1,250 and 1,380. In the classic trials of

Up Torquay and Paignton express approaching Fairwood Junction, Westbury :
engine No 6011 'King James II'

engine No 6001 in 1952, after that engine had been equipped with a 4-row superheater and modified draughting the equivalent dhp, when working at an evaporation rate of 30,000 lb per hr, with *two* firemen, was 1,500 at 50 mph and 1,370 at 60 mph. The equivalent dhp on the six runs tabulated have been very carefully calculated from the voluminous data compiled by Mr Antrobus, and in comparison with those of the Swindon diagram and of the tests with No 6001 they fairly make one rub one's eyes in wonder. Comparison of these efforts in relation to the continuous steaming results show the astonishing extent to which these Wolverhampton drivers were getting the 'extra' out of their engines. I need

hardly add that it is an achievement that would be utterly impossible with a diesel.

Every one of the runs tabulated is a classic in itself, but it is necessary to mention in particular some of their more outstanding features. On No 1, for example, look at the acceleration from 65·5 mph at Gerrards Cross to 68 mph before the Beaconsfield summit was topped, followed by 61 mph at Saunderton; but the power outputs were eclipsed on the truly phenomenal second run, with edhp values of 1,583 at Beaconsfield summit and 1,815 at Saunderton. On No 3 run, after heavy delays in the early stages, and passing High Wycombe 8 min late, a splendid attempt was made to regain lost time,

The last 'King' to be built : No 6029 'King Stephen', later renamed
'King Edward VIII'

and after another very big effort up Saunderton, 54.5 mph and an edhp of 1,785, there came the fastest sustained running of all six after Princes Risborough, with maximum speeds of 91.5 mph at Haddenham, and 91 mph at Fosse Road. Columns 4, 5 and 6 all relate to the working of loads exceeding 500 tons between Paddington and Bicester. They were all magnificent performances, and on the Gerrards Cross and Saunderton banks showed substantial 'extras' over both the theoretical and the 30,000 lb per hr figures for horsepower. Of these six runs it was only on the occasion that permanent way checks put the train 8 min late in passing High Wycombe that a late arrival occurred at Leamington.

One could continue discussion of these results indefinitely, following a variety of modes of analysis; but I think the figures themselves are enough to show that the 'King' class, in its original form, was an outstandingly successful locomotive design. It is important to appreciate that at the time these runs were made the locomotives had the original two-row low-degree superheaters, and the original draughting, with the jumper ring on the blast-pipe. Furthermore, Stafford Road shed, Wolverhampton, did not enjoy the choicest of coal supplies. They rarely received the finest grades of soft Welsh coal, more usually having to run with the best grades of local Staffordshire stuff. The secret of success was the tremendous spirit of pride in the job which permeated every grade of the service at Wolverhampton. I did not have the pleasure of making any footplate journeys in pre-war days, but from 1950 I rode with many drivers who had been main-line firemen in the great days of 1930-9, and in addition to the men whose driving feats are described in this chapter, Lewis, Glover, A. Smith, Jay, Brunsdon, and others, I have pleasurable memories of Curtis, the Macmillan brothers, Bert Griffiths, W. H. Shaw, and others of the post-war era.

CHAPTER 4

THE WAR YEARS

THE week-end of 2-3 September 1939 virtually marked the end of the Churchward era on the Great Western Railway. The network of high-speed express trains was suspended earlier than on other British railways because of the emergency measures needed for the evacuation of children from London, Birmingham and Liverpool; and although the subsequent 'phoney' period of the war did not result in any immediate physical disruption, such as was to come in the autumn of 1940, the fact that the railway as a whole and the locomotive department in particular were under Government control placed restraints upon the autonomy of Swindon such as had not previously been experienced. At the outbreak of war C. B. Collett was in his 69th year, but he carried on until the spring of 1941, when his retirement took place within a few weeks of the death of his great contemporary, Sir Nigel Gresley. Collett was succeeded by F. W. Hawksworth, who for many years had been Chief Draughtsman and

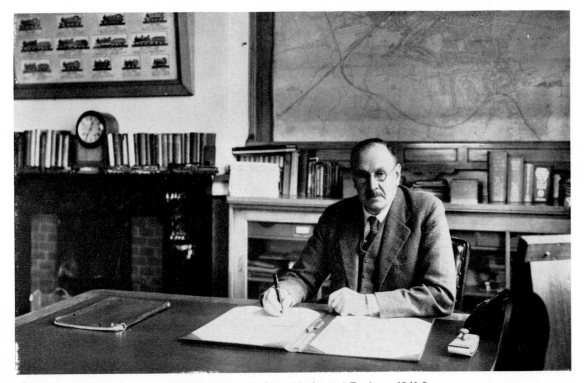

F. W. Hawksworth, Chief Mechanical Engineer 1941-9

Engine No 5071 as renamed 'Spitfire' in 1940 with the experimental 8-wheeled tender

who on John Auld's retirement became Principal Assistant to the Chief Mechanical Engineer. The succession, as always, on the GWR, was solid and secure. Hawksworth's immediate *entourage* were all men whom I came to know personally. F. C. Hall, one of the most charming of men, became Principal Assistant; W. N. Pellow was Outdoor Assistant and Locomotive Running Superintendent; K. J. Cook became Locomotive Works Manager; and H. Randle Carriage Works Manager. F. C. Mattingly was Chief Draughtsman, and a very brilliant young man, A. J. W. Dymond, became Personal Assistant to the CME, eventually to be entrusted with the nursing of various important new projects into fruition.

By the end of 1941 Hawksworth and his men certainly had their hands full of special tasks in connection with the war; but in this book, of course, I am concerned only with the story of 'Stars', 'Castles' and 'Kings'. War conditions certainly imposed a very heavy burden upon those responsible for the maintenance of all kinds of steam locomotives. At Swindon production of munitions was a first priority, and any practices that would prolong the intervals between visits to works of locomotives for repairs were adopted. There was inevitably a certain amount of 'patching up' done in repair work, and though this mainly concerned locomotives of lesser importance than the four-cylinder 4—6—0s it did affect them all to some extent. With the method of manufacture there was a certain thinning of the tubes at the bends of the superheaters, which in wartime conditions led to leaking; tubes were

The wartime livery of plain green, and crest on tender : engine No 4035 'Queen Charlotte'

The wartime livery on engine No 6029 'King Edward VIII'

patched, rather than replaced, and the butt-welding method used for insertion of new portions left flash at the joints.

On the road, much trouble was experienced with lower grades of coal. Great Western locomotives were more susceptible to the effects of poor coal than perhaps some of those on the northern lines, which had large superheaters, giving a high degree of superheat. But quite apart from fundamental causes of trouble such as this, there were difficulties arising from locomotives being sent out after inadequate servicing at the sheds, with boilers overdue for washout, smokeboxes uncleared of ashes, and blocked tubes. Against this rather gloomy picture I

*Wartime and after—austerity grime! Engine No 4043 'Prince Henry' on
Paignton - Newcastle express near Dawlish Warren*

The engine that never was ! An artist's impression of what the second Swindon 'Pacific' might have looked like

must record that even during the very worst days of the war I logged a number of excellent runs, with both 'Stars' and 'Castles', principally on the West to North route via the Severn Tunnel. A few of these runs are mentioned briefly at the end of this chapter. As the war years passed by there was ample evidence that no speedy return to a semblance or normality was likely once hostilities ended, and it appeared that some changes from traditional Great Western design were desirable. Experience was obtained, for the first time in the lifetime of most Swindon men, with locomotives of other than Great Western design: with the American-built Austerity 2—8—0, and with the LMSR Stanier 2—8—0, which all British railway companies were required to build in large quantities by the Ministry of War Transport.

The first outcome was the design of a superheater quite new to Swindon practice, and applied first on the new 'Hall' class engines of the '6959' class. This new design, with three rows of elements, was similar to the Schmidt, but incorporated the cherished Swindon feature of the regulator valve in it. In certain quarters outside the railway itself there was considerable doubt as to whether such a valve could be made steam-tight in high-temperature heaters, but this particular problem was satisfactorily settled. An improved feature was the elimination of the flat metal-to-metal joints by which the elements were attached to the heater in the standard 'Swindon' type of superheater. Initial reports from the running inspectors were very favourable. The 'Halls' with larger superheaters were reported to steam more freely, and the shed and works staff appreciated the new type of joints with the elements. The first batch of these engines was put into traffic in the summer of 1944, but in the meantime there had been stirrings in another direction altogether.

The Locomotive Committee of the Board had always included a number of directors who were genuinely interested in locomotives as such. Churchward, who was always on good terms with them, once said, in argument with Sir Aubrey Brocklebank: 'You're the only b—— director I've ever met who knew everything about valve gears!' The same august body had less success with Collett, and the 'sales resistance' he put up against their suggestions for a streamlined locomotive had the farcical result related in Chapter 2. In Hawksworth's time Captain Hugh Vivian was chairman of the committee, and as indicating his locomotive interests he was also chairman of Beyer, Peacock & Co Ltd. There is no evidence to suggest that he ever tried to get Hawksworth to try a Garratt; but war or no war there was

a feeling that the Great Western Railway ought to be making some preparations towards post-war traffic, and the resumption of high-speed running with heavy trains. The more progressive of the younger men in the Chief Mechanical Engineer's department felt that in any new development the principles of André Chapelon should be carefully heeded. During the war, with the accent on munitions production, and a policy of 'make-do-and-mend' prevailing in locomotive affairs, the drawing office, once Churchward's right hand throughout his brilliant development, had rather lost caste; but when the suggestion of a new 'Pacific' engine was made the opportunity was welcomed.

At the same time it seems to have been something of a 'cloak-and-dagger' business. Those concerned have told me that they had only the sketchiest of directives, from F. C. Mattingly. They were asked to put forward their ideas for a 'Pacific', and the only positive instruction issued in those early stages was that the boiler pressure was to be 280 lb per sq in. In response to requests for more information the reply was that standard practice was to be followed. A good deal of design work was done on the boiler. While bearing in mind all the basic features of Churchward's classic development the restriction in steam flow that to some extent handicapped the 'Kings' was eliminated, and a very high degree of superheat provided for. Two different schemes were worked out, using five-row and six-row superheaters respectively. In these preliminaries standard practice was certainly not followed, because provision was made for accommodating the regulator in a steam dome on top of the boiler. While preliminary work was thus being done on the boiler another draughtsman had taken the 'King' front-end, and completely streamlined the ports and steam passages in the Chapelon style.

Then, alas, those concerned had another visit from Mattingly, only the second he had paid while the project was live, and then it was to tell them to stop work. From that moment nothing more was done, and all that remained was a preliminary line diagram of what might have been Swindon's *chef d'oeuvre*. How the project originated in the first place, and how it was stopped one can only guess. Two points only may be put forward: it was essentially an express passenger engine (unlike Bulleid's 'Merchant Navy' class, officially designated 'mixed traffic'), and Authority probably frowned upon work expended on a super-express passenger locomotive in wartime. The second point is this: it would seem that hope was not entirely dead in the hearts of those who had initiated the project, when the

Smokebox layout of the '5098' class of 'Castles' with 3-row superheater

Post-war 'Castles': engine No 7000 'Viscount Portal'

'County' class 4—6—0s appeared in 1945. These engines included two features quite out of normal context: the use of a boiler pressure of 280 lb per sq in, and the otherwise inexplicable introduction of an entirely non-standard coupled wheel diameter of 6 ft 3 in. Both these features were included in the stillborn 'Pacific'. Is it not a logical thing to guess that the 'County' was a guinea pig for the 'Pacific' which it was still hoped sometime to build?

I feel that a counter-suggestion that the 'County' was a definite attempt by Hawksworth to break away from the Churchward-Collett tradition, and that the new 4—6—0s were intended to be the post-war standard express passenger engine is quite fallacious. I have seen it suggested that 'Castle' building was resumed only after the 'Counties' had proved a 'failure'. This is quite at variance with the facts, for although the 'Counties' did not at first come fully up to expectations they did some very fine work, particularly on the more severely graded stretches of line, as in Cornwall and north of Wolverhampton. In any case the erecting shop switched straight over from 'County' to 'Castle' building within a matter of weeks.

The first post-war batch of 'Castles' was turned out in May and June 1946, bearing the numbers 5098-9, and 7000 to 7007. Except for Nos 7000 and 7003 they bore names that had twice previously been displaced. The two new names were *Viscount Portal*, the chairman of the GWR, on No 7000, and *Elmley Castle* on No 7003. Even then not all the twice displaced 'Castle' names were allowed finally to settle, as noted in the Case History of the 'Castles' (see Appendix). Engine No 7001 was renamed *Sir James Milne* in February 1948, and No 7007, the last express passenger engine to be built by the company, was renamed *Great Western*, and had the coat-of-arms on the driving wheel splasher beneath the nameplate. The thrice-displaced names *Denbigh Castle* and *Ogmore Castle* emerged once again in 1950. Almost at the end of the steam era No 7005 was renamed *Sir Edward Elgar* in August 1957 at the time of the centenary

of the great composer's birth. Apart from what might be termed the personalia of the new engines, they embodied certain important changes in design.

They were known officially as the '5098' class, and forty engines of this new series were built. Following the purely Great Western batch, in 1946, there were ten in each of the years 1948, 1949 and 1950 built to provide necessary replacements in express passenger motive power while the new British standard designs were being worked out. The principal difference from previous practice lay in the boiler, which had a three-row superheater of the type introduced on the '6959' series of 'Halls'. Engines with the modified superheater could readily be distinguished, on the right-hand side, by the longer casing over the oil pipe leading to the super-heater header. The first two engines of the new series had the standard GWR sight-feed lubricators, but all subsequent engines had mechanical lubricators. The arrangement was not at first finalised, and several types of lubricator were tried, and in various positions. One of these latter was behind the outside steampipe, which of course made access to the inside motion more difficult than ever; but in later years the lubricators on most engines were moved ahead of the steampipe.

Mechanical lubrication brought problems of its own. In concordance with prevailing fashions elsewhere it was intended to take the responsibility for regulating oil supply out of the hands of the driver, and provide a carefully metered flow precisely to suit the needs of the engine. But the sight-feed hydrostatic lubricator was 'the breath of life' to Great Western enginemen; they had grown up with it, and were expert in its manipulation, and very soon there were complaints that the new engines were sluggish in comparison. The contrast was perhaps worsened because the first two of the new engines, Nos 5098 *Clifford Castle* and 5099 *Compton Castle* with sight-feed lubricators, were exceptionally powerful and free running. It was argued that with post-war systems of engine manning a driver would have no opportunities of finding out the vagaries of individual engines, and therefore could not use the old form of lubricator to advantage. This was the talk of backroom theorists. With any experienced driver it would not take ten miles of running for him to sense that an engine was sluggish, and adjust the lubricator to give a slightly faster rate of feed. It was perhaps not without significance that in the comprehensive series of dynamometer and stationary plant trials between engines of the '5013' and '5098' series of 'Castles' that No 5098 herself represented the latter series. One feels that on this account the results may not have been entirely representative of the work of the '5098' class, at any rate in its early days.

The 'County' class had a new type of tender with flush sides, and of welded construction. This was shown on the diagram of the proposed 'Pacific', but strangely enough it was not supplied on the first batch of the '5098' class 'Castles'. These had the old type, with the traditional flared top. The new type was subsequently used on the later batches of these engines, from No 7008 onwards, from 1948. Like the 'Counties' the new 'Castles' were fully lined out in the old style, and the use once again of the coat of arms with the letters GW on either side was a much pleasanter tender decoration than the totem used in the later 1930s.

While the construction of the first engines of the '5098' class did not actually take place in wartime the change in design from the '5013' series was certainly the result of wartime experience, and the next

Tender cross-section

event in 'Castle' history also arose out of wartime and post-war austerity. It is difficult at this distance in time to appreciate the full severity of the coal situation as it came to affect all British railways in the years from 1944 onwards. It was particularly acute on the Great Western, which in pre-war years had been distinctly 'choosey' on the grades of coal purchased for locomotive purposes. Even in pre-war

The Hawksworth straight-sided tender

48

The new-style tender attached to engine No 7033 'Hartlebury Castle'

years, however, it had not been plain sailing and the famous dispute with the South Wales coal owners over the price of coal had led to the threat to electrify the entire system *west of Taunton*. In the years of austerity following the second world war the management had to stomach the extraordinary situation of seeing much of the best Welsh coal earmarked by Government decree 'for export only' while Great Western engines, in South Wales above all places, struggled to make steam on dross imported from the USA!

The notable experiment in oil-firing eventuated from this situation. There was irony in its first application, to heavy mineral 2—8—0 engines of the '28XX' class working in South Wales, but the later extension of the scheme to include 4—6—0s

of the 'Hall' and 'Castle' classes savoured less of defiant propaganda, and had the making of a semi-permanent change in fuel provisioning. The management surveyed areas where coal was most expensive, through having to be conveyed over the longest mileage, and the thought developed of making Cornwall an all-oil-fired area. The workings were then entirely self-contained, and although many engines at Laira shed, Plymouth, worked both east and west of the Tamar it would not have been difficult to rearrange matters. The arrangement of the firebox is shown in the accompanying drawing. The burner, mounted at foundation ring level in a small chamber in the front of the firebox, was of the type in which oil flowed over a weir on to a ribbon of steam by which it was caught up,

Engine No 5091 'Cleeve Abbey', oil-fired, with small tender

49

Layout of firebox : oil-fired locomotives

atomised and projected towards the back of the firebox at an inclination to the horizontal. The chamber carrying the burner had a small bottom damper door which could be preset to a suitable opening.

The floors of the firebox consisted of a steel plate in which were cut six rectangular holes giving a total air inlet of $2\frac{1}{4}$ sq ft. The normal type of ashpan was modified to provide a suitable firepan; the original damper gear was retained. The air supply to the firebox through the orifices in the floor was controlled by opening or closing the damper doors in the firepan. Firebricks with a high alumina content were used to line the floor and the lower part

Cab layout on oil-fired 'Castle' class locomotives

of the firebox. The firehole door was redesigned to form a reasonably effective seal, and although easily opened was effectively locked when in the shut position. A peep-hole with cover was also provided.

Five engines of the 'Castle' class were so equipped, namely 100A1, 5039, 5079, 5083 and 5091. The first two mentioned were stationed at Old Oak Common, while 5083 and 5091 were at Bristol. All these four engines were kept close to headquarters for observation purposes, while 5079 *Lysander* returned to her home shed, Laira, to become—as one senior locomotive inspector put it—the 'flagship' of

the Cornish oil-fired fleet. I had some good runs with 5039 and 5091, and a dreadful one behind 100A1, which judging by the amount of black smoke emitted suggested either she was in dire trouble, or the crew were not familiar with oil firing. *Lysander* was a superb engine. I rode her in both directions between Plymouth and Penzance on the Cornish Riviera Express, and she gave me some excellent runs. Her steaming was rock-steady, and several times when pounding hard up the 1 in 60 gradients the firemen remarked that one just could not knock the needle off the red line indicating full

Engine No 5083 'Bath Abbey', oil-fired, with 4,000-gallon tender

boiler pressure.

The Great Western oil-firing project, which was conceived as a conversion scheme on a limited scale, not a general changeover from coal to oil firing, was noted by the Ministry of Fuel and Power; and in the midst of their own appalling difficulties over coal supply the Great Western scheme was hailed as an inspiration, and conversion on a national scale, and at huge expense, was initiated. Official hand-outs were issued detailing long lists of locomotives to be converted; millions of pounds of public money were spent in providing oil-fuelling plants. The propaganda was so loud and so widespread that at last another government department got to hear about it, and pointed out that we had insufficient foreign exchange to buy the necessary oil. The railways were nationalised by then, and the limited, logical and essentially practical Great Western development was terminated in the general debacle.

Before closing this chapter reference must be made to the details of wartime runs over the West to North route mentioned earlier. In general the 'Castles', with Walschaerts valve gear, did not show

up so well on the heavy banks as the 'Saints', which had monopolised this route for so long. Churchward's setting of the Stephenson link motion, with negative lead in full gear, gave a splendid distribution of steam when slogging hard at 30 mph on a 1 in 100 bank, and with one exception I have never noted 'Castle' hill-climbing to equal, let alone to surpass, the best achieved with the 'Saints'. Hill-climbing became of greater importance than ever during the war years, because for a long period speeds were limited to a maximum of 60 mph and any time lost uphill could not be regained by fast

GWR: PONTYPOOL ROAD—SHREWSBURY						
Run No		1		2		3
Engine No		5032		5086		5032
Engine Name		*Usk*		*Viscount*		*Usk*
		Castle		*Horne*		*Castle*
Load, tons E/F		416/450		392/420		411/460
Dist miles		Actual		Actual		Actual
		m	s	m	s	m	s
0·0 PONTYPOOL ROAD				0	00	0	00
				pws			
1·6 Little Mill Jc				4	50	3	05
6·8 Penpergwm				12	30	9	08
9·5 Abergavenny				15	27	13	04
10·5 ABERGAVENNY JC				16	45	14	48
13·5 Llanvihangel				23	07	22	56
21·0 Pontrilas				30	15	30	45
26·8 Tram Inn				36	09	36	35
				sigs			
33·5 HEREFORD		0	00	48	25	46	50
4·2 Moreton-on-Lugg		7	35	7	50	8	12
7·5 Dinmore		11	25	11	37	12	14
10·2 Ford Bridge		14	55	14	45	16	10
12·6 LEOMINSTER		17	20	17	05	18	35
18·9 Woofferton		23	40	23	48	26	17
23·5 LUDLOW		28	50	28	42	31	45
28·1 Onibury		34	10	33	57	37	24
31·1 CRAVEN ARMS		38	05	37	47	41	27
38·2 CHURCH STRETTON		49	45	47	54	52	35
41·7 Leebotwood		53	35	51	36	56	30
46·7 Condover		58	15	55	35	61	00
				sig stop		sigs	
51·0 SHREWSBURY		63	40	64	55	68	40
Net times		63¾		41¼ + 61		46¾ + 66½

Engine No 5079 'Lysander', oil-fired, at Truro

running down the banks. I had several runs on the 7.30 pm 'Mail' out of Bristol, and one that remains particularly in my memory took place in the early autumn of 1940, when the Battle of Britain was at its height, and from Pontypool Road onwards we were running through a continuous 'Alert'. *Usk Castle* was the engine, and we got a remarkably clear road from Pontypool Road right through to Shrewsbury, where the 'Alert' was still on. In the blackout I was not able to log in detail until after Hereford, but from the accompanying table it will be seen that with a 450-ton train we were able to cover the 51 miles to Shrewsbury in 63¾ min. We certainly exceeded the temporary speed limit on the descent from Church Stretton, by momentarily touching 71 mph.

Later in the war, when the speed limit had been raised to 75 mph, I had an excellent run on this same train with engine No 5086 *Viscount Horne*. This was the rebuild of a 'Star' that had given me some grand runs in pre-war years, No 4066 *Malvern Abbey*. Despite a permanent way check at Little Mill Junction, which handicapped the start, this 420-ton load was taken up the Llanvihangel bank with no lower speed than 26 mph on the 1 in 82, recovering to 28 mph on the 1 in 95 that leads to the summit. Even so, this falls behind a 'Saint' performance that I shall always remember, when No 2949 hauling 450 tons made speeds of 29 and 31 mph on these two stretches. As will be seen from the table, *Viscount Horne* was taken briskly down to Hereford and made a net gain of 8¾ min on the easy schedule then in force. Onwards to Shrewsbury, this engine did not show any great superiority over the work of *Usk Castle*, in air raid conditions, until Craven Arms was passed, and then there came a really fine culminating pull up to Church Stretton, with a minimum speed of 37 mph, against 27 mph by *Usk Castle*. Furthermore, we had a moment of real old-time running down to Shrewsbury, with a top speed of 82 mph near Condover. Other runs in this same period, with 5014 *Goodrich Castle*, 5077 *Fairey Battle* and 5060 *Earl of Berkeley*, all showed good work.

In the autumn of 1944 I had an engine pass for the 9.45 am from Newton Abbot to Shrewsbury, a duty worked on alternate days by Newton and Salop sheds, and usually provided with engines that were

Austerity fuel! Saturdays only Wolverhampton - Paignton express at Langley Crossing, Chippenham : engine No 5055 'Earl of Eldon'

High-speed ATC test run, 12 October 1947 : engine No 5056 'Earl of Powis'
at 86 mph near Twyford

in first-class condition. I travelled on a Salop day, and once again we had *Usk Castle*, in positively regal condition. True, she was painted in unlined green, but the basic metalwork of her chimney cap and safety-valve cover had been bared, and not polished, but *burnished*. From the viewpoint of locomotive performance it was unfortunate that we had a heavy relief train just ahead, and suffered many signal checks until we were clear of the Newport area. Between Pontypool Road and Shrewsbury the conditions were somewhat different from those obtaining on the companion runs tabulated, in that this engine had worked through from Newton Abbot, and the others had come on fresh at Bristol. Thus although we were running well behind time the engine was not unduly pressed.

In view of my earlier remarks about 'Castle' performance on steep inclines, *Usk Castle* was worked in 35 per cent cut-off and full regulator from Abergavenny and yet fell to 20·5 mph on the worst part of the bank, and recovered only to 24 mph on the 1 in 95. Between Hereford and Church Stretton *Usk Castle* was working in 17 per cent with practically full regulator, and it was only when we had passed the junction with the one-time Bishops Castle line that cut-off was advanced to 25 per cent. Minimum speed at Church Stretton was 33·5 mph and maximum afterwards 76 mph.

In the up direction I had two runs with No 5072,

on the noon service from Shrewsbury, also a double-home turn. In between the two runs the engine had been renamed. In 1940 she was *Compton Castle*, and when I was on the footplate in 1944, *Hurricane*. Both runs included some good hill-climbing, and after I sent details of the second run to Swindon I learned some years later the excellence of the work caused such a surprise that a small team of engineers from the experimental section was sent to Shrewsbury to check the performance of this train and make sure I had not over-assessed the merit of the hill-climbing. Actually the 1944 run when I was on the footplate was not nearly as good as that of 1940, when No 5072 did not fall below 32 mph on the ascent to Church Stretton, against 27-8 mph, with cut-offs of 34 to 37 per cent when I was on the footplate. It was the same ascending from Hereford to Llanvihangel, with speeds at the summit of 34 and 30 mph, and most significant of all, 34 mph on that most trying 1 in 100 through Cattybrook tunnel to Patchway, against 28 mph, working in 32 per cent cut-off, on the 1944 run. Engine No 5072, as *Compton Castle*, certainly gave me some of the finest heavy-grade hill-climbing I have ever logged with a 'Castle'. The sustained speed of 34 mph maintained consistently on a successive of 1 in 100 banks involved the output of 1,350 edhp and probably needed the use of a cut-off of at least 40 per cent. This was grand for the year 1940.

CHAPTER 5

TESTING: OLD AND NEW METHODS

THE longevity of any particular locomotive class, or group of classes, is usually attributable to a variety of factors quite apart from its inherent qualities of design. In the case of the 'Castles' and 'Kings' the maintenance of those engines as first-class power units up to the final demise of steam traction on the Western Region was to a very large extent due to the energy, enthusiasm and engineering skill of one man who kept the flag of the GWR flying; yet he did so with such discretion and *bonhomie*, to back his precepts, as to carry the chief officers of the nationalised British Railways with him for much of the time. I refer, of course, to Sam Ell, who in 1947 was in charge of the experimental section of the locomotive drawing office. An extended reference to testing methods may seem a little beside the point in a history of a family of locomotive classes; but while Ell's work may not have prolonged the life of the 'Castles' and 'Kings' it most certainly kept them in top form to the very end, and effectively blocked any attempt there might have been to supersede them by alien types on the most important duties. Their eventual fall to the diesels was the result of politics, not engineering.

In the 1930s a great deal of very important spade work, little known outside Swindon, had been done towards making the process of locomotive testing more scientific. C. T. Roberts, who later became Chief Mechanical and Electrical Engineer of Scottish Region was, in dynamometer-car testing, feeling his way towards the principle of testing at constant rates of evaporation, while A. J. W. Dymond was charged with the task of modernising the stationary testing plant in Swindon Works. This latter project was an example of what one of his assistants once called the 'diabolical cunning' of C. B. Collett. Sir Nigel Gresley was a most persistent advocate of a national locomotive testing station, on the same lines as the celebrated French plant at Vitry-sur-Seine. He got the support of Stanier in this, and when the question arose of securing some agreement for sharing expenses a suggestion was made that the Great Western might join in. The old Churchward plant, as Stanier knew it, was capable of absorbing no more than about 500 hp. Although he took little or no part in inter-railway discussions, Collett took care to keep himself very well informed, and when an official approach was made to the Great Western to participate in the project for a national testing station Gresley and Stanier were invited to come, or send representatives, to Swindon, and to their astonishment saw the plant completely modernised, and absorbing the all-out effort of a 'Saint' class engine No 2931 *Arlington Court,* at 70 mph! Obviously Swindon had no need to participate in the new project!

However it may have been attained Ell had, in 1947, a first-class tool at his disposal, while the pre-war work of C. T. Roberts with the dynamometer car needed not a great deal more than some finishing touches to form the basis of all postwar road testing on the Western Region. The

The 1948 Interchange Trials: engine No 6018 near New Barnet

Engine No 6022 'King Edward III', with 4-row superheater. Tender is lettered 'British Railways'

corollary to Hawksworth's development of super-heating, first on the '6959' series of 'Halls' and then on the '5098' series of 'Castles' was the fitting of a four-row superheater on engine No 6022 *King Edward III*, and it was perhaps prophetic of things to come that this latter was the first engine I ever saw running on the Swindon stationary plant. That was in the summer of 1947, and at the beginning of the following year the Great Western, together with the other three British main-line railways, passed into national ownership, and became the Western Region. The new organisation was not three months old before the huge programme of locomotive inter-change trials was announced. Recalling the brilli-antly spectacular performances put up by Great Western engines in previous interchange trials great things were expected from the 'Kings' and 'Halls' that participated, though there was disappointment that structure gauge restrictions precluded their use on the LMS and Southern lines covered on the trials. So far as this book is concerned only the work of the 'King' class engines Nos 6001 and 6018 is

Engine No 6018 'King Henry VI' on clearance tests at Kings Cross prior to test runs to Leeds

involved.

It is very important to appreciate the background circumstances to these trials, as they affected the Western Region, before any comparison is made of the results attained with those from *Pendennis* and *Caldicot Castles* in 1925, and from *Launceston Castle* in 1926. In 1948 the Western Region management had no heart for nationalisation, a sentiment that was equally shared in the locomotive department at Swindon. There was none of the fiercely competitive spirit of some engine crews of other regions shown by the Great Western drivers in the running of any of the test trains, and superficial observers jumped to the conclusion that the 'King' class engines were past their day, and were overdue for superseding. The test trains were scheduled at the relatively slow speeds prevailing since the war. To engines in good condition they were an easy task, and the drivers of the 'King' class

engines concerned, encouraged to do no more than run their trains to time, made journeys that looked more or less of pedestrian quality. Compared with pre-war standards, and particularly with the magnificent work so consistently recorded by G. P. Antrobus on the Birmingham line, the performances were of little consequence. In the main series of interchange trials engine No 6018 was used on both the Western and on the Eastern Region lines.

Although a good deal was made of the fact that the 'King' class engine was being fired with coal having characteristics exactly the opposite of those normally used no trouble was experienced, and the official report contains this note: 'Engine steamed freely on coal having characteristics widely differing from that normally used on engines of the Western Region. Live steam injector only used, as steaming rate was usually less than the minimum supply rate of the 12 mm exhaust steam injector'. But the factor

The 1948 Interchange Trials : engine No 6018 on up Leeds express at Wakefield

PERFORMANCES OF WESTERN REGION 'KING' CLASS No 6018

Paddington—Plymouth route
DOWN: 20 and 22 April
UP: 21 and 23 April

Date	Location	Miles from Paddington	Mile post	Gradient 1 in	Speed mph	Recorded Pull tons	Recorded Dbhp	Equivalent Pull tons	Equivalent Dbhp	Cut-off per cent	Boiler pressure lb/sq in	Regulator position*
April												
20	Whiteball Tunnel	153·25	173·5	127R	26	6·7	1,082	8·1	1,253	30	235	½
20	Rattery	206·72	227	65R	31	5·0	927	7·1	1,310	30	230	1st valve 1¼
21	Hemerdon Bank	219·5	239·75	42R	15	8·95	804	12·2	1,090	50	235	¼
21	Long Sutton	128·0	128	264R	53	3·3	1,048	3·8	1,210	17	240	¼
22	Wellington Bank	149·25	169·5	170R	45	4·3	1,159	5·1	1,380	25	230	¼
22	Rattery Bank	205·75	226	90R	24	7·3	1,048	9·6	1,371	40	236	¾
23	Stoke Canon	170·25	190·5	217R	48	3·6	1,034	4·2	1,210	20	245	Just open

* 2nd valve position shown except where otherwise stated

Kings Cross—Leeds route
DOWN: 18 and 20 May
UP: 19 and 21 May

Date	Location	Miles From Kings Cross	From Leeds	Gradient 1 in	Speed mph	Recorded Pull tons	Recorded Dbhp	Equivalent Pull tons	Equivalent Dbhp	Cut-off per cent	Boiler pressure lb/sq in	Regulator position
May												
18	Wrenthorpe	177·0		91R	29·5	5·51	970	7·0	1,234	35	220	½
19	Abbots Ripton		122·3	200R	47·4	3·61	1,020	4·17	1,180	17	240	½
20	Wrenthorpe	177·0		91R	34·2	5·69	1,162	7·28	1,480	35	240	½
21	Hitchin		155·5	200R	48·3	3·65	1,053	4·20	1,212	20	235	⅝
21	Grantham		82·5	200R	36·0	4·91	1,055	5·74	1,055	25	230	⅝

RESULTS FROM MAIN SERIES OF INTERCHANGE TRIALS

	6018 DOWN: 1.30 pm Paddington—Plymouth North Road UP: 8.15 am Plymouth MB—Paddington				6018 DOWN: 1.10 pm Kings Cross—Leeds UP: 7.50 am Leeds—Kings Cross			
Engine No .								
Train and route .								
	Down	Down	Up	Up	Down	Down	Up	Up
Date .	20/4/48	22/4/48	21/4/48	23/4/48	18/5/48	20/5/48	19/5/48	21/5/48
Weight of engine (in wo) tons .	135·7	135·7	135·7	135·7	135·7	135·7	135·7	135·7
Weight of train behind drawbar tare tons . (inc dynamometer car)	Paddington 482·00 Newton Abbot 324·50	Paddington 482·00 Newton Abbot 324·50	Plym'th Mill Bay 330·15 Newton Abbot 491·80 Reading 454·80	Plym'th Mill Bay 330·15 Newton Abbot 491·80 Reading 454·80	KX 494·5 Wakefield 366·75	KX 495·0 Wakefield 367·75	Leeds 299·75 Wakefield 423·25 Doncaster 452·0 Grantham 491·0	Leeds 299·75 Wakefield 427·25 Doncaster 456·0 Grantham 492·5
Train miles (actual) .	225·1	225·1	225·8	225·8	185·7	185·7	185·8	185·8
Ton miles exc weight of engine .	103,480	103,480	104,470	104,470	90,643	90,741	86,029	86,469
„ inc weight of engine .	134,020	134,020	135,110	135,110	115,840	115,941	111,242	111,682
Time, booked running min .	287	287	287	287	236	236	241	241
„ actual running min .	282·4	288·9	287·8	282·6	238·6	238·5	235·6	232·5
„ overall (inc stops) .	322·0	323·0	330·1	326·5	262·5	255·4	265·0	264·4
Speed mph average .	47·8	46·8	47·1	48·0	46·7	46·7	47·3	47·9
Work done hp hours .	2,820	3,220	2,897	2,841	2,773	2,921	2,321	2,338
Hp min/ton mile (train) .	1·635	1·867	1·664	1·632	1·834	1·932	1·619	1·622
Coal, total wt lb .	10,730	11,730	10,602	10,966	9,630	10,023	7,451	7,996
„ lb/mile .	47·66	52·11	46·96	48·56	51·85	53·93	40·12	43·01
„ lb/ton mile (exc engine) .	0·104	0·113	0·102	0·105	0·106	0·110	0·087	0·092
„ lb/ton mile (inc engine) .	0·080	0·088	0·078	0·081	0·083	0·086	0·067	0·072
„ lb/dbhp hour .	3·81	3·64	3·66	3·86	3·48	3·43	3·21	3·42
„ lb/sq ft grate/hr running time)	66·5	71·0	64·5	67·9	70·6	73·4	55·4	60·2
Water, total gallons .	8,145	8,510	7,910	8,029	7,985	8,285	6,989	7,389
„ gallons/mile .	36·2	37·8	35·0	35·6	43·0	44·6	37·6	39·8
„ lb/ton mile (inc engine) .	0·608	0·635	0·586	0·594	0·689	0·715	0·628	0·662
„ lb/dhp/hour .	28·87	26·42	27·30	28·26	28·82	28·35	30·12	31·61
„ lb water/lb coal (actual) .	7·59	7·25	7·46	7·32	8·29	8·27	9·38	9·24
Gross calorific value of coal (as rec'd)	13,810	13,570	13,430	13,520	13,769	13,816	13,833	13,793
Btus/dhp hour .	52,600	49,400	49,200	52,200	47,800	47,400	44,400	47,200
Train miles under power .	192·9	193·1	195·6	196·1	157·2	161·5	162·4	162·4
Time under power, min .	238·0	247·7	247·0	243·8	200·6	205·3	200·8	197·1
No of signal and temporary pw checks	5	6	9	8	11	8	8	4
No of unbooked stops .			1		1			1
Average dhp (under power) .	711	780	704	699	830	854	693	712
Average db pull, tons (under power) .	2·45	2·79	2·48	2·43	2·95	3·03	2·39	2·41
Coal, lb/hour (running time) .	2,280	2,436	2,211	2,329	2,422	2,521	1,898	2,063
„ lb/hour (under power) .	2,705	2,842	2,575	2,699	2,878	2,928	2,227	2,431
„ lb/sq ft grate/hr (under power) .	78·9	82·9	75·1	78·7	83·9	85·4	64·9	70·9
Water, lb/hour (running time) .	17,310	17,670	16,490	17,050	20,080	20,850	17,800	19,060
„ lb/hour (under power) .	20,530	20,620	19,220	19,760	23,880	24,210	20,910	22,480
General weather conditions .	Fine and dry	Fine and dry	Stormy to fine	Fine and dry	Fine. Dry rail	Fine. Dry rail	Dull. Dry rail	Fine. Dry rail
Wind .	Westerly. Light air	Southerly. Fresh breeze	Easterly. Slight breeze	South Westerly. Slight breez	Easterly. Fair to strong	Easterly. Fair to fresh	Variable. Very light.	Northerly. Light

that contributed as much as anything to the difference in performance between Great Western engines of pre-war years and No 6018 in the interchange trials was the greatly reduced demands on the boiler. The 1.30 pm down from Paddington, for example, was allowed 45 min start-to-stop to Reading, and then 70 min for the ensuing 59·6 miles on to Westbury; while the 8.30 am up from Plymouth was allowed 113 min non-stop from Westbury to Paddington. Then there were start-to-stop runs of 53 min down and 55 min up over the 47·1 miles between Westbury and Taunton. If one compares

59

these with the times made on an 'ordinary' run of pre-war days, as exemplified by the log of No 6000 on the Cornish Riviera Express on p 139 of Part I, the astonishing disparity will be more than obvious! In addition to this there were numerous out-of-course checks, which interrupted the continuity of the steaming, and this affected the overall efficiency of the performance.

So much was made at the time of the difficulties under which Western Region locomotives were labouring through having to use unfamiliar coal that a second series of trials was run in November 1948 on which another 'King' class engine, No 6001, was fired with Welsh coal. Allowing for the difference in calorific value of the coals used, No 6001 showed a reduction of 6·4 per cent over No 6018 in coal consumption per dhp hr, though anyone familiar with locomotive running conditions would appreciate that such a difference, obtained in the course of runs on service trains, and trains moreover making such a modest demand on locomotive capacity, could easily arise from the difference between individual locomotives, or the driving techniques of the crews concerned, and have nothing whatever to

do with the nature of the fuel. As other observers pointed out, hard Yorkshire coal did not prevent *Pendennis Castle* from making some brilliant running in the interchange trials of 1925 on the LNER. In 1948 engine No 6018 put up some immaculate, if unspectacular, performances between Kings Cross and Leeds, and her basic coal consumption was actually better there than on her home ground between Paddington and Plymouth. Her best figure, of 3·21 lb per dhp hr on the 7.50 am up from Leeds on 19 May 1948 compares strikingly with the worst Plymouth figure, of 3·86 lb per dhp hr on the 8.30 am up on 23 April 1948. Between the two there is a 20 per cent difference, with the same engine, the same crew, and the same grade of fuel! Nevertheless the detailed reports of the interchange trials provide an interesting record of 'King' performance and they are set out in the accompanying tables. These include results from a contemporary series of tests run with the high-superheat 'King' No 6022.

In subsequent discussions with S. O. Ell, I remember how he emphasised the 'hit and miss' nature of testing on service trains without any scientific control of working on the footplate. In

Dynamometer-car test run, 19 May 1948 : No 6018 on up Leeds express leaving Hadley Wood Tunnel

RESULTS FROM TESTS WITH WELSH COAL

	'King' (low superheat) 6001 DOWN: 1.30 pm Paddington—Plymouth North Road UP: 8.15 am Plymouth MB—Paddington				'King' (high superheat) 6022 DOWN: 1.30 pm Paddington—Plymouth North Road UP: 8.15 am Plymouth MB—Paddington			
	Down	Down	Up	Up	Down	Down*	Up	Up
Date	23/11/48	25/11/48	24/11/48	26/11/48	14/12/48	16/12/48	15/12/48	17/12/48
Weight of engine (in wo) tons	135·7	135·7	135·7	135·7	135·7	135·7	135·7	135·7
Weight of train behind drawbar	Paddington 480·6 Newton Abbot 326·2	Paddington 480·6 Newton Abbot 326·2	Plymouth 329·9 Newton Abbot 485·05 Reading 452·25	Plymouth 332·25 Newton Abbot 487·4 Reading 452·25	Paddington 481·0 Newton Abbot 322·5	Paddington 445·8 Exeter 290·6	Plymouth Mill Bay 325·0 Newton Abbot 478·4 Reading 443·3	Plymouth Mill Bay 326·6 Newton Abbot 480·0 Reading 413·0
tare tons								
(inc dynamometer car)								
	(Tare)	(Tare)	(Tare)	(Tare)	(Tare)	(Tare)	(Tare)	(Tare)
Train miles (actual)	225·1	225·1	225·8	225·8	225·1	225·1	225·8	225·8
Ton miles exc weight of engine	103,270	103,270	103,320	103,760	103,230	92,280	101,770	100,990
„ inc weight of engine	133,810	133,810	133,950	134,390	133,770	122,830	132,410	131,630
Time, booked running min	287	287	288	288	287·0	259·0	288	288
„ actual running min	305·0	305·6	289·4	289	304·1	278·7	294·4	302·4
„ overall (inc stops)	334·2	337·5	326·4	329·5	340·0	293·2	332·0	350·6
Speed mph average	44·3	44·2	46·8	46·9	44·4	48·4	46·0	44·8
Work done hp hours	2,891	2,762	2,870	2,935	3,245	2,902	2,800	2,959
HP min/ton mile (train)	1·680	1·604	1·666	1·697	1·886	1·887	1·651	1·758
Coal, total wt lb	10,030	10,002	10,046	10,354	10,266	10,254	9,214	10,224
Net coal (gross less train heating)	9,426	9,402	9,502	9,795	9,718	9,765	8,620	9,559
„ lb/mile	41·88	41·77	42·08	43·38	43·17	43·37	38·18	42·34
„ lb/ton mile (exc engine)	0·091	0·091	0·092	0·094	0·094	0·106	0·085	0·095
„ lb/ton mile (inc engine)	0·070	0·070	0·071	0·073	0·073	0·080	0·065	0·073
„ lb/dhp hour	3·26	3·40	3·31	3·34	2·99	3·37	3·08	3·23
Gross coal, lb/sq ft grate/hr (running time)	57·5	57·3	60·7	62·7	59·05	64·4	54·75	59·14
Water, total gallons	9,102	9,147	9,326	9,416	9,209	9,206	8,193	8,901
Net water (gross less train heating)	8,554	8,599	8,822	8,907	8,718	8,767	7,665	8,322
„ gallons/mile	38·0	38·2	39·1	39·5	38·73	38·94	33·94	36·85
„ lb/ton mile (inc engine)	0·639	0·643	0·659	0·663	0·652	0·714	0·579	0·632
„ lb/dhp hour	29·59	31·14	30·74	30·35	26·9	30·2	27·4	28·12
„ lb water/lb coal (actual)	9·07	9·14	9·29	9·10	8·97	8·98	8·89	8·71
Gross calorific value of coal (as rec'd)	14,920	14,940	14,800	14,760	14,850	14,720	14,310	14,490
Btus/dhp hour	48,600	50,900	49,000	49,300	44,500	49,500	44,000	46,800
Train miles under power	190·7	198·3	196·0	190·4	192·5	207·8	185·4	185·8
Time under power, min	255·3	261·9	245·1	238·3	253·7	248·7	239·9	242·5
No of signal and temporary pw checks	3	4	3	5	3	3†	4	6
No of unbooked stops					1	4		2
Average dhp (under power)	680	633	703	739	767	700	700	732
Average db pull, tons (under power)	2·54	2·33	2·45	2·58	2·82	2·34	2·53	2·67
Net coal, lb/hour (running time)	1,855	1,846	1,970	2,033	1,917	2,102	1,757	1,897
„ lb/hour (under power)	2,216	2,154	2,326	2,466	2,298	2,356	2,156	2,365
Gross coal, lb/sq ft grate /hr (under power)	68·7	66·8	71·7	76·0	70·8	72·1	67·2	73·8
Net water, lb/hour (running time)	16,830	16,890	18,290	18,490	17,200	18,870	15,630	16,510
„ lb/hour (under power)	20,110	19,710	21,600	22,430	20,620	21,150	19,170	20,590
General weather conditions	Misty at start	Fine and dry	Greasy rail at start. Fine	Greasy rail at start. Fine	Stormy. Wet rail	Fine. Dry rail. Fog later	Fine. Greasy rail	Fog patches. Greasy rail
Wind	Northerly to Easterly. Light breeze	S.E. Light breeze	East. Light air—light wind	South. Light air	Southerly to Westerly. Moderate breeze	South to S.W. Light air	West. Light air—light breeze	Westerly to Northerly. Light air

* 5.30 pm train ex-Paddington   † plus continuous signal checks from Taunton to Norton Fitzwarren, and from Rattery to Wrangaton

PERFORMANCES: ENGINES 6001 AND 6022

'King' Class (low superheat) No 6001

Paddington—Plymouth route
DOWN: 23 and 25 November
UP: 24 and 26 November

Date	Location	Miles from Paddington	Mile post	Gradient 1 in	Speed mph	Recorded Pull tons	Recorded Dbhp	Equivalent Pull tons	Equivalent Dbhp	Cut-off per cent	Boiler pressure lb/sq in	Regulator position*
Nov												
23	Wellington Bank	150·75	171	90R	38	5·0	1,135	6·05	1,372	30	230	Just open
24	Hemerdon Bank	219·50	239¾	42R	14	9·4	786	12·63	1,056	55	244	1st valve full
24	Dainton Bank	198·25	218½	38R	25	6·5	973	8·83	1,318	35	250	Just open
24	Stoke Canon	168·75	189	217R	48	3·3	948	4·85	1,390	25	230	1st valve $\frac{7}{8}$
24	Silverton	166·50	186¾	219R	51	3·8	1,159	4·43	1,350	22	245	1st valve $\frac{7}{8}$
24	Bruton Bank	112·75	127	98R	48	4·0	1,148	5·08	1,457	22	240	1st valve full
24	Bruton Bank	110·75	125	140R	42	4·4	1,102	5·37	1,330	25	230	1st valve full
25	Wellington Bank	150·75	171	90R	36	4·5	967	5·39	1,160	25	230	1st valve full
26	Hemerdon Bank	219·50	239¾	42R	15	8·7	780	11·93	1,070	55	240	Just open
26	Cullompton—Tiverton S	159·75	180	155R	31	6·1	1,131	6·98	1,292	30	240	1st valve full

* 2nd valve position shown except where otherwise stated

'King' Class (high superheat) No 6022

Paddington—Plymouth route
DOWN: 14 and 16 December
UP: 15 and 17 December

Date	Location	Miles from Paddington	Mile post	Gradient 1 in	Speed mph	Recorded Pull tons	Recorded Dbhp	Equivalent Pull tons	Equivalent Dbhp	Cut-off per cent	Boiler pressure lb/sq in	Steam chest pressure lb/sq in
Dec												
14	Strap Lane	105·75	120	409R	49·9	3·45	1,030	3·89	1,160	20	236	214
14	Whiteball	152·75	173	80R	30·5	6·1	1,112	7·49	1,364	30	230	210
14	Dainton Bank	197·00	217¼	41R	33·6	5·0	1,003	7·34	1,472	35	215	185
15	Hemerdon Bank	220·25	240½	42R	20·5	7·5	921	10·42	1,281	45	232	210
15	Keinton Mandeville	120·50	120½	330F	63·5	2·75	1,042	3·18	1,206	20	240	200
15	Pewsey	76·00	76	234R	60·0	2·5	896	3·7	1,325	17	220	200
16	Aldermaston	45·00	45	480R	50·1	3·5	1,042	3·64	1,086	15	240	225
16	Clink Road Jc	99·25	113¼	151R	56·5	3·0	1,012	3·56	1,200	15	240	225
16	Whiteball	151·00	171¼	90R	42·8	4·2	1,078	4·95	1,266	22	225	203
16	Whiteball	151·75	172	86R	35·3	4·85	1,025	6·06	1,275	22	230	210
16	Whiteball Tunnel	153·25	173½	127R	29·7	5·6	995	6·84	1,213	25	225	205
17	Hemerdon Bank	219·75	240	42R	17·5	8·0	837	11·2	1,169	45	235	205
17	Dainton Bank	199·75	220	76R	46·75	3·5	978	5·06	1,440	30	240	180
17	Savernake	71·00	71	198R	56·0	2·9	968	3·59	1,197	20	230	205

The 1948 Interchange Trials : engine No 6018 'King Henry VI' on one of the preliminary runs, passing Beeston Junction with an up Leeds express

COMPARISONS WITH INTERCHANGE TRIALS
The equivalent values shown in column (3) are based on:

South Kirkby Hards, dry:	14,400 btu/lb
Blidworth Hards, dry:	13,940 btu/lb
Abergorki, dry:	15,100 btu/lb

	Interchange trials South Kirkby coal (actual) (1)	Additional tests Abergorki coal (actual) (2)	Additional tests Abergorki coal (S. Kirkby equivalent) (3)	Decrease per cent Col 3 compared with Col 1 (4)
'King' Class (low superheat)				
Lb/train mile	48·82	42·28	44·33	9·2
Lb/train ton mile	0·082	0·071	0·074	9·8
Lb/dhp/hr	3·74	3·33	3·50	6·4
Lb/sq ft grate /hr (runn'g time)	67·5	59·6	62·6	7·3
'King' Class (high superheat)				
Lb/train mile		41·23	43·23	
Lb/train ton mile		0·070	0·074	
Lb/dhp/hr		3·10	3·25	
Lb/sq ft grate /hr (runn'g time)		57·7	60·5	

marked contrast to the 'hit or miss' trials of 1948 were the fascinatingly precise results that he obtained with engine No 5098 *Clifford Castle* on the stationary test plant. It was often considered that measurement of coal consumption per dhp hr eliminated much of the variation in driving technique and effects of incidental delays, and reduced engine performance to a common yardstick by which direct comparison could be made between one locomotive and another. This was certainly not so, as clearly shown by the carefully controlled test results from

Up Worcester express near Tilehurst : engine No 5090 'Neath Abbey'

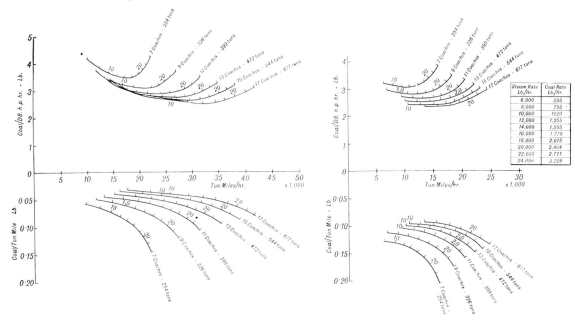

Steam Rate Lb./Hr.	Coal Rate Lb./Hr.
6,000	595
8,000	795
10,000	1,020
12,000	1,255
14,000	1,505
16,000	1,779
18,000	2,075
20,000	2,404
22,000	2,777
24,000	3,228

Performance of engine No 5098 'Clifford Castle'

one individual engine. In the graphs reproduced above the coal consumption figures are shown for running on level track and on a rising 1 in 200 gradient. From these graphs certain tables have been prepared. The first, relating to level track, shows the speed for the most economical use of fuel in a variety of loading conditions. From this table it will be seen that with a light load of 254 tons tare the most economical speed is 71 mph, whereas with a

heavy load of 472 tons it is 58·5 mph. But then notice the difference in basic coal consumption: 3·5 against 2·8 lb per dhp hr on a 1 in 200 gradient. This would be below traffic needs, and a second table shows the results with the firing rate increased to 86 lb per sq ft of grate area per hr.

Another interesting study brought out from the graphs reproduced is the coal consumption involved in the haulage of various loads at a uniform speed

Up Cheltenham express near Twyford: engine No 5057 'Earl Waldegrave'

North to West express ascending Dainton Bank : engine No 5058 'Earl of Clancarty'

of 65 mph on level track.

It is also interesting to extract the details of performance that could be expected with those same five loads when No 5098 was steamed up to her maximum rate of evaporation, namely 24,000 lb of steam per hr.

From the above it would certainly seem that on a number of celebrated pre-war occasions 'Castles' were being steamed very near to their limit, on the Cornish Riviera Express, in days before the construction of the 'Kings', and on the 'Cheltenham Flyer'.

Engine 5098: LEVEL TRACK Firing rate 57 lb per sq ft of grate area per hour			
Load behind tender (tons tare)	Speed mph	Coal per dhp hour (lb)	Coal per train mile (lb)
254	71	3·5	25
326	64·5	3·17	27·5
399	60·5	2·95	29·5
472	58·5	2·8	30·25
544	55	2·7	32·5

Engine 5098: 65 mph ON LEVEL TRACK		
Load behind tender (tons tare)	Coal per dhp hour (lb)	Coal sq ft of grate area per hour (lb)
254	3·6	49·5
326	3·2	49·5
399	3·0	56
472	2·95	67
544	2·95	77

Engine 5098: RISING 1 in 200 GRADIENT Firing rate 86 lb per sq ft of grate area per hour			
Load behind tender (tons tare)	Speed mph	Coal per dhp hour (lb)	Coal per train mile (lb)
254	60	3·6	45
326	55	3·3	49
399	50	3·15	54
472	45	3·0	60
544	40	2·85	67·5

Engine 5098: 24,000 lb of steam per hour LEVEL TRACK			
Load behind tender (tons tare)	Speed mph	Coal per dhp hour (lb)	Coal per train mile (lb)
254	86·5	4·3	37·5
326	82	3·8	39·2
399	78·75	3·5	41·8
472	73·75	3·2	45·0
544	69·5	3·1	45·0

OCEAN MAIL SPECIALS: 1949 Engine: 5098 *Clifford Castle*				
Date . . .	26/8/49		13/9/49	
Load ton tare .	303		338*	
Dist miles	Time min	Av sp mph	Time min	Av sp mph
0·0 Plymouth Dock Gates .	0		0	
0·9 North Road .	3	18·0	3	18·0
24·0 Totnes . .	36	42·0	37	40·8
32·8 Newton Abbot .	49 (pass)	40·6	49 *arr*	43·8
			52 *dep*	
52·9 Exeter . .	73	50·3	76½	49·3
83·7 Taunton . .	104	59·6	110	55·2
111·2 Castle Cary .	129	66·0	134½	67·4
131·8 *Heywood Rd Jc*	153	51·4	154½	61·8
160·0 Bedwyn . .	179	65·0	182	61·5
190·4 Reading . .	208	62·9	209½	66·4
226·4 Paddington .	243†	61·7	247½	56·9

* Bank engine No 5060 Plymouth to Newton Abbot
† Net time 239 min

Reverting to engine No 5098 there was no doubt she was a star engine at that time and these details of test performance can be supplemented by some details of her work in regular service. In 1949 she was much in demand for 'Ocean Mail' specials from Plymouth, and on 26 August 1949 she made the first post-war run from North Road to Paddington in the even four hours. There was another very fast run just over a fortnight later, with a heavier train that required an assistant engine over the South Devon line. Mr Hawksworth was kind enough to give me copies of the inspectors' reports on these two journeys, and from the accompanying table it will be seen that the times were 170 min (167 min net) from Exeter to Paddington with 303 tons tare, and 171 min with 338 tons.

Only a few days after the second of these two runs I had the opportunity of riding this same engine myself on the 9.45 am West to North express throughout from Newton Abbot to Shrewsbury. I have set out the logs in full detail, but a summary of the running gave the following interesting results.

Some examples of actual working are interesting in view of the test performances recorded in the comprehensive series of Swindon trials.

1. Stoke Canon to Sampford Peverell: average speed 56·3 mph; cut-off 24 per cent full regulator.
2. Level track, Brent Knoll: 64 mph; cut-off 19 per cent full regulator.
3. Acceleration up Filton bank, 1 in 75 from dead start at Stapleton Road: 21 mph; cut-off 45 per cent full regulator.

Plymouth - Liverpool express leaving Teignmouth : engine No 7000 'Viscount Portal'

WESTERN REGION:
9.45 am NEWTON ABBOT—BRISTOL

Load: 13 coaches, 421 tons tare, 460 tons full
Engine: 4-cyl 4—6—0 No 5098 *Clifford Castle*
Driver: Nickless; Fireman: Williams (Salop shed)

Dist miles		Sch min	Actual m s	Speed mph
0·0	NEWTON ABBOT .	0	0 00	
1·0	*Milepost 213* .		3 06	
4·8	Teignmouth Old Quay		7 55	54 (max)
5·1	Teignmouth .	8	8 50	
0·0		0	0 00	
1·3	Parsons Tunnel Box .		2 54	
2·8	Dawlish . .	6	5 39	
0·0		0	0 00	
1·7	Dawlish Warren .		3 21	43·5/48
3·7	Starcross . .		5 53	45 (slack)
7·4	Exminster . .		10 04	59 (max)
11·3	St Thomas's .		14 15	
12·2	EXETER ST DAVID'S .	18	16 15	
0·0		0	0 00	
1·3	Cowley Bridge Jc .		2 58	
3·4	Stoke Canon .		5 58	49·5
7·2	Silverton . .		10 17	56/54·5
8·4	Hele . . .		11 33	57·5
12·6	Cullompton .		15 51	60
14·8	Tiverton Jc .		18 14	55/60·5
16·6	Sampford Peverell .		20 03	59·5
18·9	*Milepost 175* .		22 37	48·5
			sigs pw	
19·9	Whiteball Box .	26	24 50	
20·9	*Milepost 173* .		27 02	28
23·7	Wellington . .		29 43	78
26·9	*Milepost 167* .		32 06	84
28·8	Norton Fitzwarren .		33 38	70·5
30·8	TAUNTON .	38	37 08	
0·0		0	0 00	
4·7	Cogload . .		6 47	55·5
			pw slack	15
10·6	*Milepost 152* .		15 38	58
11·5	BRIDGWATER .	15	17 10	
0·0		0	0 00	
2·5	Dunball . .		4 37	50
6·3	HIGHBRIDGE .	9	8 33	60·5
9·1	Brent Knoll .		11 15	63
12·5	*Milepost 139* .		14 36	64·5
13·6	Uphill Jc .	17	16 05	
15·2	WESTON-SUPER-MARE	21	19 59	
0·0		0	0 00	
2·3	Worle Jc . .	5	4 47	
7·1	YATTON . .		10 51	58 (max)
13·2	Flax Bourton .		17 42	49
				45·5
15·4	Long Ashton .		20 30	58 (max)
17·2	Parson Street .		22 48	
			sigs	
19·1	BRISTOL (TEMPLE MEADS)	26	27 45	

WESTERN REGION:
12.34 pm BRISTOL—SHREWSBURY

Load: 13 coaches, 421 tons tare, 460 tons full
Engine: 4-cyl 4—6—0 No 5098 *Cliffo.d Castle*
Driver: Nickless; Fireman: Williams (Salop shed)

Dist miles		Sch min	Actual m s	Speed mph
0·0	BRISTOL (TEMPLE MEADS)	0	0 00	
1·6	Stapleton Road .	6	5 12	
0·0		0	0 00	
0·9	Ashley Hill . .		2 53	
2·1	Horfield . .		6 43	21
3·2	Filton Jc . .	8	9 33	slack
8·0	Pilning . .		15 47	67·5/61·5
				66
14·1	Severn Tunnel West Box .	23½	22 54	
14·9	SEVERN TUNNEL JC .	26	25 11	21
20·9	Llanwern . .		33 23	57
			pw slack	10
24·0	Maindee East Jc .	38	37 53	
26·4	Caerleon . .		43 09	45
29·2	Llantarnam . .		47 28	34·5
			pw slack	10
31·0	Pontynewydd . .		53 18	26
33·4	*Milepost 32½* . .		59 32	23
33·7	PONTYPOOL ROAD	56	60 55	
0·0		0	0 00	
1·6	Little Mill Jc .		2 42	59
4·2	Nantyderry . .		5 29	51/56
6·8	Penpergwm . .		8 29	60/46
9·5	Abergavenny .	12	12 23	
13·5	Llanvihangel .	22	23 00	17·5/22
15·9	Pandy . .		25 54	74 (max)
21·0	Pontrilas . .	31	30 22	57 (min)
26·8	Tram Inn . .		36 20	63
30·1	Red Hill Jc .	41	39 52	
33·5	HEREFORD .	47	45 15	
0·0		0	0 00	
1·7	Shelwick Jc .	4½	4 30	
4·2	Moreton-on-Lugg .		7 31	55·5
				58
7·5	Dinmore . .		11 02	46 (min)
10·2	Ford Bridge .		14 14	63
			pw slack	
12·6	LEOMINSTER .	16½	18 22	15
15·8	Berrington . .		23 47	50
18·9	Woofferton .	23½	27 19	65
23·5	Ludlow . .	29	32 00	53
25·7	Bromfield . .		34 20	53·5
			sigs	40
28·1	Onibury . .		37 10	43·5
				36
31·1	CRAVEN ARMS .	38	41 33	49
34·0	*Milepost 17* .		45 29	41
35·6	Marsh Brook .		47 47	42·5
36·7	*Milepost 14½* .		49 27	38·5
			pw slack	15
38·2	CHURCH STRETTON .	49	52 40	
			sig checks	
51·0	SHREWSBURY .	71	73 52	

4. Llanvihangel bank, 1 in 95: speed 22 mph;
cut-off 38 per cent full regulator.

The above data shows both the strength and the weakness of the 'Castle' engine particularly when it came to climbing a heavy bank.

Some of the starts from the many intermediate stops showed off to remarkable effect the surefootedness of Great Western 4—6—0 locomotives; from Teignmouth, in heavy rain, we passed Parsons

Tunnel Box, 1·3 miles in 2 min 54 sec, and the working was thus:

Start	75 per cent cut-off
In 150 yd	45 „
In ½ mile	35 „
In 0·9 mile	25 „

During this start there was no suspicion of slipping. Another factor that must be taken into account in assessing this interesting performance was the extremely 'intermittent' character of the demands

---

Engine 5098: NEWTON ABBOT—SHREWSBURY

Length of journey	216·5 miles
Booked time, including stop . .	367 min
Left Newton Abbot . . .	3 min late
Arrived Shrewsbury . . .	6½ min late
Actual time including stops . .	370½ min
Booked running time . . .	312 min
Actual running time . . .	319 min
Net running time	295 min
Net average speed . . .	44 mph
Water consumption . . .	38 gall per mile
Coal consumption (estimated) . .	40-42 lb per mile
Coal per sq ft of grate area per hour of running time .	56 lb
Max estimated dhp at 61 mph .	1,450

---

upon the locomotive. From Taunton to Pontypool Road, for example, we covered only 81·1 miles in 154 min and during that time the regulator was open for only 100 min. That our average coal consumption was only 40-42 lb per mile in working a 460-ton train in these circumstances was a remarkable tribute to the efficiency of the locomotive. Of course I could quickly sense, from my footplate experience, that *Clifford Castle* was quite a 'star' engine, and her working was impeccable throughout; but even with this reservation the run, following up the test details previously recorded, is a great tribute to the latest version of the 'Castle' class. With the hydrostatic lubricator she was very free running, as instanced by the maximum speed of 84 mph down Wellington bank and the rapid acceleration from Llanvihangel summit to 74 mph before Pandy. At the same time one notes, with significance, the rather laboured ascent from Abergavenny to Llanvihangel.

The tests in which engine No 5098 was pitted against the 'standard' engine No 5087, and the first 'Castle' to be fitted with a 4-row superheater, No

Paignton - Manchester express on Teignmouth sea wall : engine No 4000 'North Star'

5.55 pm Paddington - South Wales express near Cholsey : engine No 5049
'Earl of Plymouth' with the author on the footplate

5049 *Earl of Plymouth* paved the way for the full-scale testing carried out later under the auspices of the British Railways Board. The alteration of No 5049 did not materially improve the performance. The heating surface of the superheater was increased to 393 sq ft, and the final steam temperature was raised to about 660 deg F. I was able to make a round trip from Swindon to Paddington and back on this engine, and these gave the following results:

Engine 5049: SWINDON—PADDINGTON		
Train . . .	2.11 pm up	5.55 pm down
Distance . .	77·3 miles	77·3 miles
Gradient (average) .	1 in 1,510 (falling)	1 in 1,510 (rising)
Booked time . .	89 min	87 min
Load tons tare . .	400	439
Load tons gross .	430	470
Actual time . .	86 min 42 sec	88 min 50 sec
Checks (number) .	ONE	ONE
Net time . .	$83\frac{1}{2}$ min	$86\frac{3}{4}$ min
Net average speed .	55·7 mph	53·5 mph
Maximum speed .	65 mph	62 mph
Water consumed (tender gauge) .	1,650 gall	2,300 gall
Water per train/mile .	21·3 gall	29·7 gall

It will be seen that the booked speeds of the two trains were in inverse ratio to the loads and haulage effort involved, though on the down journey in making a running average of 58 mph over the 55·7 miles from Slough to Marston East Box the cut-off

was not advanced beyond 17 per cent and the regulator was kept about 3/5ths open on the main valve. It will be noticed also how closely the speed corresponded with the most economical working rate for this weight of train as given in the table on page 65. If the performance of No 5049 can be considered similar to that of the 'King' class engine with a 4-row superheater, and an evaporation of about $8\frac{3}{4}$ lb of water per lb of coal taken as typical, the coal consumption on this round trip of mine can be taken as $24\frac{1}{2}$ lb per train mile on the 2.11 pm up, and 34 lb per mile on the 5.55 pm down. Nevertheless, the performance of No 5049 did not justify any further conversions at that time, and the engine merely remained as one of the 'star' performers at Canton (Cardiff) shed.

Arising from the methods used in carrying out the tests, and the comprehensive nature of the performance data secured and collated, their practical application was demonstrated in what was then termed 'scientific train timing', and a supplement to the report on the trials with engine No 5098 showed the results of such timing applied to non-stop running between Newport and Paddington in various conditions of loading. Bearing in mind that any 'scientifically' prepared schedules must serve day-to-day conditions, an explanation of the 'basic' and 'recovery' classes of duty must be noted. The

'5098' CLASS
TIME SCHEDULES: NEWPORT—PADDINGTON
Load: 11 cars, 363 tons tare, 400 tons full

Duty	Basic	Recovery	High
Steam rate lb/hr under power*	16,000	18,000	20,000
Coal rate lb/hr under power*	1,779	2,075	2,404

Dist miles		Time min	Time min	Time min
0·0	NEWPORT	0	0	0
9·8	Severn Tunnel Jc	13½	13	12¾
10·6	Severn Tunnel West	15	14½	14¼
20·3	Patchway	32½	31	29¾
21·4	Stoke Gifford	34½	33	31¼
33·4	Badminton	50½	47¾	45¼
50·5	Wootton Bassett	66¾	63¼	60
56·1	Swindon	73	69¼	65½
76·9	Steventon	91¾	87	82¼
80·3	D.dcot	94½	89¾	84¾
97·4	Reading	109¾	104	98½
102·4	Twyford	114½	108½	102¾
109·2	Maidenhead	120¾	114½	108½
114·9	Slough	126	119½	113¼
124·3	Southall	135	127¾	121
132·1	Westbourne Park	142¼	134¾	127¼
133·4	PADDINGTON	146¼	138½	131½

Max speed at Little Somerford	mph	77·0	81·0	83·0
Average speed Swindon-Southall	mph	66·0	70·0	73·8

* Time under power taken as 97 per cent total running time

'5098' CLASS
TIME SCHEDULES: NEWPORT—PADDINGTON
Load: 13 cars, 429 tons tare, 470 tons full

Duty	Basic	Recovery	High
Steam rate lb/hr under power*	16,000	18,000	20,000
Coal rate lb/hr under power*	1,779	2,075	2,404

Dist miles		Time min	Time min	Time min
0·0	NEWPORT	0	0	0
9·8	Severn Tunnel Jc	13¾	13½	13
10·6	Severn Tunnel West	15¼	15	14½
20·3	Patchway	34¾	33½	31½
21·4	Stoke Gifford	37	35½	33½
33·4	Badminton	54½	51¼	48¼
50·5	Wootton Bassett	71	67¼	63½
56·1	Swindon	77¾	73¾	69½
76·9	Steventon	97¼	92¼	87
80·3	Didcot	100	95	89½
97·4	Reading	116½	110¼	103¾
102·4	Twyford	121½	115	108
109·2	Maidenhead	128¼	121¼	113¼
114·9	Slough	133¼	126½	118½
124·3	Southall	143¼	135½	126¾
132·1	Westbourne Park	150¾	142¾	133½
133·4	PADDINGTON	154	146½	137¼

Max speed at Little Somerford	mph	75·0	77·0	82·5
Average speed Swindon-Southall	mph	62·5	66·2	71·4

* Time under power taken as 97 per cent total running time

*North to West express near Penpergwm:
engine No 5073 'Blenheim'*

'basic' is the rate which shows the greatest economy in working, and which is two-thirds of the practical maximum continuous steaming rate of the engine. It was then considered that all locomotives of the class which were fit for the road should have been able to recover time to the extent shown by the difference between the 'basic' and 'recovery' duty. Thus on the Newport—Paddington run a 'Castle' worked at 18,000 lb per sq in should have been able to make up roughly 8 min on the basic non-stop timing of the 146 min with a 400-ton load. Engines in good condition, working to 5/6ths of the maximum steaming capacity could make a non-stop run in 131½ min. The schedules are set out herewith, for both 400- and 470-ton trains, and it is the average speeds from Swindon that make such interesting reading. Average speeds of 73·8 mph are striking examples of the expectancy of performance in high steaming conditions, and will be referred to later in this book in connection with the accelerated services of 1954.

CHAPTER 6

NATIONALISATION UNDER WAY

MR Hawksworth remained in office at Swindon for the first two years of nationalisation, but on his retirement at the end of 1949 the organisation was completely changed, in accordance with the precepts being applied to British Railways as a whole. Instead of the one supreme head of the locomotive department the organisation was split into three, with a mechanical and electrical engineer, a carriage and wagon engineer, and a motive power superintendent. At first K. J. Cook, H. Randle and W. N. Pellow filled these offices. There had been much gratification among Great Western enthusiasts at the continuance of 'Castle' building after nationalisation; but until new standard designs were ready there was really no other course, in providing replacements for superannuated express passenger engines, unless of course British Railways had wanted really to set the heather on fire around Swindon by planting pre-grouping engines of alien design upon the Western Region. In authorising the construction of more 'Castles', and also 'Halls' and 'Manors' high authority left Swindon to its own devices to the extent of permitting the continued use of the Great Western style of numberplate on the cab side, though on the engine front the painted figures on the buffer beam were replaced by cast numberplates on the smokebox door, in the Midland and LMS style. It so happened, however, when working express trains that were carrying their reporting numbers the large

Falmouth - Paddington express passing Teignmouth : engine No 4081 'Warwick Castle'

71

Engine No 6028 'King George VI' in bright blue livery, at Bath

plates mounted on the smokebox door hid the engine number, and with its removal from the buffer beam the engines of these trains looked anonymous from the front.

There was also the vexed question of painting. Very soon after nationalisation Lord Hurcombe asked R. A. Riddles what colour he was going to paint the BR engines. As a good North Western man Riddles replied 'black'. The noble lord was horrified, and so there began the series of experiments with different colours. Some of the 'Kings', in common with engines of other regions in the '8P' power classification, were painted in Prussian blue with red lining—reminiscent of the Great Eastern; while some of the 'Castles' appeared in a pale green. This latter was set off by a lining out scheme in the LNWR style, and looked positively bilious! At first the basic idea was to have something different from anything that had gone before. Riddles tried to get his black by having one of the LMS 'Princess Royal' Pacifics magnificently turned out in the full LNWR style, but the first decision was that the '8P' engines should be in Caledonian blue, though with black underframes. On the 'Kings', retaining their polished brass safety valve covers and copper chimney tops, the famous blue

looked a thorough misfit. Sir Felix Pole, who by that time was quite blind, said he was glad to be spared of the sight of a 'King' in blue! But to the delight of all Western supporters the historic Brunswick green of the GWR was chosen for the second-line express passenger engines, though with just enough variation in the lining out for it to be said that it was *not* Great Western. After a relatively short time the 'Kings' also reverted to Brunswick green—and so did the 'Pacifics' of the other regions.

The 1948 batch of 'Castles', Nos 7008 to 7017, in addition to having the straight-sided tender, included one non-Castle name that gave great satisfaction, No 7017 *G. J. Churchward*. In a book like this I need not enlarge upon the appropriateness of such a name. Engine No 7013 *Bristol Castle* became the object of some controversy in February 1952. In that month King George VI died, and it was desired to use the engine *Windsor Castle* for the Royal funeral train. Unfortunately the historic 4082 was not at that time in a suitable condition for so important a duty, and so the name and numberplates were transferred to No 7013, together with the commemorative plaques relating to the Royal visit to Swindon in 1924 when King George V drove the engine from the works to the station. It

Engine No 7011 'Banbury Castle' in experimental pale green livery

Up South Wales express near Llanharan : engine No 5027 'Farleigh Castle'

was, of course, immediately noticed that the engine hauling the funeral train of King George VI was not the real 4082, but an engine belonging to the '7000' series, and the management of the Western Region had some awkward moments explaining what they had done! To them, no doubt, one 'Castle' was as good as another; but it needed no more than a schoolboy spotter, let alone an adult locomotive enthusiast to note the deception. The name and number remained on the real 7013 until that engine was withdrawn in February 1965, but the commemorative plaques were removed a little time after the special Royal Train working. The real 4082, as 7013, survived almost as long, and was not with-

Engine No 7017 'G. J. Churchward' showing the earlier WR tender style

*The last 'Castle' built, No 7037, prior to the naming ceremony on 15 November 1950
by HM the Queen, when Princess Elizabeth*

drawn until September 1964, after a life of forty years.

The 1949 batch, 7018 to 7027, all had true 'Castle' names, and all retained their bestowed names during their comparatively short lives. The last lot, 7028 to 7037, came out in May-August 1950, and the last one of all was the subject of a special naming ceremony on 15 November 1950. Until that day the engine ran without a name. On that day Queen Elizabeth II, when Princess Elizabeth, paid a visit to Swindon Works on the occasion of the golden jubilee of the borough of Swindon, and Her Royal Highness not only performed the naming ceremony of engine No 7037 *Swindon*, but also followed the precedent set by her grandfather,

in 1924, by driving a locomotive from the works to the station. This latter engine was appropriately No 4057 *Princess Elizabeth*. 'Stars' were getting a little scarce by that time, but with the exception of No 4051 all the 'Princesses' were still running. At the time it was thought that No 4057 would probably be among the last to go, though in actual fact it was her last overhaul and she was withdrawn in February 1952.

Mention of No 4057 brings me back to the 'Stars' in general, and the story of their last twenty-odd years must now be recorded. Although the changes were no more than superficial their appearance altered considerably. Many engines of the class acquired 4,000-gallon high-sided tenders. In 1936

Engine No 7037

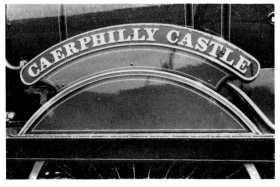

Engine No 4073

for a short time the old eight-wheeled bogie tender built for *The Great Bear* ran attached first to No 4045 and then to No 4022, while shortly after World War II No 4043 had the experimental eight-wheeled Collett tender which had been built in 1931. Then there was a change in chimneys. The chimney originally put on to the 'Grange' class was also used on 'Stars' from 1939 onwards. This was 1 ft 9 in high, as compared with the true 'Star' chimney which was 1 ft 11¾ in. The 'Grange' chimney looked much better in combination with the shorter variety of safety-valve cover which was coming into general use; but what with shorter chimneys, outside steam pipes and 4,000-gallon tenders, the 'Stars' began to look like 'Castles'. The distinguishing feature remaining was, of course, the cab.

During the war the 'Stars' were painted plain black, while the original 'King' series, renamed 'Monarchs' in 1927, were the victims of the changing pattern of the war itself. In 1940 seven of the original ten engines remained, and they bore names as follows:

4021	*British Monarch*	
4022	*Belgian Monarch*	(5/40)
4023	*Danish Monarch*	(11/40)
4025	*Italian Monarch*	(6/40)
4026	*Japanese Monarch*	(1/41)
4028	*Roumanian Monarch*	(11/40)
4030	*Swedish Monarch*	(11/40)

The figures in brackets indicate when these names were removed, and from these dates one can identify events connected with the war. Eventually only No 4021 retained a name. The others spent their last ten to twelve years nameless, with the legend 'Star Class' painted in small letters on their central splasher. After the war the remaining 'Stars' were eventually repainted in the lined green used on the 'Castles', 'Counties', and later on the 'Halls' as well.

Engine No 7007

A total of forty-seven 'Stars' remained to enter national ownership in January 1948, though eight engines of the class were withdrawn sufficiently early after that date as not to receive smokebox numberplates. Engine No 4004 *Morning Star* was the only one to be withdrawn in 1948, only the second of the class since September 1940, when No 4067 *Tintern Abbey* had been converted to 'Castle' class and renumbered 5087. The only post-war withdrawal in Great Western days was No 4014 *Knight of the Bath* in 1946. Three more, all 'Knights', were all that the year 1949 claimed; but more general withdrawal began in 1950, with seven scrapped in that year, and sixteen in 1951.

In 1950 the allocation of the class was:

Bristol (Bath Road)	9
Gloucester	1
Laira (Plymouth)	1
Landore (Swansea)	5
Oxford	1
Shrewsbury	5
Stafford Road (Wolverhampton)	6
Swindon	6
Westbury	3

By that time 'Stars' were rarely to be seen on first-

The last 'Castle' built: No 7037 'Swindon', carrying the arms of the borough

Engine No 4042 'Prince Albert' as running with 'elbow' steampipes in 1949

class express work, though in the immediate post-war period, before there were many of the new 'Castles' at work, certain engines which were in first-class condition were put on to some important turns. A case in point was the Stafford Road engine No 4031 *Queen Mary*, which for several weeks in 1946 worked the Wolverhampton-Penzance express, when it was restored after the war, as between Wolverhampton and Newton Abbot. The engine worked through, but was re-manned in each direction at Bristol. The Bath Road engines were perhaps the exception to the general rule, and in those post-war years were frequently on the London expresses. In the autumn of 1949 I made the round trip from Bristol to Paddington and back on the footplate of No 4042 *Prince Albert* with the impressive results to be described later; but in those years of austerity one of the finest and most unexpected of all my journeys with 'Stars' came one Friday evening in the summer of 1947 when I was

bound for Cardiff and joined the 5.55 pm from Paddington at Swindon. This was usually a 'Castle' turn, worked moreover by engines in the immaculate condition then characteristic of the Canton top-link; but on this occasion an enormous train of fourteen coaches, absolutely packed and weighing at least 510 tons behind the tender, arrived from Paddington behind No 4030 looking very shabby and dilapidated.

I feared the worst, although the train arrived very little behind time; and then the driver proceeded to coax a marvellous performance out of this old 'crab'. The 5·6 miles to Wootton Bassett, where speed was reduced for the junction, took 9 min 37 sec, and then, after touching 67 mph at Little Somerford, the $8\frac{1}{2}$ miles of continuous 1 in 300 to Badminton were climbed at a minimum speed of 48 mph before the stop. Over the last four miles speed averaged 52, 50·5, 49·5 and 49 mph respectively. The 22·7 miles from Swindon took 28 min 45

9 am Bristol - Paddington express : engine No 4091 'Dudley Castle'

Liverpool - Plymouth express near Dawlish : engine No 5078 'Beaufort'

76

The up 'Dutchman', 8.30 am Plymouth to Paddington, passing Teignmouth:
engine No 6024 'King Edward I'

sec. Speed rose to 67 mph again down the descent from Badminton, but with such a load the driver was not risking an unassisted climb out of the Severn Tunnel and we stopped at Pilning Junction to take a bank engine. The run finished with a smart spurt on the level from Newton to Cardiff, 11·7 miles in 16¼ min start-to-stop. The edhp on the Badminton ascent was about 1,100—very good indeed for an obviously run-down 'Star'.

Reverting to the gradual demise of the class, by the end of 1951 there were no engines of the 'Star' and 'Knight' series left in traffic, though fortunately No 4003 *Lode Star* had by that time been scheduled for preservation. The year 1952 saw another twelve of them withdrawn, and by the end of 1954 there were only three left: the two unrebuilt 'Abbeys' 4061 *Glastonbury Abbey* and 4062 *Malmesbury Abbey*, and No 4056 *Princess Margaret*. These three engines led a remarkably active life in their

last year, and in the following chapter there are details of some splendid runs I was able to make on their footplates. *Princess Margaret* in particular was a great favourite among the enginemen at Bath Road; in fact one driver once remarked to me: 'She's the best "Castle" we've got!' She was so good that I tried to persuade High Authority to put her on the up 'Bristolian', but it would not be risked. Eventually, as the last working 'Star', she was withdrawn in October 1957, and with her ended one of the greatest locomotive sagas in history. She was not the longest lived of them all, despite her 43 years and 3 months; *Lode Star* and *Rising Star*, each with 44 years 5 months held the record, while *Knight of the Grand Cross* and the original 'Kings' *Edward* and *George* each just topped 43 years. Engine No 4021, the first of the two last mentioned, held the record for mileage covered, 2,035,000, a notable achievement.

CHAPTER 7

LAST WORK OF THE 'STARS'

In the years 1949 to 1956 I had eight unforgettable footplate runs, and although the engines concerned were allocated to enable me to study their workings no special preparations were otherwise made. The engines were working in the links concerned; it was just that the locomotive authorities were kind enough to see that they were on the jobs selected on the days I had my footplate passes. In this way I rode *Prince Albert* on the 9 am Bristol to Paddington, returning with the 1.15 pm; *Princess Charlotte* on the 7.15 am Plymouth to Paddington; *Malmesbury Abbey* on the up 'Merchant Venturer', returning with the down West of England 'Postal' special; and finally *Princess Margaret* on various turns from Bristol, to Paddington and to Newton Abbot.

It was as long ago as 1949 that I imagined I was making my last footplate journey on a 'Star' engine. No 4042 *Prince Albert* was then newly out-shopped from Swindon, and allocated to Bath Road shed, Bristol, she was doing some fine work. It was arranged for me to ride her on the morning round trip from Bristol to Paddington and back. The return working on the 1.15 pm down was then quite a hard turn with a train of 350 to 400 tons, and allowed 114 min for the 106·9 miles non-stop from Paddington to Bath. It was this latter run that provided the principal source of interest, because the up run, though also made non-stop from Bath, was allowed 5 min more. The engine was as near-perfect as one could expect a steam locomotive to be, and

Last duties : engine No 4038 'Queen Berengaria' on Westbury - Swindon stopping train near Chippenham

on the eastbound run we made the journey in 118 min 26 sec with a load of 430 tons. This included a bad signal delay at Reading, and the net average speed was 57 mph. Details of the down journey are set out in the accompanying table, and although a load of ten coaches weighing 365 tons gross behind the tender would not be considered a heavy load for a 'Star', in the circumstances that developed it was substantial enough.

We got a bad start out of Paddington, with signals causing a slowing to 10 mph at Old Oak East, and a permanent way check at West Drayton. From there onwards, however, we got an absolutely clear road to Bathampton. As will be seen from the log the combined effect of the two initial checks was to put us 5 min late through Slough. Just beyond that station the driver used 18 per cent cut-off for a while, with full regulator; but this did not give the speed required and a mile beyond Maidenhead he advanced to 20 per cent. From this change the controls remained completely unchanged for 50 miles. I cannot recollect ever having seen running conditions on a steam locomotive remain constant for so long. The boiler pressure was maintained between 210 and 225 lb per sq in, though I must add these were the extremes; the more usual variation was between 215 and 220 lb per sq in. This steady and excellent working was gradually regaining lost time, and we passed Swindon only 1 min late.

Then the steaming was eased. Cut-off was reduced to 15 per cent just after Swindon, and at Hay Lane, adjacent to the 80th milepost and the summit of the line, the driver changed over to the first valve of the regulator. This gave us a splendid concluding spurt, with a top speed of 92 mph at Dauntsey. The finish was hindered by signal checks, though we were able to stop in Bath just short of the public arrival time of 3.10 pm. The net time,

Engine No 4062 'Malmesbury Abbey', with straight-sided tender temporarily attached

WESTERN REGION: 1.15 pm PADDINGTON—BRISTOL

Load: 10 coaches, 340 tons tare, 365 tons full
Engine: 4-cyl 4—6—0 No 4042 *Prince Albert*
Driver: Clark; Fireman: Bishop (Bristol Bath Road shed)

Dist miles		Sch min	Actual m s	Speed mph
0·0	PADDINGTON	0	0 00	
1·3	Westbourne Park		3 10	
			sigs	10
5·7	Ealing Broadway		10 37	50
9·1	Southall	12½	14 27	54·5
10·9	Hayes		16 28	57·5
			pw slack	
13·2	West Drayton		20 20	10
16·2	Langley		24 25	55
18·5	SLOUGH	22	27 07	59
21·0	Burnham (Bucks)		29 36	61
24·2	Maidenhead	28	32 55	58·5
31·0	Twyford	35	39 45	62
36·0	READING	40	44 27	66
38·7	Tilehurst		46 53	65
44·8	Goring		52 32	64·5
48·5	Cholsey		55 57	66
53·1	DIDCOT	58	60 13	66
56·5	Steventon	61½	63 25	63
60·4	Wantage Road		67 09	62
66·5	Uffington		73 13	60
71·6	Shrivenham		78 17	61·5
77·3	SWINDON	83	83 56	62
82·9	Wootton Bassett		89 10	68
85·3	Incline Box		91 15	70·5
87·7	Dauntsey		93 12	82
91·0	*Milepost 91*		95 45	76
94·0	CHIPPENHAM	100	98 19	67
98·3	Corsham		102 33	58·5
101·9	Box		105 54	71·5
			sigs	
104·6	Bathampton		108 25	
			sig stop	
106·9	BATH	114	114 43	
1·0	Oldfield Park		2 27	
4·5	Saltford		6 51	53·5
6·9	Keynsham		9 27	61
9·8	St Anne's Park		12 36	
			sigs	
11·4	BRISTOL	18	17 10	

however, was no more than 106½ min, and I was most interested to see that our point-to-point time of 53 min 52 sec for the 58 miles from Reading to Chippenham was a shade faster than the sectional timing of this train in 1939, when the schedule was 102 min from Paddington to Bath, with a load generally much under 300 tons. The water consumption was 31 gallons to the mile, with a coal consumption of about 35 lb per train mile. The average consumption of the complete round from Bristol to Paddington and back was only 31 gallons of water per mile, and this was enough to give us net average speeds between Paddington and Bath of 57·2 mph going up, with 430 tons, and of 60·2 mph on the return, with 365 tons. This was indeed an excellent all-round performance.

In 1950 engine No 4054 *Princess Charlotte* was

stationed at Laira. She was newly overhauled and was in spanking condition. She was frequently used on the 7.15 am from Plymouth to Paddington, and on one of these occasions I rode on the footplate. While I was unfortunate with the weather, which was very wet and miserable, I was very fortunate in my driver and fireman. Fred Gould was one of those born enginemen who never wasted a pound of steam, while Eric Warr was one of those enthusiastic souls who was prepared to shovel his heart out if necessary, but had also the innate sense of enginemanship that enabled him to match his efforts to his driver. Between them they treated me to a performance that was astonishing in its economy in fuel. The engine was in perfect mechanical condition, and with a load of 345 tons we could have made some quite record running; but there was no need, and there was nothing of the exhibitionist about Fred Gould. The only spell of any length where the engine was worked at all hard was on the rise to Whiteball, and then only in 20 per cent cut-off, increased to 25 on the final pitch past Burlescombe.

After Taunton the engine was worked in 15 per cent cut-off the whole way to Paddington, except for a brief increase on the later stretches of the Bruton bank. Even with this there were lengthy stretches where the regulator was very far from fully opened. As will be seen from the log we were keeping very closely to our booked point-to-point times. The signal checks descending the Kennet Valley were not severe and did not affect our running times by more than about $1\frac{1}{4}$ min. We had a comfortable minute in hand at Reading, and with easy running and observance of the slight speed restriction then in force through Slough we were $2\frac{1}{2}$ min early at Southall. We did not need the lavish amount of recovery time then provided on the last stretch and so stopped in Paddington $6\frac{3}{4}$ min early. There was nothing spectacular about this fine run except the coal and water consumption. A careful check on the tender gauge indicated a usage of about 24 gallons per mile, the coal consumption was about 27 lb per mile—a perfect exposition of a Churchward locomotive at its finest.

In the 1950s those of us with an eye to the older locomotives of the Great Western stud were constantly delighted as successive engines of the 'Star' class were given 'heavy-general' overhauls at Swindon, and came out glittering as if brand new. Such apparitions were certainly growing fewer, but those that did emerge could certainly show a good deal of their finest form. By the year 1952 I felt that the time had probably come to make a 'last journey' on a 'Star', and one summer evening Authority kindly put No 4062 *Malmesbury Abbey* on to the Bristol evening round trip to Paddington and back. Going

7.15 am Plymouth - Paddington express in Sonning Cutting : engine No 4054
'Princess Charlotte'

8.54 am EXETER—PADDINGTON

Load: 10 cars, 324 tons tare, 345 tons full
Engine: 4054 *Princess Charlotte*
Driver: F. Gould; Fireman: E. Warr (Old Oak)

Dist miles		Sch min	Actual m s	Speed mph
0·0	EXETER . .	0	0 00	—
3·5	Stoke Canon . .		7 07	43·5
7·2	Silverton . .		11 30	53
12·6	Cullompton . .		17 17	60
14·8	Tiverton Jc . .		19 47	51/58
19·9	*Whiteball Box* .	25	25 37	44·5
23·7	Wellington . .		29 11	75
30·8	TAUNTON . .	38	36 37	
2·4	*Creech Jc* . .	4	4 38	47·5
8·0	Athelney . .		10 47	60·5
11·9	*Curry Rivel Jc* .		14 50	60
17·2	Somerton . .		20 42	50
25·5	Alford . .		28 44	69
27·6	CASTLE CARY .	30	30 44	60·5
31·0	Bruton . .		34 24	50·5
34·4	*Milepost 122¾* .		39 05	34
40·4	*Blatchbridge Jc* .	45	45 33	67·5
42·4	*Clink Road Jc* .	47½	47 29	57
45·7	*Fairwood Jc* .	51	50 39	65·5
48·1	*Heywood Road Jc* .	54	53 14	eased
55·8	Lavington . .		61 29	60·5
61·6	Patney . .	69	68 13	48·5
67·4	Pewsey . .		74 13	61·5
72·6	Savernake . .	81	80 04	53·5
76·3	Bedwyn . .	85	83 54	61·5
84·2	Kintbury . .		91 29	66
			sigs	40
89·6	NEWBURY . .	98	97 07	
97·9	Aldermaston . .		105 30	67
			sigs	
106·7	READING . .	116	114 51	
111·7	Twyford . .	122	121 01	60
118·5	Maidenhead . .	129	127 32	66
124·2	SLOUGH . .	135	133 04	60*
129·5	West Drayton . .		138 10	64
133·6	Southall . .	145	142 27	57
137·0	Ealing Broadway .		145 42	64
142·7	PADDINGTON .	160	153 12	

Net time: : Taunton—Paddington 152 min
Estimated coal consumption 27 lb per mile
* Speed restriction

5.25 pm BRISTOL—PADDINGTON

'The Merchant Venturer'
Load: 9 cars, 294 tons tare, 315 tons full
Engine: 4062 *Malmesbury Abbey*
Driver: W. Hares; Fireman: D. Howlett (Bristol)

Dist miles		Sch min	Actual m s	Speed mph
0·0	TEMPLE MEADS	0	0 00	
1·7	St Annes Park . .		4 20	48
			pws	40
4·6	Keynsham . .		8 12	55 (max)
11·5	BATH . .	17	16 40	
2·3	Bathampton . .		4 16	50
5·0	Box . .		7 12	63
8·6	Corsham . .		11 16	46·5
11·9	*Milepost 95* . .		14 36	65
12·9	CHIPPENHAM .	19	16 07	
3·0	*Milepost 91* . .		4 49	55·5
6·3	Dauntsey . .		8 19	58
			sigs	15
11·1	Wootton Bassett .		15 15	
			sigs	
16·7	SWINDON . .	24	23 05	
5·8	Shrivenham . .		8 04	64·5
10·8	Uffington . .		12 37	72
			pws	47
				60
16·9	Wantage Road .		19 02	
			pws	15
21·8	Steventon . .	25	25 30	55·5
24·2	DIDCOT . .	28½	28 51	64·5
28·8	Cholsey . .		33 07	66
38·6	Tilehurst . .		42 05	69
			sigs	
41·3	READING . .	46	45 40	
3·0	*Milepost 33* . .		5 17	55
			pws	40
5·0	Twyford . .	8	7 36	
11·8	Maidenhead . .	15	14 05	68
15·0	Burnham . .		17 24	71
17·5	SLOUGH . .	21	19 46	56*
22·8	West Drayton . .		25 01	64·5
26·9	Southall . .	30	29 32	60*
30·3	Ealing Broadway .		32 18	70·5
34·7	Westbourne Park .	39	36 18	
36·0	PADDINGTON .	45	39 05	

* Speed restrictions

up on the 'Merchant Venturer' the load was not so heavy as I could have wished for; but there were several permanent way slacks in operation and there were still restrictions to full speed running at both Slough and Southall. Again I was fortunate in having another splendid pair of enginemen in W. Hares and D. Howlett of Bath Road shed, Bristol.

In making a number of footplate runs on up expresses from Bristol I have always found it traditional to take things very easily to Bath, while the fire is still a bit 'green'; but having got the boiler conditions nicely settled down Hares made a thrilling run to Chippenham. Less than a mile from the start the cut-off was fixed at 25 per cent, and there it stayed till we emerged from Box Tunnel. The result was a rapid acceleration to 63 mph at

Box, and a climb through the tunnel, with its awkward 2 miles at 1 in 100, without speed falling below 46½ mph. Cut-off was reduced to 15 per cent at Corsham, and we made a very smart run into Chippenham. On restarting, the cut-offs were 25 per cent after one mile, and 15 per cent in another mile, which produced a rapid acceleration to 55·5 mph at the crossing of the River Avon, at Milepost 91.

From Swindon onwards 15 per cent was the normal running position, and Driver Hares used longer cut-offs only for brief moments in accelerating from checks. With so good an engine, and a load of no more than 315 tons behind the tender we naturally had things very comfortably in hand all the way. As on my run with No 4054 we gained substantially

*The up Merchant Venturer near Thingley Junction: engine No 4062 'Malmesbury Abbey',
with the author on the footplate*

on time in the final approach to Paddington, and arrived 6 min early. With the numerous intermediate stops, and various out-of-course slowings, there was not the same opportunity for continuous highly economical steaming as with No 4054. On this up journey from Bristol to Paddington the water consumption averaged 31 gallons per mile, and the coal about 36 lb per mile. This was good enough, but on the return journey I was to see the working of this splendid engine in a still more favourable light. As usual she took the West of England 'Postal', and I recall with amusement the slight air of suspicion with which police and postal officials scrutinised my footplate pass and allowed me to enter the platform!

This time we had a heavier load, while a succession of checks gave us a late start of 5½ min from Reading. This provided our driver and fireman the opportunity to give an immaculate display of 'Star' performance. In getting away the cut-off was reduced to 25 per cent in one mile, and to 15 per cent at Pangbourne. After that Hares drove entirely on the regulator. From Pangbourne successive readings of boiler pressure gave 220, 218, 220, 215, 220, 215, after which I stopped taking notes of what was absolutely rock-steady steaming. The reserve capacity of the engine was shown when the regulator was opened a little wider near Uffington, and the speed which had dropped to 59 mph on the long gradual rise quickly picked up to 63 mph before Shrivenham. The downhill dash after Wootton Bassett, with its maximum speed of 82 mph on Dauntsey

bank, was made on the easiest of steaming, and with quite a quiet finish we reached Bath a minute early. The water consumption on the trip showed an average of 26 gallons per mile between Paddington and Bath, and the coal consumption was about

Dist miles		Sch min	Actual m s	Speed mph
0·0	PADDINGTON .	0	0 00	
			sigs	
1·3	Westbourne Park .	3	4 08	
5·7	Ealing Broadway .		10 28	53
9·1	Southall . .	12½	14 07	57
18·5	SLOUGH .	22	23 23	66
24·2	Maidenhead .	28	28 50	62
			pw sigs	
36·0	READING .	41	45 30	
5·5	Pangbourne .		8 05	61
12·5	Cholsey .		14 32	66
17·1	DIDCOT .	20	18 47	65
20·5	Steventon .	23½	21 51	66
24·4	Wantage Road .		25 30	64
27·9	Challow .		28 58	60
30·5	Uffington .		31 36	59
35·5	Shrivenham .		36 36	63
41·3	SWINDON .	45	42 15	61
46·9	Wootton Bassett .		47 31	68
51·7	Dauntsey .		51 30	82
58·0	CHIPPENHAM .	62	56 32	68
62·3	Corsham .		60 37	60
65·9	Box .		63 48	76
68·6	Bathampton .		66 14	
70·9	BATH .	76	69 37	

10.10 pm PADDINGTON—BATH
West of England Postal Special
Load: 11 vans, 312 tons tare, 345 tons full
Engine: 4062 *Malmesbury Abbey*
Driver: W. Hares; Fireman: D. Howlett (Bristol)

8.30 am Bristol - Paddington express at Langley Crossing, Chippenham : engine No 4056 'Princess Margaret', with the author on the footplate

30-31 lb per mile.

These runs on *Malmesbury Abbey* were made on 5 June 1952, forty-five years after the first introduction of the four-cylinder 4—6—0s, and thirty-nine years after the finalisation of the design with superheaters and 15 in diameter cylinders. Then I thought these must surely be my last runs on 'Stars' in first-class express work, and at the time I felt happy that what I expected to be the finale had been such a good one. Nevertheless, on a raw winter's morning towards the end of 1955 I was waiting on Bath station ready to board yet another 'Star', No 4056 *Princess Margaret*. It was the 8.53 am to Paddington this time, with a 325-ton load, and another fine pair of enginemen in Driver Giles and Fireman Andress. We got a bad start, and after a succession of checks were stopped dead at Box, right at the foot of that nasty ascent through the tunnel. We made an excellent restart; cut-off was back to 37 per cent in ½ mile, and was further reduced to 27 per cent soon after we had entered the tunnel. We steadily gathered speed. There was an occasional slip, but it was well controlled by the driver, and we emerged at 30 mph. Then the use of 20 per cent cut-off brought a quick acceleration to 64 mph before the Chippenham stop. The run thence to Paddington is tabulated herewith.

With a minute or so of lost time to regain the engine was hustled away, with 30 per cent cut-off after 1¼ miles, 22 per cent at Milepost 91, and a reversion to 24 per cent at Dauntsey. This gave us a truly splendid start. The engine, like all the 'Stars' featured in this chapter, was a perfect 'Rolls-Royce' of an engine, riding beautifully, and responding vigorously to every adjustment of the controls. After the checks through Swindon she was worked up in

20 per cent cut-off with the first valve of the regulator, and gave us a steady 75 mph down through the Vale of the White Horse. Then came checks: adverse signals to 30 mph in the approach to Didcot, and a very heavy permanent way check to 10 mph at Pangbourne. Then we were away again and by Reading working in 20 per cent cut-off, regulator three-quarters open, and doing 65 mph. This work-

9.19 am CHIPPENHAM—PADDINGTON
Load: 9 cars, 310 tons tare, 325 tons full
Engine: 4056 *Princess Margaret*
Driver: Giles; Fireman: Andress (Bristol)

Dist miles		Sch min	Actual m s	Speed mph
0·0	CHIPPENHAM	0	0 00	
3·0	*Milepost 91*		4 58	56
6·3	Dauntsey		8 19	61·5
8·7	*Incline Box*		10 54	51·5
11·1	Wootton Bassett		13 27	58·5
			sigs	30
16·7	SWINDON	21	20 16	
22·5	Shrivenham		26 05	67·5
27·5	Uffington		30 28	71
33·6	Wantage Road		35 30	75
39·5	Steventon	41	38 40	75
			sigs	30
40·9	DIDCOT	44	42 18	
45·5	Cholsey		47 03	67·5
48·2	Goring		50 17	71·5
			pws	10
58·0	READING	61½	62 18	65
63·0	Twyford		66 42	72
69·8	Maidenhead	73	72 11	75
75·5	SLOUGH	78	76 48	76/73*
80·8	West Drayton		81 10	72
84·9	Southall	88	84 39	71·5
88·3	Ealing Broadway		87 53	66·5
			pw sigs	
92·7	Westbourne Park		92 55	
94·0	PADDINGTON	101	96 38	

Net time 88½ min
* Speed restriction

Up Cheltenham, Gloucester and Bristol express in Sonning Cutting :
engine No 4022 unnamed (formerly 'King William')

ing continued to Maidenhead, where with the speed just topping 75 mph cut-off was reduced to 15 per cent. Thenceforward a brisk and practically undelayed finish brought us into Paddington $2\frac{1}{2}$ min early. The net time from Chippenham was, however, no more than $88\frac{1}{2}$ min—a start-to-stop average of 63.7 mph. This fast run was made on a water consumption averaging 30 gallons per mile from Chippenham to Paddington, and a coal consumption of 35-36 lb per mile.

Three weeks later on 26 November 1955 I did have my very last runs on a 'Star' class engine. Once again it was No 4056 *Princess Margaret,* and this time on the 6.45 am North to West mail from Bristol to Newton Abbot. It was a raw, frosty morning, with mist in places, and we pulled out of Temple Meads with eleven coaches and vans, a gross load of 340 tons behind the tender. There was rime on the rails, and the engine was at first inclined to slip; but Driver Connett took her gently up to Flax Bourton, on 25 per cent cut-off and a partly opened regulator, and we topped the bank at 45 mph. The first signs of dawn were showing as

we got into speed, and touched 64 mph at Yatton, and then observing the severe slack at Worle Junction we clocked into Weston-super-Mare dead on time. After the very bad permanent way check before Uphill Junction we got splendidly into speed, and along this level stretch I saw the same kind of driving as on the other 'Stars': 16 per cent cut-off, regulator just over half open, giving us 63 mph on the level. There was rather more variation in the boiler pressure on this trip, and I have notes of 200 lb per sq in; but we were running very comfortably to time, and the generous recovery allowance between Highbridge and Bridgwater more than retrieved the time by which we had overstayed our schedule at Weston.

Station business was heavy on this early-morning mail train, and we were standing for $9\frac{1}{2}$ min at Bridgwater, instead of the allotted 5 min. Furthermore, there is little margin in the run forward to Taunton, and we needed 18 per cent cut-off from about $2\frac{1}{2}$ miles out of Bridgwater. At Taunton the engine was re-manned, and we left just over 1 min late for the attack on Wellington. Our new driver

6.45 am BRISTOL—EXETER Load: 11 cars, 326 tons tare, 340 tons full Engine: 4056 *Princess Margaret* Driver, to Taunton: Connett; Fireman: Graves (Bristol) to Exeter: Palmer; Fireman: Parsons (Taunton)				
Dist miles		Sch min	Actual m s	Speed mph
0·0	TEMPLE MEADS .	0	0 00	
1·9	Parson Street .		5 40	
5·9	Flax Bourton .		11 04	45
12·0	YATTON .		16 53	64
16·8	*Worle Jc* . .	22	21 46	20*
19·1	WESTON- SUPER-MARE .	26	26 08	
			pws	5
1·6	*Uphill Jc* .	3	5 08	
6·1	Brent Knoll .		10 58	55
8·9	HIGHBRIDGE .	14	13 51	60
12·7	Dunball .		17 33	63
15·2	BRIDGWATER .	27	20 48	
3·5	*Fordgate Box* .		6 04	52/56
6·8	*Cogload* .		9 40	52·5
9·1	*Creech Jc* .		11 59	61·5
11·5	TAUNTON .	16	15 30	
2·0	Norton Fitzwarren .		4 15	45·5
7·1	Wellington .		10 52	52
8·9	*Milepost 172* .		13 08	
			sigs	28
9·9	*Milepost 173* .		15 25	
10·9	*Whiteball Box* .	17	17 40	26·5
15·9	Tiverton Jc .		23 02	70·5
18·2	Cullompton .		25 04	63/58*
23·6	Silverton .		30 23	65
27·3	Stoke Canon .		33 49	68
			sig/stop 4½ ft	
30·8	EXETER .	40	44 04	

           * Speed restrictions

used 20 per cent from Norton Fitzwarren, and 25 per cent from Poole siding (a mile short of Wellington). We were going splendidly up the bank when we sighted Beam Bridge 'distant' on. After closing the regulator speed dropped to 28 mph before the signal cleared, and then with 45 per cent cut-off at first, reduced to 35 at the entrance to Whiteball tunnel we made a lovely ascent: surefooted, with a thrilling, staccato exhaust and holding 26½ mph through the tunnel. This was excellent work with a load of 340 tons. An easy run down to Exeter, on 15 per cent cut-off with the first valve only, would have given us an early arrival, but for a prolonged signal stop outside. I have not tabulated the continuation of the run round the coast to Newton Abbot: we had two permanent way checks and took 28 min 37 sec for these 20·2 miles in place of the 26 min scheduled. The intermittent character of the performance demanded on this turn, and the heavy work needed on Wellington bank are reflected in the coal and water consumption, which were estimated at 42 lb per mile and 35 gallons per mile.

I returned from Newton on No 4056 working the 11.34 pm West to North express, with a load of 375 tons behind the tender, with yet a third crew. Those who claim that the immaculate performance of Great Western locomotives was the

Wolverhampton - Weymouth (Saturdays) express near Castle Cary : engine No 4061 'Glastonbury Abbey'

West to North express entering Temple Meads, Bristol : engine No 4056 'Princess Margaret', with the author on the footplate

outcome of the most selective manning may well be confounded by the results I noted with *Princess Margaret* in that one day! We kept exact time round the coastal section in this direction—26 min 3 sec to be precise—and then set out on the remarkable run tabulated. Driver Iles had opened out to full regulator by Exeter Riverside box. Cut-off was 25 per cent from Cowley Bridge Junction and 21 per cent from Stoke Canon. After that the working was

12.7 pm EXETER—BRISTOL
Load: 11 cars, 350 tons tare, 375 tons full
Engine: 4056 *Princess Margaret*
Driver: Iles (Bristol)

Dist miles		Sch min	Actual m s	Speed mph
0·0	EXETER . .	0	0 00	
3·5	Stoke Canon . .		6 07	48
7·2	Silverton . .		10 16	56·5
12·6	Cullompton . .		15 37	63
14·9	Tiverton Jc . .		17 56	54·5/61
19·9	*Whiteball Box* . .	26	23 29	44·5
			pws	30
23·7	Wellington . .		29 12	72
			pws	30
30·8	TAUNTON . .	37	37 13	
2·4	*Creech Jc* . .		3 55	55
4·7	*Cogload* . .		6 20	60
8·0	*Fordgate* . .		9 21	67
11·5	BRIDGWATER .	15	13 05	
2·5	Dunball . .		4 40	50
6·3	HIGHBRIDGE .	9	8 37	60
9·1	Brent Knoll . .		11 18	65
13·6	*Uphill Jc* . .	17	15 48	
			pws	5
15·2	WESTON-SUPER-MARE .	20	20 58	
2·3	*Worle Jc* . .	4	4 30	20*
7·1	YATTON . .		10 39	63
13·2	Flax Bourton . .		16 35	57
15·4	Long Ashton . .		18 50	62
			sigs	
19·1	TEMPLE MEADS .	25	25 05	

unchanged until we were over Whiteball summit. The most telling comment I can make about this ascent is to refer readers to Part I of this book, where on page 114 I detailed the record run of *Caldicot Castle* with the up Cornish Riviera Express during the Interchange Trials of 1925. The times achieved on that rather exceptional occasion were 6 min 14 sec to Stoke Canon; 15 min 33 sec to Cullompton; and 23 min 31 sec to Whitehall Box. More than thirty years later with an almost identical load (375 against 380 tons) *Princess Margaret* fractionally *surpassed* those times! All the way up the bank the boiler pressure was well sustained, never below 210 lb per sq in, and mostly at 215 to 220 lb per sq in.

After that remarkable exhibition we had the usual succession of 'fits and starts'. The level running after Taunton was all made on 15 per cent cut-off, mostly with full open regulator; but we had a magnificent finish, from Weston. After the usual slow negotiation of Worle Junction the driver worked in 20 per cent cut-off with full regulator—hard going!—and this took us up to 63 mph at Yatton, prior to clearing the Flax Bourton bank at the fine minimum speed of 57 mph. Signals were slightly against us in the approach to Bristol, but we had the satisfaction of finishing dead on time. And this really was my last footplate trip on a 'Star'. The fuel and water consumption was naturally heavier on a run of this quality, and the average water consumption between Newton Abbot and Bristol was exactly 40 gallons per mile; the coal consumption was 47 to 48 lb per mile. The veteran locomotive had nevertheless showed herself mistress of the job, and in equalling *Caldicot Castle* between Exeter and Whiteball had an outstanding piece of work to her credit.

The last line-up? Engines 2920 'Saint David' and 4056 'Princess Margaret'
outside Swindon works. Actually it proved not to be the
last time for No 4056

Engine No 4003 'Lode Star' on road transporter en route for
Swindon Municipal Museum

CHAPTER 8

IMPROVED DRAUGHTING

IN the years immediately following the retirement of F. W. Hawksworth 'Castles' and 'Kings' continued to do good work on the schedules then prevailing. At times, indeed, some of the newest 'Castles' put up some performances that could be called phenomenal. But for a variety of reasons such standards of performance could not be relied on always. Difficulties in servicing and the quality of coal supplies made necessary some intensive research work to improve the steaming of the whole stud of ex-Great Western locomotives. As a matter of policy the accent was to be on increased steam production. The quality of performance that I have described in the foregoing chapter, dealing with the 'Stars', showed Great Western working at its pre-war finest. It was certainly not attainable by *any* engine, on *any* fuel that might be supplied. As a supplement to those farewell performances of the 'Stars', in ideal conditions, I must describe in detail an altogether exceptional performance with a 'Castle' that I logged personally in 1950. It indicates what was probably the optimum working rate of the '5098' class, as originally built. The engine in question was, of course, fitted with the then standard mechanical lubricator.

I had a footplate pass for the 3.30 pm from Paddington to Plymouth, and secured an excellent record. There was nothing unusual about it; just top-class performance by an engine in first-class condition. It was nothing more than one would expect from a good 'Castle'. I stayed overnight in Plymouth and returned next morning to Chippenham, travelling by the 8.30 am London express as far as Westbury. This was the return working of the crew with whom I had ridden the previous day, but normally provided with a 'King'. Engine No 7036 *Taunton Castle* had done us so well that Driver Cook asked for her again. He was reminded that the load would be 'fourteen' from Newton Abbot, but that caused neither him nor Fireman Hughes any concern. So, from Exeter, with a load

of exactly 500 tons behind the tender, I commenced to log the running. My footplate pass did not apply to the up journey but in good conditions I was able to record a maximum of data.

The opening run to Taunton was good enough in all conscience, with an attained maximum speed of 59 mph at Cullompton, and a speed of 50 mph held to within 2 miles of Whiteball summit. After that, with a fast run down the bank and a maximum speed of 82 mph below Wellington we more than

---

10.3 am EXETER—WESTBURY
Load: to Taunton, 14 cars, 460 tons tare, 500 tons full
to Westbury, 15 cars, 490 tons tare, 535 tons full
Engine: 7036 *Taunton Castle*
Driver: A. Cook; Fireman: L. Hughes (Old Oak)

Dist miles		Sch min	Actual m s	Speed mph
0·0	EXETER .	0	0 00	
1·3	*Cowley Bridge Jc* .		3 41	
3·5	Stoke Canon . .		6 45	48·5
7·2	Silverton .		11 05	55·5/53
12·6	Cullompton .		16 45	59
14·8	Tiverton Jc .		19 16	50·5/57·5
17·9	*Milepost 176* .		22 43	51·5
19·9	*Whiteball Box* .	25	25 29	37·5
23·7	Wellington .		29 19	77·5
26·9	*Milepost 167* .		31 47	82
			pws	15
30·8	TAUNTON .	38	36 50	
2·4	*Creech Jc* .	4	4 30	51
8·0	Athelney . .		10 18	62/59
11·9	*Curry Rivel Jc* .		14 17	61·5
17·1	Somerton .		19 54	53/63·5
20·5	Charlton Mackrell .		23 14	57
22·7	Keinton Mandeville		25 26	66·5
27·5	CASTLE CARY .	31	30 03	58
29·1	*Milepost 128* .		31 39	60
30·1	*Milepost 127* .		32 42	56
31·1	Bruton .		33 44	50·5/52·5
32·1	*Milepost 125* .		35 04	48
33·1	*Milepost 124* .		36 21	46·5
34·1	*Milepost 123* .		37 45	40
	Milepost 122¾ (Summit) .			34·5
40·4	*Blatchbridge Jc* .	46	44 16	72
42·4	*Clink Road Jc* .	48½	46 01	64·5
45·7	*Fairwood Jc* .	52½	49 01	72
47·2	WESTBURY .	55	51 39	

88

Liverpool - Plymouth express just over Whiteball summit : engine No 7029 'Clun Castle'

kept time to Taunton, despite a permanent way slack to 15 mph near Norton Fitzwarren. Then, however, there was yet another coach to be added, and the locomotive staff at Taunton had an assistant engine ready to couple on ahead of No 7036. But Driver Cook and his fireman disdained any such assistance, and we went forward with the tremendous load of 535 tons. It was then that the work became so completely outstanding. I was very sorry not to be on the footplate, and so able to record every detail of the working, but it was evident from the times and speeds that Cook was to some extent conserving his efforts so as to make maximum performance uphill. For example, the running from Creech Junction to Curry Rivel Junction, largely on level track, was good though not unusual; but then came the astounding climb of Somerton bank where the minimum speed of 53 mph on 1 in 264 was steadily sustained for more than a mile. The edhp rose from 800 at Curry Rivel Junction to 1,360 at the top of the bank.

After Castle Cary the engine was worked in 25 per cent cut-off, with full regulator, and the ascent of the Bruton bank was a masterpiece in itself. As will be seen from the log the 5 miles between mileposts 128 and 123 occupied only 6 min 6 sec, and yet the average gradient between these two points is 1 in 122. Making careful allowance for the loss in kinetic energy in the train, due to the decelera-

tion from 60 to 40 mph, the average edhp during that strenuous 6 min works out at 1,600. The experimental section at Swindon has reported that the maximum they had noted with a 'King' when making up time in revenue-earning service was 1,440. *Taunton Castle* surpassed this, and it is probable that the actual cut-offs used were greater than those indicated on the scale, and reported to me by Driver Cook. In any case, the run provides yet another example complementary to those with 'Kings' on the Birmingham route detailed in Chapter 3, of a steam locomotive being worked intermittently at far higher steaming rates than the boiler could continuously sustain. The practical result was that this enormous train was brought into Westbury $3\frac{1}{4}$ min inside schedule time. It will be appreciated with what regret I left the train at Westbury, to catch the local connection to Chippenham.

The research into methods of increasing the steaming capacity of locomotives was directed towards both 'Castles' and 'Kings', and also to the 'Hall' and 'Manor' classes of two-cylinder 4—6—0. It was later applied to the 'Counties' as well. But in view of the very comprehensive test data subsequently published in S. O. Ell's paper to the Institution of Locomotive Engineers principal interest, so far as this book is concerned, centres upon the 'Kings'. As originally designed, with a jumper top to the blastpipe, this latter was 7 in below the centre

'King' class : the original 4-row superheater layout as applied to engine No 6022 'King Edward III'

line of the boiler. The throat of the chimney, 1 ft 4 in diameter, was 2 ft 11 in above this, and above the throat the chimney tapered out to 1 ft 8 in diameter at the top. This was the arrangement on the 4-row superheater boiler fitted to engine No 6022 in 1947. At that time there were no arrangements for self-cleaning in the smokebox. For servicing the latter were considered essential in British Railway days, and as the wire mesh would necessarily offer some resistance to the flow of flue gases from the tubes to the chimney it was evident that means had to be provided for sharpening the blast. At first it was thought that this would seriously interfere with the economical work of the engine, but careful studies indicated that any such deterioration would be more than counteracted by the improved steaming capacity effected. The drawings on pages 90 and 92 show successive stages in the development of the blastpipe and chimney proportions.

In the studies that took place at Swindon it was found that in single blastpipe designs the upper limit of the boiler was approached, and sometimes actually fixed in good designs by the limiting discharge rate of the orifice. It proved so in the re-draughted 'King'. It was estimated that when the self-cleaning plates were fitted the draughting limit

and the front-end discharge limit would approximately coincide. The blastpipe and chimney proportions used as a first-approximation in design proved remarkably accurate, and the modified arrangements fitted to two 'King' class engines, 6001 and 6017 in the autumn of 1952, won golden opinions from the operating staff in ordinary revenue-earning service. A similar change was also made to engine No 5025 of the 'Castle' class. The design was, however, not ultimately finalised so far as the 'Kings' were concerned until engine No 6001 *King Edward VII* was put on to the stationary test plant at Swindon, for 'full dress' trials, in the spring of 1953. Ell's work in this respect is an object lesson for all time in the history of locomotive design. By small, well-considered changes, very cheaply carried out, the boiler limit of continuous evaporation was advanced to more than 30 per cent above its normal working rate. On the heaviest pre-war duties the 'Kings' had been required to steam continuously at rates of about 25,000 to 26,000 lb per hr for periods of about one hour on end; against this the modified 6001, with the small adjustment shown desirable in the stationary tests, had a front-end limit of no less than 33,600 lb per hr. The 'runs' on the stationary plant, some of which I was able to observe per-

Engine No 6001 'King Edward VII' at 75 mph on the stationary plant

'King' class : modified smokebox layout with improved draughting developed on No 6001

*Engine No 6001 'King Edward VII' with dynamometer car ready for the
classic controlled road tests of 1953*

sonally, were impressive enough; but the interpretation in the form of load haulage on the road was thrilling beyond measure. The tests runs were made between Reading and Stoke Gifford sidings, and as the special trains had to be given paths amid the ordinary traffic of the day they were timed at con-

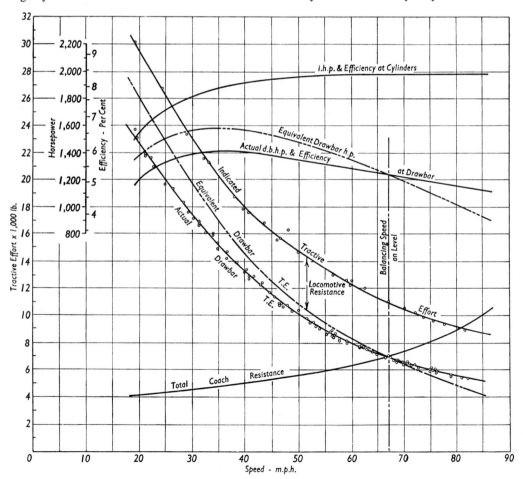

Test results : steam rate 28,700 lb per hour

93

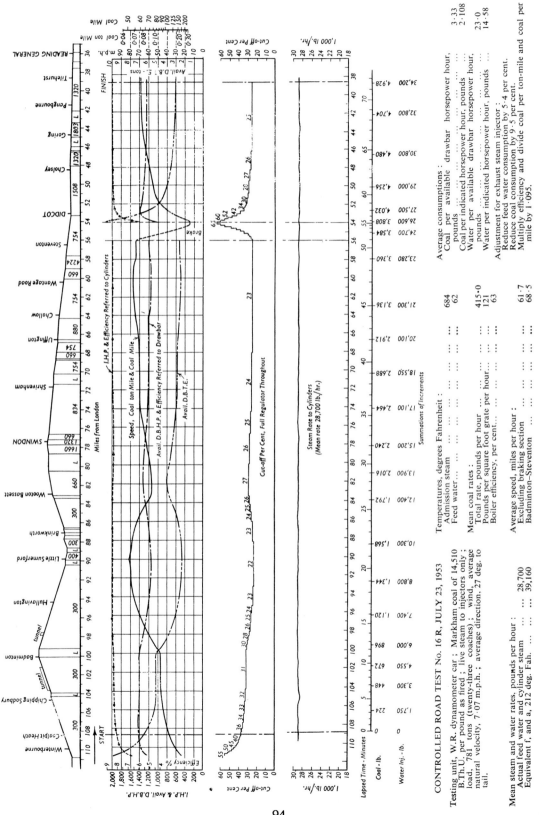

temporary express passenger speed, and loaded so as to demand high rates of steaming. In these circumstances the test trains reached a maximum formation of 25 coaches, and a little short of 800 tons tare.

The accompanying diagram shows in graphical form the performance on a run from Stoke Gifford to Reading with a load of 23 coaches, 781 tons tare, when the steaming rate was 28,700 lb per hr. The test at constant steaming rate began on passing Coalpit Heath station, at a speed of about 38 mph, and it finished near Tilehurst. The average speed, excluding the section on which the train was being braked to observe a 15 mph speed restriction, was 61·7 mph; and this tremendously hard work, including a maximum speed of 81 mph at Little Somerford, was performed on a coal consumption of 3·33 lb per dhp hr. The complete analysis of the

performance is given in a second diagram, which shows a series of inter-related graphs prepared from this one test. It will be seen from this latter graph that the maximum indicated hp was a little below 2,000, while the relation between the actual dhp measured in the dynamometer car and the 'equivalent' value, after a correction for gradient, is clearly shown. In these steaming conditions the balancing speed on level track with this particular train was 67 mph. In comparing this with the actual speed run down the slight gradients in the Vale of the White Horse it will be appreciated how markedly those gradients can assist the running. The speed in the neighbourhood of Wantage Road was 77 mph.

It was my privilege to ride in the dynamometer car when an even heavier load was conveyed, and the steam rate was a full 30,000 lb per hr. There was an admixture of some lighter stock, however,

Mr S. O. Ell (right) with the author at Stoke Gifford prior to the run detailed on page 96

Engine No 6001 with 25-coach test train approaching Swindon at 60 mph

and the 25 coaches included in the rake had a tare weight of 796 tons. On both these runs we had a clear road throughout. They were made on weekdays amid the ordinary traffic, and a considerable wait was necessary at Stoke Gifford before a path was available for the return trip. In anticipation of this the outward test was ended at Badminton so that opportunity would be available to let down the fire before the long period of waiting. The outward run was thus of approximately one hour's duration, and to provide roughly comparable conditions the return test was ended at the 49th milepost. Remark-

WR DYNAMOMETER CAR CONTROLLED ROAD TEST
Load: 25 cars, 796 tons tare, 798 tons full
Engine: 6001 *King Edward VII*

Dist miles		Time m s	Speed mph
0·0	*Scours Lane Jc* . .	0 00	Pass slowly 10 mph
0·9	Tilehurst . . .	2 25	
2·7	*Milepost 39½* . .	Start of test	
3·8	Pangbourne . . .	6 48	47
7·0	Goring . . .	10 40	53·5
10·7	Cholsey . . .	14 44	56
15·3	DIDCOT . . .	19 32	58
18·7	Steventon . .	23 03	58
22·6	Wantage Road .	27 02	60
26·1	Challow . .	30 36	59
28·7	Uffington . .	33 16	59
31·2	*Knighton Crossing* .	35 51	58·5
33·8	Shrivenham . .	38 26	61·5
39·5	SWINDON . .	44 09	60
42·2	*Hay Lane Box* .	46 45	64·5
45·1	Wootton Bassett .	49 43	66/50*
51·9	Little Somerford .	56 14	72
56·4	Hullavington .	60 36	57·5
58·2	*Milepost 96* . .	62 30	54
60·2	*Milepost 98* . .	64 44	53
62·2	Badminton . .	67 02	52 end of test
70·7	Coalpit Heath .	75 22	65·5
74·2	*Stoke Gifford West* .	80 02	

* Speed restriction

WR DYNAMOMETER CAR CONTROLLED ROAD TEST
Load: 25 bogies, 796 tons tare, 798 tons full
Engine: 6001 *King Edward VII*

Dist miles		Time m s	Speed mph
0·0	*Stoke Gifford East Box* dep	0 00	
0·75	*Milepost 110¾* . .	3 48	
1·5	*Milepost 110* .	5 25	
1·6	Winterbourne .	5 45	
3·0	Coalpit Heath .	8 09	
4·3	*Westerleigh Jc* . .	10 18	40
6·9	Chipping Sodbury .	13 58	42·5/45
11·5	Badminton .	20 06	45·5
17·3	Hullavington .	25 58	72
21·8	Little Somerford .	29 32	78
24·5	Brinkworth . .	31 47	71
28·6	Wootton Bassett .	35 43	58
31·5	*Hay Lane Box* .	38 48	56
34·2	SWINDON . .	41 34	60
35·5	*Milepost 76* . .	42 52	62
37·8	*Marston East* . .	45 00	64
40·0	*Milepost 71½* . .	47 00	68
42·5	*Knighton Crossing* .	49 13	67
45·0	Uffington . .	51 24	69
47·6	Challow . .	53 40	69·5
51·1	Wantage Road .	56 38	70·5
55·0	Steventon . .	59 57	71
58·4	Didcot . .	62 48	71
62·5	*Milepost 49* . .	66 20	69
65·0	*South Stoke Box* .	68 30	68·5
66·7	Goring . .	70 03	67
70·0	Pangbourne (41½) .	72 57	67
71·5	*Milepost 40* . .	74 25	60
72·8	Tilehurst . .	75 50	
73·5	*Scours Lane Jc* up Home . arr	76 55	

ably fine and steady running was performed on both tests, as will be seen from the accompanying logs. The firing rate was approximately 4,000 lb per hr, and as this was well above the figure of 3,000 lb per hr generally considered the maximum for one fireman in continuous working, two firemen were carried. The enginemen concerned, all from Swindon shed, were Driver Hinder, with Firemen Shurmer and Green. The former did *all* the actual firing on the outward journey, and the latter on the return. The second fireman was available on each occasion to do all the various odd jobs that normally came within the duties of a steam locomotive fireman.

It was, of course, not envisaged that duties would regularly be undertaken by engines with the 'improved draughting' involving such efforts as these. It was that the enhanced maximum capacity with good coal provided a margin for recovery, and a margin for working on inferior fuel, and still possessed the capacity to operate service trains punctually. As mentioned earlier in this book a considerable point was made at the time of the 1948 interchange trials of the difficulties under which Great Western engines were working in having to use unfamiliar coals. The following results are therefore of great interest, as showing the difference in performance of the modified 'King' No 6001 when using a grade 1A soft coal and a grade 2B 'hard'.

R. A. Smeddle, Chief Mechanical and Electrical Engineer to 1962

Engine No 6001: IMPROVED DRAUGHTING			
Coal:			
grade	. . .	1A	2B
pit	. . .	Markham	Blidworth
gross calorific value Btu/lb .		14.510	12.740
Steam rate, lb/hr . . .		24.900	22.730
Max ihp		1.770	1.630
at speed mph . .		70–80	70–80
at cut-off per-cent .		20–23	18–19
Max edhp . . .		1.340	1.210
at speed mph . .		35	33
at cut-off per-cent .		30	28
Coal per ihp hr/lb .		1·70	1·84
Coal per dhp hr/lb .		2·24	2·48

With the re-draughted engines at their disposal accelerated schedules were planned to require continuous steaming rates of around 20.000 lb and from the foregoing table it will be appreciated that even with a grade 2B hard coal of much reduced calorific value a 'King' should have a comfortable margin in reserve. Not many weeks after the conclusion of this comprehensive series of 'full-dress' trials I had an opportunity of riding on engine No 6001 in ordinary service. The train was the up 'Cornish Riviera Express', nominally non-stop from Plymouth to Paddington; but with a substantial

summer load an assistant engine had to be taken over the South Devon line, and the actual non-stop run to London was from Newton Abbot West. Details of the running are set out in the accompanying log. With a gross load of 425 tons behind the tender the effort required was naturally far below that put forth on the maximum test occasions. Furthermore, except for a momentary sight of an adverse 'distant' at Norton Fitzwarren the road was clear throughout, and the run was thus an exposition of economy in working.

In making an actual time of 174 min over the 173·5 miles from Exeter to Paddington a cut-off of 17 per cent was used throughout, except for two spells of about 5 min each: 20 per cent for the last 3 miles up to Whiteball summit, and 22 per cent from Bruton up to Brewham summit. Over the harder initial stage of the journey, between Exeter and Fairwood Junction the evaporation rate was approximately 18.000 lb per hr for an average speed of 62·25 mph, while on the remaining 97 miles to Paddington, using an average of only 23 gallons per mile the evaporation rate was only about 14.000 lb per hr. As will be appreciated from the log much of this 97-mile stretch was covered under very easy steam, and indeed the last appreciable firing took

Up Cornish express near Castle Cary, with 14-coach Saturday load : engine No 6009 'King Charles II'

UP CORNISH RIVIERA EXPRESS
NEWTON ABBOT WEST—PADDINGTON
Load: 12 cars, 396 tons tare, 430 tons full
Engine: 6001 *King Edward VII*
Driver: Hammett; Fireman: Henwood (Laira)

Dist miles		Actual m s	Speed mph
0·0	*Newton Abbot West* .	0 00	
0·2	NEWTON ABBOT .	1 20	
5·4	Teignmouth . .	8 52	50
8·2	Dawlish . .	12 42	54
15·7	Exminster . .	20 53	62
20·4	EXETER . .	26 12	30*
23·9	Stoke Canon .	30 27	54
27·6	Silverton . .	34 23	60
33·0	Cullompton . .	39 42	64·5
35·2	Tiverton Jc .	41 57	57/64
40·3	*Whiteball Box* .	47 20	47·5
44·1	Wellington . .	50 48	85
		sigs	60
51·2	TAUNTON .	56 57	64·5
53·6	*Creech Jc* .	59 10	67
59·2	Athelney . .	64 20	63·5
62·9	*Curry Rivel Jc* .	68 04	67
68·4	Somerton . .	73 11	59
73·9	Keinton Mandeville .	78 18	72
78·8	CASTLE CARY .	82 42	58*/60
85·6	*Milepost 122¾* .	90 31	44
91·6	*Blatchbridge Jc* .	96 17	73/65
96·9	*Fairwood Jc* .	100 59	69
99·3	*Heywood Road Jc* .	103 15	62
107·0	Lavington . .	110 23	68
112·5	Patney . .	116 17	56
118·6	Pewsey . .	122 20	64·5
123·8	Savernake . .	127 42	58
127·5	Bedwyn . .	131 31	69
140·8	NEWBURY .	143 47	easy
152·1	Theale . .	154 50	
157·9	READING .	160 55	40*
169·7	Maidenhead .	173 37	60
175·4	SLOUGH . .	179 19	60
184·8	Southall . .	189 01	
193·9	PADDINGTON .	200 08	

* Speed restrictions

place at Newbury. From Reading inwards, indeed, we were just killing time. It must be added, however, that the running conditions were virtually perfect on a hot and calm summer's day and the engine fired with good quality Welsh coal. The average evaporation between Exeter and Paddington was about 15,500 lb per hr. It is, of course, not possible to relate this directly to the Swindon test results and read off from the graphs the corresponding coal consumption. On this service run the steaming was not uniformly maintained throughout; but making some allowance for the varying and intermittent character of the performance demanded the coal consumption would have been something less than 30 lb per mile. From my observations at Swindon stationary plant, from my journeys in the dynamometer car, and finally from personal experience on the footplate I formed the impression that No 6001 in her modified form was an extremely good engine.

I must mention also at this stage the work of some of the modified 'Castles', and particularly No 5025 *Chirk Castle* and No 7034 *Ince Castle*. I have tabulated three runs on Paddington-Bath non-stops made in 1953-4, on which some very fine work was done. Until June of the latter year the 1.15 pm down was allowed 106 min for the run, with a minimum load of ten coaches, and with two 15 mph permanent way checks en route it needed some smart work to keep time. Actually we did not quite manage it, but the main feature of the run was the very fast finish, with its maximum of 90 mph at Dauntsey and a time of only 24 min 48 sec for the last 29·6 miles from Swindon. This was the first post-war occasion on which I had noted a maximum speed of 90 mph in ordinary service on the Western, though from June 1954, when the substantial accelerations came into force, they became common enough.

The 5.5 pm down had an easier timing, but the tremendous energy shown on this trip arose from a slightly late start, because of the bursting of a carriage-warming hose at the last minute, and the need for its replacement. Driver Wilkins was one of the finest of all the Bristol enginemen of the day, and with such an engine as *Chirk Castle* we had wiped out the late start by the time we passed Reading. Despite two bad checks he was through Swindon in $81\frac{3}{4}$ min, and there was no need for undue haste afterwards. In making 75 mph on the level at Reading the engine was developing about 800 dhp. Wilkins was also the driver on the third run tabulated, which was made just before the accelerated times of June 1954 came into force. Then the 1.15 pm had its time cut to 97 min for the Paddington-Bath run, but with a normal load of only seven coaches. The succession of checks on this journey would have discouraged the majority of drivers, but not Wilkins!

First of all, through bad operating, we got a succession of checks out to West Drayton through a much slower train running ahead of us, and the time to Slough was as much as 25 min 25 sec. We

WR PADDINGTON—BATH

Train				1.15 pm		5.5 pm		1.15 pm	
Engine No				7034		5025		7034	
Engine Name				*Ince Castle*		*Chirk Castle*		*Ince Castle*	
Loads tons E/F				335/350		341/370		360/380	
Driver (BRD)				Flowers		Wilkins		Wilkins	
Dist miles				Actual m s	Speeds mph	Actual m s	Speeds mph	Actual m s	Speeds mph
0·0	PADDINGTON	.		0 00		0 00		0 00 sigs	
9·1	Southall	. .		12 24 pws	64·5 15	12 36	61	14 55 sigs	
18·5	SLOUGH	.	.	24 26	62	20 57	74	25 25	62
24·2	Maidenhead	.	.	29 52	66	25 47	71	30 42	67
31·0	Twyford	.	.	35 56	67·5	31 32	69·5	36 40	69
36·0	READING	.	.	40 18	70·5	35 45	75	40 57	72
41·5	Pangbourne	.	.	45 08	68	40 24 sigs	69·5 10	45 38	70·5 69
48·5	Cholsey	.	.	51 23	67	49 34	57	51 38 pw sigs	70 5
53·1	DIDCOT	.	.	55 36	64·5	54 06	64	59 20	
60·4	Wantage Road	.	.	62 17	65·5	60 59 sig stop	63·5	68 01	63·5
66·5	Uffington	.	.	68 03 pws	63·5 15	71 03	52	73 33 pws	69 25
71·5	Shrivenham	.	.	74 12		76 22	64·5	78 41	
77·3	SWINDON	.	.	82 08	63·5	81 45	66/58	85 39	64·5
82·9	Wootton Bassett	.		87 00	75	87 08	67·5	90 27	75
87·7	Dauntsey	.	.	90 35	90	91 04	81	94 01	92
91·0	*Milepost 91*	.	.	92 49	88	93 35	77	96 16 sigs	86·5 47·5
94·0	CHIPPENHAM	.		94 56	80	96 00	69·5	99 35	
98·3	Corsham	.	.	98 23	72/69	99 54	62·5	104 11	61
101·9	Box	.	.	101 24	74	103 10	69	107 23	72
104·5	Bathampton	.	.	103 57		105 35	67·5	109 44 sigs	68
106·9	BATH	.	.	106 56		108 12		113 15	
	Net times, min	.	.	$99\frac{1}{2}$		100		$97\frac{1}{2}$	

The Pembroke Coast Express in Sonning Cutting : engine No 7009
'Athelney Castle', with improved draughting

ran well thereafter, but it was after the very bad checks approaching Didcot that Wilkins really began to extend *Ince Castle*. Having been delayed thus far, and with the knowledge of another permanent way check ahead, any driver might have given up; speed was worked up to 69 mph on the rise to Uffington, requiring an edhp of about 950, and then having observed the Shrivenham restriction we simply *flew*. My previous maximum with this engine down Dauntsey bank was eclipsed by a top speed of 92 mph, but even then we did not get a clear road. The net time on this most enterprising trip was, however, not more than $97\frac{1}{2}$ min—an average of about 66 mph start to stop. These runs with engines having the improved draughting were certainly the shape of things to come, after the June accelerations of 1954.

The practical results of all the work done at Swindon in 1953, and previously, on the subject of draughting were seen in the summer of 1954. The General Manager of the Western Region, K. W. C. Grand, was very anxious to restore pre-war speed,

and particularly by the 'Bristolian' express to a non-stop schedule of $1\frac{3}{4}$ hours between Paddington and Temple Meads in each direction. R. A. Smeddle had given the utmost encouragement to Ell in all the development work carried out, and by the summer of 1953 he was quite confident that the 'King' class engines with improved draughting could do the job, in any ordinary conditions of weather and fuel that were likely to occur. But the operating authorities were very sceptical, and a good deal of 'sales resistance' was offered to the proposed accelerations. The general manager was, however, quite resolute, and for the summer service of 1954 a number of other accelerations were planned on the Bristol route, to be worked by 'Castle' class engines with improved draughting. The schedules were worked out in detail by the staff of the experimental department at Swindon, under S. O. Ell, and while the normal point-to-point times were laid down in accordance with steaming rates now shown to be eminently practical recovery margins were also built in, at intervals, to provide for permanent

The Sunday Cornish Riviera Express, diverted via Chippenham :
engine No 6023 'King Edward II'

way slowings, and other occasional delays. The general principle adopted was that 4 min recovery time should be included at approximately 50-mile intervals. On the Bristol service, therefore, the 105-min 'Bristolian' schedule would include 8 min recovery time, and thus envisage a running time of 97 min as regularly practicable. With the seven-coach train proposed no difficulty was anticipated with 'King' class engines in making a 'net' average of 73 mph start-to-stop.

In May 1954 what could be termed as a 'dress rehearsal' for the accelerated 'Bristolian' was staged, except that the working conditions were in certain respects more strenuous. The run was to be virtually a continuous one, with a special train routed via Bath, North Somerset Junction and Stapleton Road, and returning to Paddington via Filton and Badminton. Brief stops were scheduled in the Bristol area; but for engine and crew it was a continuous working. It was planned to run at a maximum recovery level, and to make the test as representative of ordinary conditions as possible no special arrangements for engine or crew were permitted. The first top-link Old Oak crew available

Another view of the diverted Sunday Cornish Riviera, approaching Chippenham :
engine No 6004 'King George III'

*High-speed dynamometer-car test run, 30 April 1954, passing West Ealing at 70 mph :
engine No 6003 'King George IV'*

for a special train was allocated, and similarly the first available 'King' with improved draughting. I was invited to join the party in the dynamometer car that day, and enjoyed yet another enlivening experience of Western Region running. Although no special arrangements were made the crew actually called, Driver Wasley and Fireman French, were very much on their mettle, and Mr Grand himself rode on the footplate on the outward half of the journey.

The logs of these interesting runs are set out in the accompanying tables. The load was slightly heavier than that proposed for the restored $1\frac{3}{4}$-hour 'Bristolian' timing, which was to be seven coaches, with a tare weight of 235 tons; but with full passenger loading the gross load of the service train was expected to be about 250 tons, whereas the test train carried only the staff of the experimental department, and a number of other railway officers.

On the outward journey 4 min recovery time was included in the schedule between Reading and Didcot, and also between Bath and the terminating point at Dr Days Bridge Junction. Generally speaking, the train was run very closely to the planned schedule, having regard to the unfamiliarity of the driver and fireman with the continuous high-speed running of this kind. There was a certain unevenness in the effort, which resulted from variations in the steaming; but taken all round it was a splendid first try. With only one check we should, according to the planned schedule have been 4 min early at Dr Days Bridge Junction. As it was we were $3\frac{1}{4}$ min early. Notable speeds were the maximum of 84 mph on the level at Didcot, an acceleration to 81·5 mph up the slight rise to Uffington, and the maximum of 96·5 mph on Dauntsey bank.

Dr Days Bridge Junction was reached at 12.35 pm and after a brief stop there we proceeded to

HIGH SPEED TEST RUN: 30 APRIL 1954
10.55 am PADDINGTON—BRISTOL
Load: 8 cars, 253 tons tare, 260 tons full
Engine: 6003 *King George IV*
Driver: Wasley; Fireman: French (Old Oak)

Dist miles		Sch min	Actual m s	Speed mph
0·0	PADDINGTON .	0	0 00	
5·7	Ealing . . .		7 26	68·5
9·1	Southall . .	11	10 18	72
13·2	West Drayton .		13 43	75
18·5	SLOUGH . .	17½	17 51	75
24·2	Maidenhead .	21½	22 14	80
31·0	Twyford . .	27	27 24	82/74*
36·0	READING . .	31	31 23	75
41·5	Pangbourne .		35 54	72
48·5	Cholsey . .		41 21	80
53·1	DIDCOT .	48	44 44	84
60·4	Wantage Road .		50 04	79·5
66·5	Uffington . .		54 38	81·5
			pws	18
71·5	Shrivenham .		59 39	
77·3	SWINDON . .	67	65 44	72
82·9	Wootton Bassett .		70 03	82
87·7	Dauntsey .		73 20	96·5
94·0	CHIPPENHAM .	79	77 33	78
98·3	Corsham . .		80 51	80
101·9	Box . . .		83 30	82
106·9	BATH . . .	88½	88 17	35*
113·8	Keynsham . .		94 57	75
117·9	*Dr Days Bridge Jc* .	102½	99 19	

Net time 96 min
* Speed restriction

HIGH SPEED TEST RUN: 30 APRIL 1954
12.53½ pm STAPLETON ROAD—PADDINGTON
Load: 8 cars, 253 tons tare, 260 tons full
Engine: 6003 *King George IV*
Driver: Wasley; Fireman: French (Old Oak)

Dist miles		Sch min	Actual m s	Speed mph
0·0	STAPLETON ROAD . .	0	0 00	
3·2	Filton Jc .	5	5 10	
11·4	Chipping Sodbury .		13 30	66
16·0	Badminton . .	18	17 47	63·5
26·3	Little Somerford .		25 25	93
33·1	Wootton Bassett .	30½	30 22	65*
38·7	SWINDON . .	35½	35 03	79
49·5	Uffington . .		42 51	87
55·6	Wantage Road .		46 59	90/88·5
62·9	DIDCOT . .	56	51 52	92·5
67·5	Cholsey .		54 57	86
71·3	Goring . . .		57 56	eased
80·0	READING . .	68	64 31	82/77
91·8	Maidenhead . .	76½	73 01	90
			eased	81
97·5	SLOUGH . .	81	77 08	84
102·7	West Drayton .		80 52	86
106·9	Southall . .	87½	84 13	73
110·3	Ealing . .		86 53	77·5
			pws	
114·7	Westbourne Park .		92 55	
116·0	PADDINGTON .	101½	95 35	

Net time 93½ min

Stapleton Road, from which we started away on our high-speed return trip to Paddington only 18½ min after our arrival at Dr Days Bridge Junction. This proved to be another splendid run, despite certain incidental difficulties with steaming—not different, however, from conditions that might be expected in ordinary service. The initial timing requiring speeds of no more than 64·6 mph up the 1 in 300 to Badminton was planned to give a little respite to the crew of an engine starting from cold from

The high-speed test run of 30 April 1954, passing Hullavington on the return journey at 86 mph

The down Bristolian passing Chippenham : engine No 6015 'King Richard III'

Bristol, as in the case of the up 'Bristolian' in normal service, and the maximum speed subsequently attained at Little Somerford was frequently exceeded later in regular working. From Swindon onwards, however, a most competent display of sustained fast running was made. The average speed of 83·8 mph over the 64 miles from Swindon to West Drayton included the observance of slightly restricted speed between Goring and Reading, and again through Twyford station. The final permanent way check cost 2 min, and left a net time of $93\frac{1}{2}$ min—exactly corresponding to the 8 min recovery time included in the $101\frac{1}{2}$-min schedule. While the day's round in which we travelled from Paddington to Bristol and back between the hours of 10.55 am and 2.29 pm was an exhilarating experience—an overall average speed of 66·2 mph inclusive of the stops in the Bristol area—the exact-

The up Bristolian near Hullavington : engine No 6009 'King Charles II'

ness of the timekeeping was a triumph for the testing staff at Swindon, no less than for the enginemen who thus had the opportunity of participating in this dress rehearsal. The accelerated times came into force in June 1954, and with the exception of the down and up 'Bristolian' they were all worked by 'Castle' class engines. The principal onus fell upon Bath Road shed, Bristol, in those first months and several 'Castles' in specially good condition were drafted thence. These included 5027, 5057, 5063, 5077 and 5096, and added to engines like 5025 and 7034 made a fairly puissant stud. As expected the 'Kings' handled the accelerated 'Bristolian' with ease. In the very first week I clocked No 6015 *King Richard III* from Temple Meads to Paddington in 96 min 12 sec start-to-stop, and although running thus at maximum recovery standard was neither usual nor necessary the train was frequently 5 min early in arriving at Paddington. The temptation to enginemen to attain very high speeds when recovering time was stimulated by the lifting of the speed limit altogether on certain stretches of the line where the permanent way was in particularly good shape. The working timetables included the statement, referring to these stretches, that the speed might be 'as high as necessary'. This was a plain invitation to 'have a go', and over the years a number of instances were recorded of speeds closely approaching 100 mph by both 'Castle' and 'King' class engines.

Dist miles		Sch min	Actual m	Actual s	Speed mph
77·3	SWINDON .	. 67	65	31	69
80·0	*Hay Lane Box*	.	67	38	79
82·9	Wootton Bassett	.	69	44	85
84·0	*Milepost 84* .	.	70	30	88
85·0	*Milepost 85* .	.	71	11	89
86·0	*Milepost 86* .	.	71	50	95
87·0	*Milepost 87* .	.	72	27	102·5
87·75	Dauntsey .	.	72	53½	
89·0	*Milepost 89* .	.	73	39	98
90·0	*Milepost 90* .	.	74	16	95
91·0	*Milepost 91* .	.	74	55	91·5
			eased		
94·0	CHIPPENHAM	. 79	77	00	80

The highest speed I noted personally with a Great Western four-cylinder 4—6—0 was on the down 'Bristolian' with the normal seven-coach train and engine No 6018 *King Henry VI*. The accompanying log shows the relevant part of this journey, following recovery from a permanent way slowing east of Swindon. The maximum was 102·5 mph and very fortunately Kenneth Leech was at Dauntsey on this occasion and photographed the train, 'in the act' as it were. I am aware that several claims have been made subsequently of considerably higher speeds for 'King and 'Castle' class engines fitted with twin blastpipes and chimneys; but none of these claims have the supporting weight of evidence to enable them to be accepted as absolute fact. They are discussed in Chapter 9.

The up Bristolian near Hullavington at 85 mph : engine No 5076 'Gladiator', with the author on the footplate

CHAPTER 9

VITAL DYNAMOMETER CAR TESTS

IN studying what proved to be the final series of dynamometer car test runs with the Great Western four-cylinder 4—6—0s it is extremely important that the practical background should be fully appreciated. By some observers of locomotive performance it has been assumed that they were carried out principally to determine the ultimate capacity of the 'King' and 'Castle' class engines, but this is certainly not so. They were conducted on an urgent basis by practical railwaymen faced with the need to provide enhanced and more reliable all-round motive power, and if possible to devise alterations to design that could be made within the provisions of a strictly limited budget. They were definitely not a series of academic studies conducted in the style of remote back-room researches. Time was vital, and throughout the entire series the operating, motive power and chief mechanical engineer's departments worked in the closest liaison. Furthermore, it was

essential in providing for the working of the traffic that the accelerated timings proposed should be capable of achievement by *any* engine of the class— not by a few picked, carefully nursed units. This principle was, of course, not so readily applicable to the entire 'Castle' class, but the aim was certainly to make it applicable to all thirty of the 'Kings'. The schedules had to be capable of observance by an engine in the most run-down condition that was permitted in traffic.

To provide the necessary data for working out the new schedules the engine chosen for the original series of tests with the improved draughting had been one with not the best of reputations, No 6001. The draughting alterations described in Chapter 8 turned it into an extremely puissant machine, if not an exceptionally speedy one, by the standards set by other engines of the class, and when the time came for the 1955 trials another 'run of the mill'

'King George IV' with final form of single chimney
Down Saturday West of England express near Castle Cary: engine No 6003

Dynamometer car test, 10 March 1955, with Cornish Riviera Express near Reading West : engine No 6013 'King Henry VIII'

engine—very far from a 'star' performer—was chosen for the exceedingly arduous tests with the 'Cornish Riviera Express'. The high management of the Western Region wished to accelerate that most famous of trains to a four-hour schedule between Paddington and Plymouth, and the operating department were of the opinion that no existing Western Region locomotives were capable of the job, with the maximum load desired, of fourteen coaches from Paddington to Heywood Road, and twelve from there to Plymouth. Mr Smeddle and his staff were quite confident that the 'Kings' with improved draughting could do it; but to prove the point a series of dynamometer car test runs was arranged, in which the 'Kings' were to be pitted against 'Pacifics' of other regions. It was originally proposed to have both Eastern and London Midland 4—6—2s on test, and in addition to run the 'BR8' 4—6—2 No 71000 *Duke of Gloucester*, which was then on trial at the Swindon stationary testing plant. Eventually, however, the only stranger to run the 'Limited' was the LMR 'Duchess' class 4—6—2 No 46237 *City of Bristol*; the performance of the 'BR8' 4—6—2 on the stationary plant provided

ample data for her likely performance between Paddington and Plymouth to be accurately assessed.

In this book, it is, of course, the performance of 'King' class engine No 6013 *King Henry VIII* with which I am concerned. The runs made on the four successive days 8-11 March 1955 are of immense importance, not only including the hardest sustained efforts ever made by a 'King' class engine in all the history of the class, but including features of such deep significance as to initiate the further development which was ultimately to prove the final phase of the 'Castles' and 'Kings'. There were to be no unduly favourable conditions in these trials. The choice of a week in early March ran the risk of rough weather, and the engine chosen for test was an average member of the class, with a considerable mileage since last overhaul. As will be apparent from the photograph of the down train on 10 March she had a bad steam leak from the left-hand outside cylinder valve gland. I rode down to Plymouth in the dynamometer car and witnessed the magnificent performance detailed in the accompanying table. It was at that time the fastest run ever made between Paddington and Exeter, and the details of coal and water consumption show that it was made with good economy. My invitation was extended to the final up journey on the following day; but unfortunately an engagement on Tyneside necessitated my returning to London on the same evening, and I therefore missed the experience of witnessing the altogether extraordinary run that was made on Friday 11 March 1955. Then the load was one of twelve coaches throughout from Plymouth to Paddington but a strong easterly wind made those twelve coaches pull like fourteen in normal weather conditions, and the task of maintaining the accelerated schedule was made exceedingly onerous. The gross load behind the tender was actually 420 tons, but the equivalent load, in calm weather, would have been nearer 480 tons.

From all previous accounts of engine performance on the up road between Exeter and Paddington the task of working such a load over that 173·5 miles in 165 min will be appreciated as an extremely

CORNISH RIVIERA EXPRESS
Dynamometer Car Test Run
Load: to Heywood Road, 14 cars, 460 tons tare, 490 tons full
to Newton Abbot, 12 cars, 393 tons tare, 420 tons full
Engine: 6013 *King Henry VIII* (ID)
Driver: Shave; Fireman: Mitchell (Old Oak)

Dist miles		Sch min	Actual m s	Speed mph
0·0	PADDINGTON .	0	0 00	
1·3	Westbourne Park .		3 16	
5·7	Ealing . .		8 55	57·5
9·1	Southall .	12½	12 20	61
13·2	West Drayton .		16 22	63
18·5	SLOUGH .	21	21 00	70
24·2	Maidenhead .	26	25 51	71
31·0	Twyford .	32	31 31	70
36·0	READING .	37	35 58	40*
			pws	20
44·8	Aldermaston .		46 37	64·5
53·1	NEWBURY .	55	54 10	66/62·5
58·5	Kintbury .		59 02	66
61·5	Hungerford .		61 49	62
66·4	Bedwyn .	68	66 17	67
70·1	Savernake .	72½	70 04	50
75·3	Pewsey .		74 48	78/75
81·1	Patney . .	82½	79 14	82
			pws	40
86·9	Lavington .		84 00	
94·6	*Heywood Road Jc* .	93	91 08	72/65
97·0	*Fairwood Jc* .		93 10	72
100·3	*Clink Road Jc* .		96 04	62
102·3	*Blatchbridge Jc* .	100½	97 48	71
108·5	*Milepost 122¾* .		103 11	60
115·1	CASTLE CARY .	113½	108 49	77/65*
122·0	Keinton Mandeville .		112 46	77·5/74
125·8	Somerton .		117 00	82/75
130·8	*Curry Rivel Jc* .		120 53	83
138·0	*Cogload* .		126 25	72/73
142·7	TAUNTON .	136½	130 18	70·5
146·6	*Milepost 167* .		133 39	66
148·6	*Milepost 169* .		135 30	62·5
149·8	Wellington .		136 45	60
151·6	*Milepost 172* .		138 39	46
152·6	*Milepost 173* .		140 02	39
153·6	*Whiteball Box* .	149	141 37	37·5
158·6	Tiverton Jc .		146 18	77
160·9	Cullompton .		148 15	eased
166·4	Silverton .		153 01	80 (max)
170·0	Stoke Canon .		155 54	
173·5	EXETER .	167½	159 14	45*
			pws	15
178·2	Exminster .		165 59	
			pws	30
188·5	Teignmouth .		178 44	
193·7	NEWTON ABBOT	192	186 15	

Net times: to passing Exeter, 156 min
to stopping at Newton, 178 min
* Speed restrictions

CORNISH RIVIERA EXPRESS
Dynamometer Car Test Run
Load: 12 cars, 393 tons tare, 420 tons full
Engine: 6013 *King Henry VIII*
Driver: F. Bolt; Fireman: E. Knapman (Laira)

Dist miles			†Actual m s	Speed mph
0·0	EXETER .	.	0 00	pass slowly
3·5	Stoke Canon .		4 13	52·5
7·2	Silverton .		8 22	58·5
12·6	Cullompton .		13 34	65
14·9	Tiverton Jc .		15 40	60/66
19·9	*Whiteball Box* .		20 38	53·5
23·7	Wellington .		23 52	80
28·8	Norton Fitzwarren .		27 49	71
30·8	TAUNTON .		29 27	74
38·8	Athelney .		35 45	77·5
42·5	*Curry Rivel Jc* .		38 40	75
48·0	Somerton . .		43 29	65/71·5
53·5	Keinton Mandeville .		48 15	67/75
58·4	CASTLE CARY .		52 31	53
			pws	17
61·8	Bruton . .		59 00	46
65·2	*Milepost 122¾* .		63 32	42
71·2	*Blatchbridge Jc* .		68 53	78
73·2	*Clink Road Jc* .		70 29	73
76·5	*Fairwood Jc* .		73 02	81
78·9	*Heywood Road Jc* .		75 02	70
86·6	Lavington .		81 28	76
92·1	Patney .		86 41	64·5
98·2	Pewsey .		91 41	73
103·4	Savernake .		96 20	61
107·1	Bedwyn .		100 00	easy
112·0	Hungerford .		104 35	62*
115·0	Kintbury .		107 19	70
120·4	NEWBURY .		111 43	79
123·9	Thatcham .		114 27	80
126·7	Midgham .		116 52	58*
132·3	Theale .		121 46	74·5
137·5	READING .		127 45	37*
142·5	Twyford .		132 52	68
149·3	Maidenhead .		138 28	74
155·0	SLOUGH .		143 07	74·5
160·3	West Drayton .		147 28	71
164·4	Southall .		151 12	70
167·8	Ealing .		153 51	71·5
			sigs	
172·2	Westbourne Park .		159 38	
173·2	PADDINGTON .		162 04	

Overall time from Plymouth, 241 min
† Times from passing Exeter slowly
* Speed restrictions

The Swindon dynamometer car in 1955, looking rearwards showing dials
for direct indicating of horsepower

difficult one. It entailed the almost unprecedented firing rate of 4,000 lb of coal per hour between Exeter and Reading. Had not the engine crew thrown themselves into the task with might and main it would have been impossible. More than this, it would, even so, have been impossible had not Inspector Andress, who was riding on the footplate, worked like a Trojan in getting coal forward. This is one case where the running details, as given in the accompanying log, are not self-explanatory; but a comparison of the performances on 10 and 11 March go some way towards clarification.

Diagrams plotted in the drawing office of the experimental section at Swindon, showing the working over three sections where the engine was being steamed continuously hard for long periods, are reproduced herewith, namely from Exeter to Whiteball, from Taunton to Castle Cary, and from Heywood Road Junction to Savernake. On these diagrams are plotted the speed, the actual dhp

DOWN CORNISH RIVIERA EXPRESS: 10/3/55 Paddington—Newton Abbot	
Average net steam produced by boiler .	26,950 lb/hr
Firing rate	3,245 lb/hr
Average dhp	
under power	978
actual	828
Coal per dhp/hr	
inclusive of auxiliaries . . .	3·32 lb
exclusive of auxiliaries . . .	3·21 lb
Average speed (actual) . . .	62·5 mph

UP CORNISH RIVIERA EXPRESS: 11/3/55 Exeter—Reading	
Running time	127·6 min
Average speed	64·7 mph
Power time	117·3 min
Total coal	8,240 lb
Firing rate	4,210 lb/hr
Net steam rate	29,835 lb/hr
Average dhp	1,020
Coal per dhp/hr	
inclusive of auxiliaries . . .	4·13 lb
exclusive of auxiliaries . . .	4·00 lb

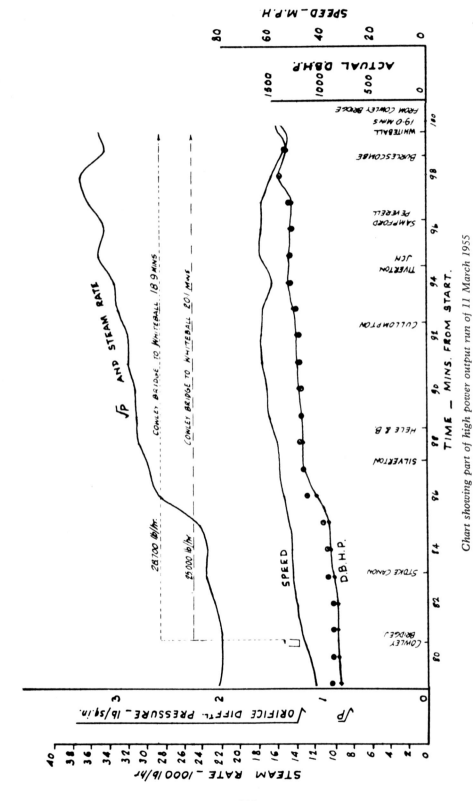

Chart showing part of high power output run of 11 March 1955

The Swindon dynamometer car in 1955, looking forward from integrator table

uncorrected from gradient, and the steam rate. Lines are drawn on the diagram to show the steam rate of 25,000 lb per hr, corresponding to the maximum firing rate it is considered that a single fireman could sustain continuously, and to a steam rate of 28,700 lb, which is considered to be attainable intermittently for recovery purposes. On clearing the area of restricted speed through Exeter, and beginning to settle down into express speed, it was soon clear that the adverse weather conditions were having a seriously hampering effect and soon after Stoke Canon a telephone message from the dynamometer car to the footplate initiated a marked stepping up of the effort. From there onwards a comparison of the actual steam rate with the 28,700 lb maximum recovery rate shows the outstanding nature of the effort developed. Near Burlescombe a peak of 37,000 lb per hr was attained, with an actual dhp, on 1 in 115, of 1,440. Corrected for gradient

this gave an equivalent figure of 1,860.

Between Creech Junction and Keinton Mandeville the steam rate was continuous above 30,000 lb per hr for 18 min, with a maximum of 34,000, with the edhp at 1,400 near Somerton. The third diagram shows the magnificent effort made between Heywood Road Junction and Savernake, when the fireman and Inspector Andress were both beginning to feel the physical strain of such an effort. On the 1 in 222 gradient from Lavington to Patney the minimum speed was 64 mph; the steam rate rose to a peak of 34,500 lb per hr, and the actual dhp recorded at 1,300 corresponded to an 'equivalent' value of 1,535. To keep up this kind of performance with little intermission, from Exeter to Reading, was a positively heroic effort on the part of Driver Bolt and Fireman Knapman of Laira shed. In addition to Inspector Andress I must also mention the engineer from the testing staff who was also on

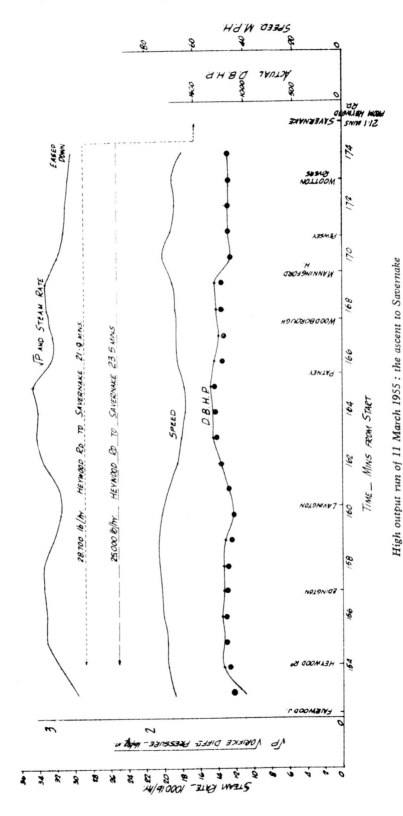

High output run of 11 March 1955 : the ascent to Savernake

Engine No 6015 'King Richard III' with double chimney

the footplate on this memorable occasion, for he became well known to enthusiasts in connection with the working of preserved locomotives: the ever-cheerful Ernest Nutty. Heroics apart, however, those graphs showed, in the greatest clarity, a weakness in the design of the 'King' class engines as re-draughted. The steam rate is proportional to the square root of the back pressure, and this can be read off, to a different scale, from the three diagrams. It will be seen that there were times when this back pressure rose to about 10 lb per sq in.

Experience was available at Swindon showing the

Engine No 6015 on the Cornish Riviera Express on the run detailed on page 118

113

H

'King' class : layout of smokebox with twin orifice blastpipe and double chimney

effect of twin orifice blastpipes, and the working of the LMR 'Duchess' class 4—6—2, and of the 'BR8' showed that the arrangement of twin blastpipe and chimney had the effect, on those engines, of permitting a high rate of evaporation with a low back pressure. The smokebox of the 'BR8' engine had in fact been worked out at Swindon, and the two blastpipes were each those of a '2301' class 0—6—0—the celebrated 'Dean Goods'—which had an outstandingly successful arrangement of draughting. Smeddle, therefore, decided to try the effect of a double-blastpipe on a 'King'.

The lay-out of the smokebox incorporating the double blastpipe as worked out by Sam Ell is shown in the accompanying drawing. It was extremely successful in removing the limitations to evaporation imposed by the former single-chimney draughting arrangement. Henceforth the maximum continous rate was limited only by the capacity of the grate to burn fuel. The efficiency of draughting was improved, enabling the orifice discharge pressure to be reduced to one-third of that of the single chimney arrangement, and this, of course, resulted in a considerable reduction in back pressure on the pistons, and a freer running locomotive. It was found possible to reduce the 'pull' on the fire and to achieve uniformity of air distribution over the firebed. Although this is to some extent anticipating the results of the test runs about to be described it was found in general that the double-chimneyed engines showed a 7 per cent economy in coal consumption over the single-chimneyed high-superheat 'Kings' with improved draughting. This economy was observed by the locomotive testing staff in the working of comparable revenue-earning express passenger services.

At this time also the 'Kings' were being fitted with new cylinders, and the historian can look back a little wistfully to what might have been achieved had the opportunity been taken of introducing the improved, internally streamlined design of cylinders sketched out for the projected 'Pacific'. The British locomotive world was already well aware of the astonishing improvement wrought by a comparable process on the LMSR 'Royal Scots', when the rebuilt version was produced, in 1943. In combination with the modified smokebox and blastpipe arrangements internally streamlined cylinders would have resulted in a veritable 'Super King'. The change would have required entirely new patterns and coreboxes, and the extra cost would have been considerable. The enhanced power might have been too much for the existing frame design to withstand, as it proved to be in the case of the Chapelon rebuilt

The original form of self-cleaning screens on the double-chimneyed 'Kings'

4—8—0s on the PO Midi Railway in France. The frames of the 'Kings' were partially renewed by welding on new front portions, ahead of the motion plate. This was, of course, just a renewal of the original design, and did not involve any strengthening or other modification.

Engine No 6015 *King Richard III* was the first to have the modified smokebox arrangement, and reports from the running inspectors were so enthusiastic that Sam Ell fixed up a trip on the Cornish Riviera Express, on which he was accompanied by Inspector W. Andress. The driver was W. Potter, the senior driver at Old Oak Common; essentially a 'safe' man, regularly entrusted with Royal Trains, but not at all the kind of man one would associate with all-out attempts on speed records. This suited Ell's purpose admirably, which was to see for himself how the modified engine performed when worked in the same way as the single-chimneyed engines were, when making maximum speeds of 85 mph. Ell and Inspector Andress rode No 6015 on Monday 26 September 1955, and on the following day Ell reported to Mr Smeddle thus:

Engines of the 'King' class have benefitted very substantially from improved draughting, but tests revealed that the internal resistance at high rates of evaporation and high speeds could be reduced by fitting a double chimney design with these special proportions. The greatest benefit would be found in the freedom with which the engine would run at high speeds and improvement in power then available.

Engine No 6015 has recently been fitted, and after an initial period on the 11.15 am ex Paddington was tried yesterday, September 26th, on the Cornish Riviera. This run revealed that the substantial improvements expected were attained. On stretches where high speeds of about 85 mph are normally obtained, speeds rose on engine No 6015 to over 100 mph with the same engine working. On stiff bank working, the reduced back pressure was reflected in a marked improvement in engine performance. Steaming in general was entirely satisfactory. Water consumption was relatively low and coal consumption reduced by the reduced tearing action on the fire by the double chimney.

I attach a log of the run, from which it will be seen that the engine was easily capable of recovering time from the several severe restrictions, and two of these signal checks. A third severe check at Totnes brought the train to a stand for 9 min, but the arrival at Plymouth was no more than 8 min late.

LOG OF CORNISH RIVIERA 10.30 AM PADDINGTON TO PLYMOUTH, MONDAY 26/9/55

Engine No 6015: Load 331 tons/10 vehicles throughout

			Booked	Actual
Paddington	.	d	10.30 am	10.30 am
Westbourne P	.	p	10.33	10.33
Southall	.	p	10.42	10.45
Slough	.	p	10.49½	10.51
Maidenhead	.	p	10.54½	10.56
Twyford	.	p	11.00½	11.01½
Reading	.	p	11.06	11.08
Newbury	.	p	11.24½	11.24
Bedwyn	.	p	11.37½	11.37
Savernake	.	p	11.41½	11.41
Patney	.	p	11.51½	11.50
Heywood Road Jc	.	p	12.02 pm	11.59
Blatchbridge	.	p	12.09	12.06 pm
Castle Cary	.	p	12.22	12.19
Creech	.	p		12.41
Taunton	.	p	12.46	12.45
Wellington	.	p		12.53
Whiteball	.	p	12.57	12.58
Exeter	.	p	1.15	1.17
Newton Abbot	.	arr	1.40	pass 1.44½
		dep	1.43	
Dainton	.	p	1.49½	1.50
Totnes	.	p	1.56½	arr 1.56
				dep 2.05
Brent	.	p	2.07½	2.18
Hemerdon	.	p	2.20	2.30
Plymouth (North Rd)	.	arr	2.30	2.38

Signal and engineering delays . . .	27 min
Late arrival at Plymouth . . .	8 min
Recovery by engine	19 min
Max recovery allowed in schedule .	9 min
Recovery above max recovery allowance .	10 min

TRS 15 mph Ladbroke Grove } 1 min
TRS 50 mph O.C.C. East

TRS 50 mph Twyford East 2 min
Signal check Reading East

TRS 75 mph Patney - Lavington
Max speed 103 mph Lavington

Max speed 100 mph Curry Rivel
TRS 30 mph Alford H 4 min
Signal check Creech 2 min
TRS 15 mph Wellington 3 min

TRS 10 mph City Basin } 4 min
TRS 30 mph Teignmouth

TRS 30 mph Totnes
Signal check stopped 9 min

The speeds were carefully observed by stopwatch, and as Ell remarks, showed that where the single-chimneyed engines attained speeds of 85 mph the modified engine was running at 100 mph. He was so pleased with these results that he suggested that his chief assistant, H. Tichener, should also have a trip. This was quickly arranged, and on Thursday 29 September Tichener and Inspector Andress arrived at Paddington to ride No 6015 on the 'Limited'. Quite fortuitously Driver Potter was again on the job, and before leaving he confided to his 'passengers' that he might be able to do even better than on the Monday. And where both observers on the Monday had clocked 103 mph—just prior to the commencement of a slight permanent way restriction to 75 mph near Patney—Andress clocked one quarter mile at 106½ and one at 108½ mph. The stop-watch was not reset after the second reading, and was taken to Swindon and shown to Ell on the following day. Then the rumours began to get around; the popular press got hold of one version, and 116 mph was quoted in print, and eventually through the exaggerations of certain ultra-ardent Great Western fans the speed got at one stage to 130 mph! In one version reported personally to myself at Swindon the locality (110 mph) was given as Langport. Recent research, how-

*St Ives to Paddington express (Saturdays) passing Wolfhall Junction, Savernake :
engine No 6017 'King Edward IV'*

ever, and fresh conversations with those actually involved, has brought this documentation to light, and the 108½ is thus revealed as a reading from one stop-watch observer. The average for ¾ mile was 107½ mph.

This reported speed has since become the subject of some controversy; certain erudite analysts have claimed that it was impossible. I was not there, and there is no supporting evidence of point-to-point times; but Sam Ell was one of the most highly disciplined experimental engineers I have ever met, and I am sure that professional etiquette would have restrained him from making any exaggerated claim. I am quite prepared to admit that a few isolated stop-watch readings might have given figures a half or even 1 mph out; but not more than that. As to the 'impossibility' of such a figure, the increased freedom of the double-chimneyed engines gives the lie to any such assertion. As described in Chapter 8

of this book I logged in great detail a rapid acceleration to 102·5 mph with a single-chimneyed 'King' on Dauntsey bank, and I certainly do not see any theoretical reason why a much freer running engine should not have travelled at higher speed between Somerton and Curry Rivel Junction. There is unfortunately no absolute proof either way—only the word of an experimentalist of the highest integrity.

In May 1956 another engine, No 6002 *King William IV*, was put through a series of trials, first on the West of England road, and later between Paddington and Wolverhampton. Through Mr Smeddle's kindness I was able to accompany three of these runs, and was able to witness at first hand not only some very fine running but also some features of the performance that were of marked significance in comparison with the working of the single-chimneyed engines. My three runs were made on the 3.30 pm Paddington to Plymouth, on

Engine No 6017 'King Edward IV' with the tapered form of double chimney

Engine No 6002 'King William IV' (double chimney) passing Teignmouth

the up 'Cornish Riviera Express', and on the 3 pm Birmingham Snow Hill to Paddington; but some

seven months earlier I had ridden on the footplate of engine No 6015 *King Richard III*, on the down 'Cornish Riviera Express', and logged a performance of outstanding merit. A reference to this personal experience may appropriately precede the description of the test runs. This was one of those occasions when the incidence of delays might well have seemed to put completely out of the question any chance of running the 'Cornish Riviera Express' to Plymouth in the even four hours. An abbreviated log of this journey is set out in the accompanying table.

Before the start it was known that three permanent way slacks were required. These were expected to cost about 9 min in running, and without unduly forcing the pace an attempt was made in the early stages to get some time in hand. With cut-offs of 15 per cent on the level to Reading, and 15 to 17 per cent up the Kennet Valley, 5 min had been gained on this fast timing to Patney. Then we ran into heavy fog, and instead of detaching our Weymouth slip coach at Heywood Road Junction we had to feel our way into Westbury and stop. This

CORNISH RIVIERA EXPRESS
Load: to Westbury, 11 cars, 362 tons tare, 390 tons full
to Plymouth, 10 cars, 327 tons tare, 350 tons full
Engine: 6015 *King Richard III* (double chimney)
Driver: Newcombe; Fireman: Hawker (Laira)

Dist miles		Sch min	Actual m s	Speed mph	Dist miles		Sch min	Actual m s	Speed mph
0·0	PADDINGTON .	0	0 00		130·9	*Curry Rivel Jc* .		132 01	82
5·7	Ealing . .		8 54	58·5	138·1	*Cogload* . .		137 32	73
9·1	Southall . .	12	12 21	64				pws	15
13·2	West Drayton .		16 04	69	142·8	TAUNTON .	136	143 54	55
18·5	SLOUGH . .	19½	20 23	75	144·8	Norton			
24·2	Maidenhead .	24½	25 00	73		Fitzwarren .		145 54	63
31·0	Twyford . .	30½	30 34	74				pws	15
36·0	READING . .	36	35 01	(slack)	149·9	Wellington . .		153 32	60
44·8	Aldermaston .		44 11	68	153·7	*Whiteball Box* .	147	157 39	47
53·1	NEWBURY .	54½	51 43	64/68	158·7	Tiverton Jc .		162 03	78·5
58·5	Kintbury .		56 23	70	161·0	Cullompton . .		163 54	eased
61·5	Hungerford .		59 05	60*	166·4	Silverton .		168 16	80 (max)
66·4	Bedwyn . .	67½	63 31	67½	170·1	Stoke Canon .		171 10	
70·1	Savernake .	71½	67 19	eased	173·6	EXETER .	165	174 41	
75·3	Pewsey . .		72 00	79/74	178·3	Exminster .		179 27	68
81·1	Patney . .	81½	76 29	83·5	188·6	Teignmouth .		191 06	eased
			fog stop		193·8	NEWTON			
94·6	*Heywood Road Jc*	92	92 56	66		ABBOT .	190	197 38	25*
95·6	WESTBURY arr		95 03		194·9	*Aller Jc* . .			56
	dep		96 53		195·6	*Milepost 216* .		200 05	
97·1	*Fairwood Jc* .	94	99 41	52	196·6	*Milepost 217* .		201 21	
100·4	*Clink Road Jc* .	97	103 24	53·5	197·6	*Dainton Box* .	197	203 20	26
	Blatchbridge .			69	202·3	Totnes .	204½	209 31	54
108·4	*Milepost 122¾*		110 35	60·5	205·2	*Tigley Box* .		213 50	26·5
111·8	Bruton . .		113 31	75	207·0	*Rattery Box* .		217 39	34
115·2	CASTLE CARY .	112	116 28	60*	209·3	Brent . .	215½	220 49	50
			pws	15	218·9	*Hemerdon Box* .	230	231 47	63 (max)
120·1	Keinton				221·8	Plympton .		234 09	72 (max)
	Mandeville .		123 02	58·5	224·1	Lipson Jc .		237 11	
125·6	Somerton . .		127 51	76/70	225·6	PLYMOUTH .	240	239 50	

* Speed restrictions

led to a delay of 12 min and made us 4½ min late on passing Castle Cary with all three permanent way slacks yet to come. Yet, as will be seen from the log, with excellent work throughout we were able to make a punctual arrival in Plymouth, having effected a net gain of no less than 21 min on schedule. This was certainly a most impressive example of the work of the double-chimneyed engines; for although the load was relatively light, by the standards of this route, in the early stages the concluding load of 327 tons tare is fairly close to the maximum permitted to an unassisted 'King' over the South Devon line. Throughout the trip No 6015 in her modified condition gave every impression of a very strong and free-running engine. The water consumption was a total of 7,800 gallons, equal to 35 gall per mile, and an evaporation of 19,500 lb per hr. This, of course, was a long way below the maximum capacity of the locomotive.

Coming now to the full dress trials of engine No 6002, in May 1956, detailed logs are shown of the journeys that I experienced personally. These do not show in the bare times speeds achieved any features of performance that would not have been expected, either with the single-chimneyed engines with improved draughting or indeed from the original design in pre-war conditions of fuel and maintenance; but in the dynamometer car there were some points of significance. Furthermore, the results obtained a year earlier with the 'Duchess' class 4—6—2 of the London Midland Region were available for comparison. The latter was by common consent one of the most advanced designs in regular service in Great Britain at the time, and in the heavy duty imposed by test conditions on the Cornish Riviera Express both the 'Pacific' and the 'King' were well extended. The first test run with 6002 was made on the 3.30 pm express, which had a rather easier timing, but conveyed the full load as far as Exeter. There was the additional interest that with the reduced load from that station onwards no assistance was taken over the South Devon line, and one could see from the dynamometer car the effects of the Dainton and Rattery inclines.

To Taunton the train was run at the point-to-point times of the four-hour Cornish Riviera Express reaching Taunton stop in 133 min 14 sec against the 136 min to pass of the latter train. The engine appeared to develop the effort easily, and as will be seen from the log there was no actual dhp in excess of 1,150. From the restart a fine effort was made up Wellington bank, with 475 tons, and the 1,200 actual dhp approaching Whiteball Tunnel was equal to 1,540 'equivalent'—an excellent figure at 42 mph.

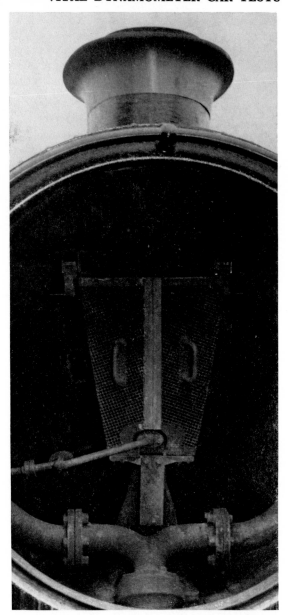

The later form of self-cleaning screen developed at Swindon

Over the South Devon line very consistent outputs of 1,100 to 1,250 actual dhp were shown on the banks, and with a load of 278 tons tare, 295 tons full this gave us minimum speeds of 30 mph at Dainton, 29·5 mph at Tigley, after a maximum of only 48 mph through Totnes, and an attained maximum of 40 mph at Rattery summit. With very easy running afterwards and a bad signal check at Plympton, we ran the 61·8 miles from Exeter to Plymouth in 69 min 33 sec instead of the 75 min booked to this train.

THE GWR STARS, CASTLES & KINGS

On the return journey by the Cornish Riviera Express on the following day we were double-headed as far as Newton Abbot, and then made the excellent run tabulated. We were working to the regular 4¼-hour schedule, and in good weather conditions had no particular need for hurry. The point that interested me above all others on this run was the striking difference in back pressure, as compared with that on the single-chimneyed 'Kings'. On the Bruton bank, where the engine was being worked hard the maximum difference in pressure across the orifice did not exceed 1¾ in of mercury. This represented a smokebox vacuum of 9 in and a pressure of 4½ lb per sq in. In recovering from the Lavington permanent way check, where for a brief period the engine was being worked really hard, developing 1,300 actual dhp on a 1 in 222 gradient,

3.30 pm PADDINGTON—EXETER
Dynamometer Car Test Run
Load: 449 tons tare, 475 tons full
Engine: 6002 *King William IV* (double chimney)

Dist miles		Sch min	Actual m s	Speed mph	Actual dhp
0·0	PADDINGTON	0	0 00		
1·3	Westbourne Pk .	4	3 07		
5·7	Ealing . .		8 37	59	
9·1	Southall . .	13	11 51	66	
13·2	West Drayton .		15 31	69	
18·5	Slough . .	21	19 53	74	
24·2	Maidenhead .	26½	24 35	72	
31·0	Twyford . .	33	30 17	71	
36·0	READING .	38	34 43	40*	
			pws	15	
41·3	Theale . .		42 58	59/64	1,150
46·8	Midgham .		48 12	60*	1,000
53·1	NEWBURY .	57½	54 28	64/61	
58·5	Kintbury .		59 35	66	1,000
61·5	Hungerford .		62 24	60*	
66·4	Bedwyn . .	71½	67 07	64	1,100
70·1	Savernake .	76	71 05	45†	950
75·3	Pewsey . .		75 39	79/75	1,050
81·1	Patney . .	87	80 23	80·5	1,000
			pws	75*	
86·9	Lavington .		84 43	87	950
94·6	*Heywood Rd Jc*	98	90 14	75	nil
100·3	*Clink Rd Jc* .		95 08	61·5	1,000
102·3	*Blatchbridge Jc* .	105	96 49	70·5	900
108·3	*Milepost 122¾* .		102 32	58	
115·1	CASTLE CARY		108 50	67/56*	
120·0	Keinton				
	Mandeville .		113 10	72/68	870
125·5	Somerton .		117 46	76/70	1,000
130·8	*Curry Rivel Jc* .		121 49	84	
138·0	*Cogload* . .		127 21		
142·7	TAUNTON .	148	133 14		
2·0	Norton				
	Fitzwarren .		3 43	51	1,100
7·1	Wellington .		9 16	58	1,200
9·9	*Milepost 173* .		12 32	42	1,200
10·6	*Whiteball Box* .	16	14 00	41·5	
15·9	Tiverton Jc .		18 46	74/68	
18·2	Cullompton .		20 37	74	
			pws	15	
27·3	Stoke Canon .		31 15	66	1,200§
29·5	*Cowley*				
	Bridge Jc .	35	33 23		
30·8	EXETER .	37	35 38		

* Speed restrictions, regular
† After slack to 50 mph at Grafton
§ In accelerating from slack

UP CORNISH RIVIERA EXPRESS
Dynamometer Car Test Run
Load: 12 cars, 391 tons tare, 420 tons full
Engine: 6002 *King William IV* (double chimney)

Dist miles		Sch min	Actual m s	Speed mph	Actual dhp
0·0	*Newton Abbot West* .	0	0 00		
0·2	NEWTON ABBOT .		1 10		
5·4	Teignmouth .		7 55	50	
8·2	Dawlish . .		11 14	52	
15·7	Exminster .		19 20	62	800
20·4	EXETER .	24½	24 50	10*	950
23·9	Stoke Canon .		30 07	54	
27·6	Silverton .		34 07	60/55	
33·0	Cullompton .		39 08	61	1,000
35·3	Tiverton Jc .		42 00	54/58	900
40·3	*Whiteball Box* .	48½	47 37	46	1,200 (max)
44·1	Wellington .		51 01	82/79	
49·2	Norton				
	Fitzwarren .		54 47	84	
			sigs	58	
51·2	TAUNTON .	59	56 42		
53·6	*Creech Jc* .		58 52	72	800
59·2	*Athelney* .		63 34	68	820
62·9	*Curry Rivel Jc* .		66 57	72	
68·4	Somerton .		71 45	60/70	950
71·6	Charlton				
	Mackrell .		74 43	64	930
73·9	Keinton				
	Mandeville .		76 42	70·5	800
78·8	CASTLE CARY	85	81 00	63	1,100
85·6	*Milepost 122¾* .		88 18	45	1,000
91·6	*Blatchbridge Jc*	100	93 55	76	850
93·6	*Clink Road Jc* .	102	95 32	72·5	
96·9	*Fairwood Jc* .	105	98 07	77·5	
99·3	*Heywood Rd Jc*	107	100 03	70	1,000
107·0	Lavington .		106 30	71·5	1,000
			pws	25	
112·5	Patney . .	121	115 18	56	1,300 (max)
118·6	Pewsey . .		120 54	66	1,000
123·8	Savernake .	131	126 10	56	750
127·5	Bedwyn . .	136	129 45	70	
132·4	Hungerford .		134 18	60*	700
135·4	Kintbury . .		137 04	71	
140·8	NEWBURY .	147	141 27	77/73	
144·3	Thatcham .		144 16	75·5	
147·1	Midgham . .		146 47	60*	
152·7	Theale . .		151 54	69	800
			sigs	30	
157·9	READING .	163½	159 31		800
162·9	Twyford . .	169	165 09	69	900
			pws	15	
169·7	Maidenhead .	174½	173 37	45	850
175·4	SLOUGH .	179½	179 32	66	800
184·8	Southall . .	189	187 54	68	880
188·2	Ealing . .		190 52	68	
193·9	PADDINGT'N	202	199 10		

Net time 192 min
* Speed restriction

*Dynamometer car tests with engine No 6002, having double chimney :
the 3.30 pm ex-Paddington passing Reading*

the back pressure was less than 6 lb per sq in, and for the rest of the ascent to Savernake it was approximately 3 lb per sq in. This clearly indicated a much freer running engine than the single-chimneyed type, and fully justified the predictions made for the change. A considerably faster run was made on the dynamometer car test run two days later, with the same engine and load. There were little differences in time to Exeter, but after that the second journey drew ahead, with overall times of 53 min 51 sec to Taunton; 76 min exactly to Castle Cary; 94 min 2 sec to Heywood Road; and 152 min 57 sec to Reading. Although the effort was then somewhat eased the arrival at Paddington was in 188 min 25 sec from the Newton start—thus practically observing the special four-hour schedule operated in the 1955 trials with engine No 6013. In calm weather, however, there was a great difference in the effort required, as will be seen from the accompanying table.

Within my own experience in the dynamometer car, by far the hardest work demanded of No 6002 came on the trip with the 3 pm up from Birmingham. Schedule-wise this could have been an easy duty, but through a piece of faulty operating we were stopped for 13 min at Banbury Junction, and so left Banbury on our 67·5-mile run to Paddington some 16 min late. With a load of 434 tons tare this gave plenty of opportunity for some hard running. The immediate start out of Birmingham was quite gentle, but then we got away in great style, reaching 78 mph at Lapworth, passing Hatton somewhat faster than usual, and then touching 88 mph before Warwick. Climbing the Southam Road bank we did well, showing a back pressure of less than 4 lb per sq in, when developing 1,320 edhp at 50 mph, and then there came the succession of checks from Ironstone sidings onwards. On the continuation run to Paddington an allowance of 86 min would have been absurdly easy in comparison with pre-war running standards on the Birmingham route, even with two

UP CORNISH RIVIERA TESTS

				1955	1956
Year	.	.	.	1955	1956
Engine No	.	.	.	6013	6002
Type	.	.	.	Single Blastpipe	Double Blastpipe
Load, tons tare	.	.	.	393½	391
Average speed mph	.	.	.	64·7	64·7
Firing rate lb/per hr	.	.	.	4,210	2,800
Net steam rate lb per hr	.	.	.	29,835	20,800
Average dhp	.	.	.	1,020	799
Coal per dhp hr (lb) exclusive of auxiliaries	.	.	.	4·0	3·5

'KING' AND LMR 'DUCHESS' CLASS COMPARISON OF TESTS RESULTS OF WR LOCOMOTIVES ON 'CORNISH RIVIERA'—WESTERN REGION

Date		WR 'King' Class No 6002				LMR 'Duchess' Class No 46237			
		28/5/56	29/5/56	30/5/56	31/5/56	17/5/55	18/5/55	19/5/55	20/5/55
Total coal	lb	11,083	10,232	11,997	10,460	13,601	12,759	14,427	12,859
Trip coal	lb	9,761	8,910	10,675	9,138	11,758	10,916	12,584	11,016
Trailing ton miles		98,500	97,100	103,800	97,100	104,700	97,700	96,380	105,200
Total water	lb	77,000	69,000	83,500	70,800	91,050	91,400	99,400	94,100
Work done on trailing load dhp	hrs	2,706	2,709	3,213	2,675	3,263	3,052	3,074	3,349
Total coal/trailing ton mile	lb	.112	.106	.116	.108	.130	.130	.150	.122
Total water/trailing ton mile	lb	.783	.711	.804	.729	.870	.943	1.032	.895
Total coal/dhp hr	lb	4.09	3.78	3.73	3.91	4.17	4.18	4.7	3.84
Total water/dhp hr	lb	28.4	25.5	26.0	26.5	27.9	30.0	32.4	28.1
Trip coal/dhp hr	lb	3.60	3.29	3.33	3.41	3.50	3.58	4.12	3.29

bad permanent way checks to be observed; but the late start was, for test purposes, fortuitous, and we had some really hard running.

The first significant item was the descent from Ardley to Blackthorn, where the engine was steamed hard. The figure of 1,150 dhp shown in the log was on topping Ardley summit, but the effort dwindled only a little as the speed rose from 56 mph at Ardley station to 86 mph at Blackthorn. At the latter point the back pressure was only 2 lb per sq in. A careful observance of the speed restriction was made at Ashendon Junction following which a big effort was transiently registered: 1,400 actual dhp and a back pressure of $4\frac{1}{2}$ lb per sq in. Some of the hardest work of all came in recovering from the Princes Risborough slack, up the 1 in 167 to Saunderton. At the summit speed was 35 mph; the actual dhp showed an equivalent value on this gradient of 1,470, and the back pressure was $7\frac{3}{4}$ lb per sq in. This was one of the highest registered with No 6002; but even this was low compared with the figures shown on certain stretches by No 6013 in the 1955 tests. Perhaps the most significant comparison between the single- and double-chimneyed engines, so far as these tests are concerned lies in the 900 dhp developed by No 6002 at 86 mph at Blackthorn, and the closely similar figure of 950 at 87 mph at Lavington on the down 3.30 pm express. In the full dress trials on No 6001 the actual dhp figure at 86 mph when 'all-out', two firemen and making a steam rate of 28,700 lb per hr was only 900. At Blackthorn No 6002 had the regulator eased back to give only 190 lb per sq in steam chest pressure. This shows clearly the great improvement in performance at high speed made by the introduction of the double chimney.

One of the most interesting results of the several stages of improved draughting on the 'Kings' is the comparison that the performance of the final version affords with the LMSR 'Duchess' class 'Pacific'. The overall results of the Cornish Riviera tests, in May 1955 with the 4—6—2 *City of Bristol* and in May 1956 with No 6002, are tabulated herewith, and on the strength of trip coal per dhp hour the advantage lies slightly with the 'King'. It was these results that convinced the Western Region management that there was no need to look beyond the indigenous Swindon design for locomotives to work the accelerated services. Authorisation was given for the whole class to be rebuilt with double chimneys, and the work was completed with No 6008 *King James II* in December 1958.

For some time previous to the 'King' trials, 'Castle' class engines had taken over the working

3 pm BIRMINGHAM—PADDINGTON
Dynamometer Car Test Run
Load: 434 tons tare, 470 tons full
Engine: 6002 *King William IV* (double chimney)

Dist miles		Sch min	Actual m	s	Speed mph	Actual dhp
0·0	BIRMINGHAM (SNOW HILL)	0	0	00		
3·2	Tyseley	5½	5	18	54	1,200
7·0	Solihull	12½	9	10	60	900
10·4	Knowle	12½	12	12	69	800
12·9	Lapworth		14	16	78	500
17·1	Hatton	18	17	38	72	700
21·3	Warwick		20	40	88	
23·3	LEAMINGTON	24	23	19		
1·1	*Milepost 105*		3	10		1,200
6·1	Southam Road		9	25	50/49	1,000
11·2	Fenny Compton		14	42	63/54·5	950
16·2	Cropredy		19	42	72	700
			sig stops			
19·8	BANBURY	25	41	37		
3·5	King's Sutton		5	48	56	
5·1	*Aynho Jc*	9½	7	29	60	
			pws		25	
10·3	Ardley	18¼	15	38	45	1,150
14·1	BICESTER		18	58	80	950
17·1	Blackthorn		21	02	86	900
20·1	Brill		23	14	73/77	
23·4	*Ashendon Jc*	33½	26	00	61*	1,150
27·4	Haddenham		29	38	71	1,400
32·8	PRINCES RISBORO'	44	35	08		
			pws		15	
	Summit				35	1,300
36·0	Saunderton		42	30	53	1,250
38·7	West Wycombe		45	30	62 (max)	
41·0	HIGH WYCOMBE	54	48	28	40*	1,100
45·8	Beaconsfield		54	11	56	900
50·1	Gerrards Cross		58	11	73	600
52·7	Denham	68	60	12	82	500
57·2	Northolt Jc	72	63	41	75	500
59·7	Greenford	74	65	35	78	
62·9	*Park Royal*		67	58	65	
64·2	*Old Oak West Jc*	78	69	36	45*	
66·2	Westbourne Pk	82	72	23		
67·5	PADDINGT'N	86	75	18		

Net time 68¼ min from Banbury
* Speed restrictions

ABOVE. Engine No 7018 'Dryslwyn Castle' being fitted with twin blastpipe and chimney

BELOW. Engine No 6000 'King George V' in final form

Engine No 7018 'Drysllwyn Castle' as first fitted with double chimney, and 3-row superheater

of the 'Bristolian' express in both directions. This gave much better utilisation of motive power, as the engine of the down train returned to London on the 12 noon up express from Temple Meads, and the engine of the up express returned on the 7.50 pm down from Paddington. Such was the success attained with the first 'Kings' fitted with double chimneys that a parallel development was commenced with the 'Castles'. Engine No 7018 *Drysllwyn Castle* was selected as the 'guinea pig'. She had been very much of a black sheep, but was taken in hand by Sam Ell and his staff, and as fitted with a double chimney in May 1956, showed vastly improved performance, while retaining her original three-row superheater. The black sheep thereupon became a veritable 'flower of the flock', and following dynamometer car tests on the Torbay Express was allocated to Bristol Bath Road shed to work the up 'Bristolian'. Once again I had the privilege of personal participation in these notable developments. On 26 July 1956 I rode down from Paddington to Torquay in the dynamometer car behind No 7018, and on 9 August 1956 rode the engine from Bristol to Paddington in 97 min 8 sec start-to-stop. The log of the dynamometer car test run on the Torbay Express is appended herewith.

Dynamometer car test run with the Torbay Express : engine No 7018
ascending Goodrington bank

124

THE TORBAY EXPRESS
Dynamometer Car Test Run
Load: 9 cars, 310 tons tare, 330 tons full
Engine: 7018 *Drysllwyn Castle* (double chimney)
Driver: Way; Fireman: Rutherford (Newton)

Dist miles		Sch min	Actual m s		Speed mph
0·0	PADDINGTON .		0	00	
5·7	Ealing . . .		9	04	60 (max)
			sigs		45
9·1	Southall . .		12	26	
18·5	SLOUGH . .		21	49	71
			sigs		20
			pws		20
36·0	READING . .	38	47	35	
44·8	Aldermaston .		56	59	65
53·1	NEWBURY . .		64	39	68/64
58·5	Kintbury . .		69	27	71
61·5	Hungerford . .		72	05	61*
66·4	Bedwyn . .		76	39	66
70·1	Savernake . .		80	40	46
			pws		10
75·3	Pewsey . .		86	10	
81·1	Patney . . .		93	28	70·5
86·9	Lavington . .		97	52	87
94·6	Heywood Road Jc .	94½	103	18	77/72
97·0	Fairwood Jc .		105	12	74
100·3	Clink Road Jc .		108	02	60
102·3	Blatchbridge Jc .		109	55	71
108·5	Milepost 122¾ .		115	18	63
115·1	CASTLE CARY .		120	52	78/62*
122·0	Keinton Mandeville .		124	57	76/71
125·8	Somerton .		129	23	78/74
130·8	Curry Rivel Jc .		133	08	88
138·0	Cogload .		138	30	79
142·7	TAUNTON . .	140	142	12	72
144·7	Norton Fitzwarren .		143	52	70·5
149·8	Wellington . .		148	38	62
152·6	Milepost 173 .		151	40	47·5
153·6	Whiteball Box .	152	152	58	46
158·6	Tiverton Jc . .		157	16	84/70
160·9	Cullompton .		158	55	83
			eased		65
166·4	Silverton .		163	28	78
170·0	Stoke Canon . .		166	27	74
173·5	EXETER . .	170	169	54	

Net time 156 min
* Speed restriction

There were a couple of severe permanent way checks in operation on the London side of Reading and with reaction from the slow running of other trains with close margins ahead we began getting signal checks no further out that Southall, and eventually we passed Reading 9½ min late. Then, except for a permanent way check near Pewsey we

got a clear road right through to Exeter and covered that 137·5 miles in 122 min 19sec to arrive on time. Quite apart from the pleasure of logging an exciting run the double-chimneyed 'Castle' gave ample evidence of her improved performance. Up the Kennet Valley we were registering 750 to 900 actual dhp, but one of the most remarkable demonstrations was that during the high speed sustained on the level after descent of the Lavington bank we registered a drawbar pull of 3·8 tons, and an actual dhp of 800 at 88 mph. The drawbar pull rose again to nearly 4 tons on the rise to Milepost 122¾, that time at 67 mph and developing an actual dhp of 950. During the fast running across the Langport cut-off with full regulator, and showing a steam and 3·8 tons, though the maximum of 88 mph on this stretch was attained under easier steam than the corresponding one on the level between Lavington and Edington: a 2·1 ton drawbar pull, and an actual dhp of 500.

The effort was stepped up to some purpose after Taunton, and the drawbar pull increased from 1·6 tons at Norton Fitzwarren to 3·5 tons at Wellington and finally to 4·5 tons entering Whiteball Tunnel. The engine was there working in 30 per cent cut-off line the drawbar pull varied between 1·8 temperature of 750 deg F. From Wellington to the tunnel the actual dhp lay between 1,000 and 1,050, with the equivalent value at 1,450 on the 1 in 80 gradient. A fast run down to Exeter wound up a most excellent performance. The principal comment to make is that this engine, with double blastpipe and chimney, showed herself capable of a power output at high speed little below that of the re-draughted single-chimneyed 'King' No 6001, when going 'all-out' on a steam-rate of 28,700 lb. *Drysllwyn Castle* as finally rebuilt was certainly an exceptional engine. When I rode her on the up 'Bristolian', only a fortnight later, she had a much easier task, even though running at full recovery rate throughout and arriving 8 min early. The water consumption was a little under 30 gallons per mile, and the firing rate only about 2,400 lb per hr. The impact of the 'King' tests with No 6002 and the successful running of No 7018 are discussed in the following chapter.

CHAPTER 10

1958 AND AFTER

In February 1958 the Western Region of British Railways took delivery, from the North British Locomotive Company, of the first of an entirely new type of express passenger locomotive, the diesel-hydraulic D600. The fact that this particular class proved unsuccessful, and that the name of the pioneer engine *Active* proved something of a misnomer, is apart from the general theme of this book. But the fact remains, that the arrival of D600 at Swindon marked the first step in a programme involving the complete replacement of steam traction by diesel in the Western Region. This metamorphosis had been long foreseen, and all but the most diehard reactionaries were resigned to its inevitability. Few however foresaw the precipitous haste with which the change would ultimately be made. In February 1958 no 'Stars' remained in traffic; but only five Churchward engines rebuilt as 'Castles' had been withdrawn. The entire 'Castle' class proper was still in service, plus one rebuild, No 4037, and of course the 'King' class was then intact. Taken together there were, at that date, 196 four-cylinder 4—6—0 express locomotives in service. Eight years and four months later the last survivor of that famous stud was taken out of traffic.

There is a good deal of evidence to suggest that the 'plan' for the replacement of steam included a great number of loose ends. When substantial orders were placed for diesel-hydraulic locomotives it was announced that it was part of a plan for the complete replacement of steam *west of Newton Abbot*. It revived memories of the ill-fated Great Western scheme for oil-firing. But so far as the present book is concerned it seems quite evident that in 1958, and even later, a considerable life was envisaged for the 'Castle' and 'King' class locomotives, if only from the amount of money that was spent in keeping a high proportion of them tuned virtually to concert pitch.

During their later years the 'Kings' fell victims to a number of troubles, arising directly from their longevity. They were never anything but top link engines. Apart from the brief periods when they were running in, after visits to Swindon for overhaul, they were consistently on the heaviest mainline work, and after thirty years troubles of a purely mechanical kind were almost inevitable. One of the most serious was the crop of fatigue cracks that developed in the bogies from January 1956. Repairs had been made by welding from time to time, but at this period the failures were sufficiently numerous for the whole class to be temporarily withdrawn from service until additional stiffening strips had been welded to the bogie frames. They were not out of traffic for long. Engine No 6012 was returned to service in the first week in February and the others followed quickly. During the emergency four Stanier 'Pacifics' were borrowed from the London Midland Region. There had been 'Duchesses' before on the Western Region; but this time the visitors included two engines of the 'Princess Royal' class.

While the repairs to the bogies were in the nature of 'patching up'—albeit, a thoroughly good and lasting job—other modifications were considered which were intended to prolong the life of the class for a further dozen years at least. Their early replacement did not appear to be foreseen in 1957-8. One of the most interesting developments was the proposal to fit roller bearings to all axles, and it went so far as the placing of an order with British Timken for complete sets of bearings for eight engines. The material was delivered at Swindon in 1957-8. Whether the substitution of roller bearings for the well-designed Swindon plain bearing would have increased the free-running qualities of the locomotives is a moot point; but it would almost certainly have reduced casualties from overheated bearings, which were becoming more frequent with the increased age of the locomotives. Unfortunately the work was never done.

The renewal of the front portion of the frames has been briefly mentioned previously. This had always been a source of some weakness in all the

Great Western four-cylinder 4—6—0 locomotives, though in stating this it must be appreciated that it is said in a relative sense only. The design as a whole was very sound, but when locomotives are in continuous heavy service for the number of years enjoyed by the 'Castles' and 'Kings', any weakness, however relative, will begin to show up in old age. When the front section of the frames needed renewal the remainder was usually fit for further use, and it was therefore the practice to cut the frames ahead of the leading coupled axle, and to weld on a new front section. By official reckoning this was considered to make the locomotives fit for a further twenty-five years of service! All thirty engines of the 'King' class had this renovation carried out, together with new cylinders. Another modification was the fitting of new outside steampipes. Movement of the outside cylinders, caused by flexing of the frames, caused breakages of the outside steampipes, and these were therefore redesigned to make them more flexible by omitting the original straight section, and increasing the radius of the end sections. The change was quite apparent, and with a modified front casing over the inside cylinders, associated with the renovated front frames, and the double chimneys, the 'Kings' certainly had something of a new look about them in their latter days.

Another interesting change concerned certain of the 'King' class engines stationed at Wolverhampton. From 1954 onwards these engines were fitted with 'Alfloc' water treatment equipment; this enabled them to run for thirty days between boiler washouts, and provided for more consistent steam-

The 1955 bogie contretemps : engine No 6013 minus bogie

ing because the heating surfaces collected less scale. Eventually the fitting of 'Alfloc' equipment extended to seventeen 'Kings': all the 1927-8 batch except 6003, 6004, 6010, 6018 and 6019, plus Nos 6020 and 6022. I had a footplate pass to ride No 6014, so equipped, on the 9 am up two-hour express; but on

Up West of England express climbing Bruton bank : engine No 6018 'King Henry VI'

*The up Mayflower near Dawlish Warren : engine No 6004 'King George III'
with double chimney*

the particular day there was unfortunately a derailment at Bicester which necessitated our diversion via Oxford. 'Kings' were not allowed to run between Ayhno and Didcot, and so we had to give up No 6014 at Banbury, and take instead a high-mileage 'Hall'.

Over the years the general scheme of allocation to sheds of the 'King' class engines had not varied very much. Until the end of World War II they had been divided, in varying numbers, between Old Oak, Newton Abbot, Laira and Stafford Road, and in 1947 it was interesting to find that the London allocation was at its smallest ever, while Newton Abbot and Laira were at their maximum. The figures were then 9, 5, 12 and 4. In December 1948 however Nos 6000, 6018 and 6019 were transferred

*Kingswear - Paddington express leaving Whiteball Tunnel :
engine No 5055 'Earl of Eldon'*

128

The down Torbay Express at Whiteball summit : engine No 7000
'Viscount Portal'

to Bristol. They were frequently on the 9 am up express to Paddington, while one of them worked on a triangular diagram from Bristol to Shrewsbury, Shrewsbury to Paddington and thence back to Bristol. The three engines did not stay at Bristol very long. In the summer of 1959 No 6019 was transferred to Newton Abbot for two months, and during that brief sojourn was the last 'King' to be stationed there. It was returned to Bristol in September 1949, and then with No 6018 went to Old Oak Common in July 1950. The pioneer engine No 6000 remained longest at Bristol and went to Old Oak Common in September 1952. From then until the autumn of 1961 the class was divided only between Old Oak, Stafford Road and Laira. In the exciting summer of acceleration on the West of England route, 1955, the allocation was Old Oak 14, Laira 10, Stafford Road 6.

When the diesels really began to get a hold on the West of England services the 'Kings' were gradually transferred away from Plymouth, and by the autumn of 1959 there were only two left, Nos 6013 and 6016. In February 1960, however, these were reinforced by the arrival of No 6002, though this was followed by the almost immediate transfer of No 6013 to Old Oak. In September 1960 No 6019 went to Cardiff Canton shed, and this was the prelude for the general transference of 'Kings' to Cardiff. In August 1961 six more of them arrived in Wales. This was their last home, and it lasted for less than a year, because in February 1962 withdrawal began, and by the end of that year the whole class had been taken out of traffic. The final allocation, as in January 1962, has a melancholy interest but is worth quoting:

Engine No	Shed
6000	Old Oak
6001	Stafford Road
6002	Laira (SRD 7/62 to 9/62)
6003	Canton
6004	Canton
6005	Old Oak
6006	Stafford Road
6007	Stafford Road
6008	Old Oak
6009	Old Oak
6010	Canton
6011	Stafford Road (OOC 9/62-12/62)
6012	Old Oak (SRD 4/62 to 9/62)
6013	Stafford Road
6014	Stafford Road
6015	Stafford Road
6016	Laira (SRD 7/62 to 9/62)
6017	Stafford Road
6018	Canton (OOC 6/62 to 12/62)
6019	Canton (SRD 3/62 to 8/62)
6020	Stafford Road
6021	Old Oak
6022	Stafford Road
6023	Canton
6024	Canton
6025	Old Oak
6026	Old Oak
6027	Stafford Road
6028	Old Oak
6029	Old Oak

The large accumulation at Stafford Road came to include some engines that were in store. Others came to be stored at Swindon. The last three, 6000, 6011 and 6018, were withdrawn in December 1962.

Down Saturday relief Cornish Riviera Express on Ratte y incline : engines 6002
'King William IV', which had worked the first part to Newton Abbot,
and 5099 'Compton Castle'

Of these No 6000 was saved for preservation, while No 6018 was taken out of store in April 1963 to work enthusiasts' special. Otherwise this was the end, and the end of one of the most famous steam locomotive classes the world has ever known. Engine No 6013 showed the highest total mileage, 1,950,162.

If the 'Kings' were approaching their end when the year 1958 opened, the last phase of the remarkable history of the 'Castles' was only just beginning, and it was a phase clearly intended to last a great deal longer than actually proved to be the case. The excellent results obtained with the double-chimneyed engine No 7018, and its fast running in regular service on the 'Bristolian', prompted a further development, in the combination of a double chimney with a 4-row superheater, on engine No 4090 *Dorchester Castle*. There had in the meantime

been another rebuild with double chimney, No 5043 *Earl of Mount Edgcumbe*; but it was the performance of *Dorchester Castle* that really sparked off the final phase of 'Castle' history. After conversion No 4090 went back to her former shed, Old Oak Common, and was soon put on to the down 'Bristolian'. While there was not a great deal of difference in the maximum steaming capacity of the engine the increased freedom in running was most marked and made her very popular on that fast train. The running inspectors at Bristol, who were using No 7018 on the corresponding up train, also watched her performance. The earlier reputation of No 7018 as a black sheep had not entirely been effaced, and there were some inspectors who considered she was still not ideal. Bath Road shed certainly had some very splendid single-chimneyed engines, both of the 2-row and 3-row superheater varieties, and No 7018 was against strong competition.

Smeddle himself took a keen personal interest in the working of the double-chimneyed engines, and the success of No 4090 led to a further rebuilding of No 7018. In April 1958 that engine left Swindon not only with a four-row superheater but also with a lubricator setting that gave about 50 per cent more oil that standard. She then became a 'flyer' beyond compare, though so far as can be traced no other 'Castle' had this lubricator setting. Between the end of 1957 and December 1961 no fewer than sixty-four further 'Castles' received double chimneys, the last to be so modified being

A distinguished nameplate : engine No 5017

OUTSIDE STEAM PIPES

Original shape on No 5017   *Modified shape on No 5018*

No 5078 *Beaufort*. The actual dates of the engines so converted are given in the Appendix dealing with the case histories of the three classes of four-cylinder 4—6—0. In view of the gathering impetus of dieselisation it was remarkable that conversions were continued during the year 1961, for by then withdrawal of the 'Castles' had begun, and by January 1961 eight of the '4073' and '5013' classes had been withdrawn, in addition to five of the re-builds from 'Stars'. During 1961 three more of the '4073' class were scrapped, while fifteen others were equipped with double chimneys. At that time, faced with the impending withdrawal of the entire 'King' class Smeddle envisaged the retention of a

Paignton to Paddington express climbing Bruton bank : engine No 5044
'Earl of Dunraven'

'Castle' class: arrangement of smokebox with twin-orifice blastpipe and chimney; 4-row superheater

The standard '5013' class as running in early BR days:
No 5016 'Montgomery Castle'

reduced stud of 'Castles' equipped with every aid to efficiency that he could provide.

Looking at the double-chimneyed 'Castles' in more detail, the accompanying drawing shows the layout of the smokebox, and it is rather curious to notice the lack of internal streamlining of the passages leading to the twin-blastpipes. The flat surfaces, and almost square corners are very marked. This drawing also shows the form of spark-arrester devised at Swindon. It had been claimed that the original Churchward type of smokebox was partially self-cleaning on account of the spark-arresting baffles; whatever claims might have been made for it in this direction an enormous amount of ash used to collect, and I shall always remember seeing the smokebox door opened on the engine that had worked the up Cornish Riviera Express on arrival at Old Oak shed, and the deposit was almost up to the top of the blastpipe! After nationalisation a number of 'Castles' and 'Kings' were fitted with the LMSR type of self-cleaning baffles. These proved difficult to clean, and caused a slight loss of draught. Superficially also they were very unwelcome because they caused the train and the surrounding

Engine No 4087 'Cardigan Castle' at Laira sheds, June 1960

133

The up Bristolian passing Hullavington at 90 mph plus : engine No 7018
'Drysllwyn Castle'

countryside to be covered with a deposit of smoke-box char. The Great Western had always paid a high regard to the amenities of the countryside through which it passed, and the risk of crop fires and such like had always received the most serious consideration. At Swindon, therefore, an indigenous type of spark-arrester was developed, in the form of a basket round the blastpipe. It allowed small particles of char to pass but arrested the larger ones.

The double chimney, as originally fitted was not a handsome device. It was a built-up affair with flat sides, although incorporating the characteristic lip-top and copper adornment. These were later replaced by a cast design of slightly elliptical cross section. It tapered outwards from the base, and some students of locomotive history have connected this detailed feature with Mr Smeddle's personal influence, recalling that he was a North Eastern man by training, and son of a North Eastern officer of long standing and high status. Quite apart from its shape, however, the double chimney sadly impaired the graceful appearance of the 'Castles', particularly when seen broadside. The setting forward of the chimney caused this effect; but as will be appreciated from a study of the cross-sectional drawing it could not have been avoided. One must be content with the axiom 'handsome is as handsome does', and the double-chimneyed 'Castles' in their freedom of running certainly had the advantage over the standard ones of the post-war era. Whether or not any of them, even including the exceptional 7018 with her extra oil supply, could have surpassed an outstanding pre-war engine with hydrostatic-lubricators, and the jumper in pristine condition, is another matter.

The jumper ring could well have been a governing factor if any deliberate attempt at a maximum speed record had been made with an engine of the '5013' class. This device was intended to lift at each exhaust beat when a locomotive was working hard at low speed, and lessen the chance of disturbance of the firebed. Experience suggested that the jum-

Outside cylinder, showing detail of original
form of steampipe

North to West express near Onibury: engine No 7017 'G. J. Churchward'

per-top was apt to remain lifted whenever a loco-motive was working hard, at whatever speed, and to remain lifted. One can well imagine that when 'Stars' and 'Castles' were working fourteen-coach trains of 500 gross tons or more, on the Cornish Riviera or Torbay Expresses, the going could be tremendously hard, continuously, for the first 1¼ hours out of Paddington. It is true that the blast

The down Torbay Express at Wolfhall Junction, Savernake:
engine No 7000 'Viscount Portal'

135

The up Cornishman climbing Hemerdon bank : engine No 7015
'Carn Brea Castle', with double chimney

might be softened at a time when the demand for steam was at a maximum, but the exhaust would be freer, and by lessening the back pressure permit of a higher indicated hp to be developed in the cylinders. The truth was that if the jumper ring remained continuously raised for any length of time it would become jammed with smokebox char and

Engine No 7004 'Eastnor Castle' on train carrying official mourners to Windso at the funeral of King George V

seriously impair the steaming by keeping the blast-pipe orifice at its increased area just at a time when the smaller area was needed to produce draught.

The withdrawal of the 'Castles' began in March 1950 with No 100 A1 *Lloyds*. This, of course, was not a true 'Castle' in originally having been a rebuild of No 4009 *Shooting Star*. Three more rebuilds went in 1951-3, namely 111, 4016 and 4032. The historic No 4000 *North Star* was withdrawn in May 1957, and before she went I had enjoyed a brief but excellent run on her footplate from Wolverhampton to Shrewsbury, with the heavy 2.9 pm express. The last of the rebuilds, No 4037, survived until 1962. This engine had received new frames and almost to the end she was a favourite on the double-home turns between Newton Abbot and Shrewsbury. An excellent example of her work is quoted on p 144. The first true 'Castle' to be scrapped was No 4091 *Dudley Castle* in January 1959, though Nos 4073 and 4074 had actually been included in the Western Region withdrawal programme for 1955. Far from being withdrawn No 4073 continued in traffic until May 1960, while No 4074 got a double chimney in April 1959!

While R. F. Hanks was Chairman of the Western Region Board, and the succession of general managers were ex-Great Western men the old traditions were as secure as anything could be under nationalisation, and Smeddle received staunch backing from Paddington. But in January 1962 there was a

Saturdays only West to North express near Whiteball summit :
engine No 7029 'Clun Castle'

great change. Roy Hammond went to the Eastern Region and in his place there arrived the fiery, iconoclastic S. E. Raymond. Within a matter of days cherished relics of former Great Western prowess were consigned to the vaults, and from the general manager's room there came an all-out campaign to try and eradicate all memories of the past. One important feature of this campaign was to secure for the Western Region the distinction of being the first region of British Railways to eliminate steam traction completely. Quite apart from any technical questions of motive power the chief mechanical engineer, for the first time in Swindon's history since the great Churchward-Inglis feud, found himself seriously at variance with the general manager, and in 1962 after only a few troubled and bitter

months Smeddle retired, to be stricken immediately with what proved to be a fatal illness.

In 1962 no fewer than fifty-four 'Castles' were withdrawn, including four, Nos 5008, 5019, 5027, and 5078, which had received double chimneys in 1961. In 1963 the slaughter was almost as great, with a further forty-nine condemned, and the year 1964 opened with only forty-six of the class still in service. A historian of the future, comparing this rate of demise with other features revealed in the case history of the 'Castle' might well rub his eyes and wonder what the impecunious nationalised British Railways were really about in those years from 1958 to 1963. But when propaganda gets a really firm hand logic and sound economics are apt to be cast to the winds.

CHAPTER 11

SWAN SONG

THE story of the elimination of steam traction on the express train services of the Western Region as told in Chapter 10 makes remarkable, if sad, reading; but 'Castles' and 'Kings' alike went down with flying colours, and in this final chapter an account must be given of some outstanding performances put up in those last eight years. In those years I was travelling regularly between Paddington and Bath, and quite apart from the interesting details of engine performance that I collected the reliability of the service in general was such as to be taken for granted in arranging business appointments, often with fairly tight margins. The series

of travel diaries that I kept during those years gives the complete lie to the somewhat nauseating anti-steam propoganda issued from official circles in those years of transition. Whatever reasons may have been advanced for the superseding of steam it was certainly not unreliable on the London-Bath route. I have, nevertheless, written enough to place the capacity of the 'Castles' and 'Kings' beyond any doubt, and in this chapter I am concerned with certain performances in those last years that have features of special significance.

At that time the 7.45 am up from Bristol was something of a prestige business train. It had a 60-

Penzance - Wolverhampton express descending Dainton bank : engines No 5066 'Sir Felix Pole' (double chimney) and No 5065 'Newport Castle'

8.26 am CHIPPENHAM—PADDINGTON

Engine No	6023	6003
Engine Name	*King Edward II*	*King George IV*
Load: to Didcot		
Coaches	12	13
Tons E/F	426/460	443/480
Load: to Paddington		
Coaches	11	11
Tons E/F	391/420	373/405

Dist miles		Actual m s	Speed mph	Actual m s	Speed mph
0·0	CHIPPENHAM	0 00		0 00	
		sig stop			
6·3	Dauntsey	15 45*	0	8 25	61
11·1	Wootton Bassett	24 15		13 44	47/55
16·7	SWINDON	29 45		19 20	
22·5	Shrivenham	34 30	77	24 19	74
27·5	Uffington	38 15	82	28 18	77·5
33·6	Wantage Road	42 48	80	32 58	79
40·9	DIDCOT	48 07	83·5	38 54	64†
45·5	Cholsey	51 29	82	42 54	76·5
52·5	Pangbourne	56 42	78·5	48 53	64†
58·0	READING	60 57	69†	53 34	71·5
63·0	Twyford	65 13	72	57 50	73
69·8	Maidenhead	70 49	73·5	63 11	76·5
75·5	SLOUGH	75 27	75	67 37	77
80·8	West Drayton	79 48	70·5	71 47	75
84·9	Southall	83 27	67	75 08	73·5
88·3	Ealing	86 22	69	78 08	
		sigs			
90·7	*Old Oak West Jc*	89 05		80 42	
92·7	Westbourne Park	93 07		84 31	
				sig stop 4 min	
94·0	PADDINGTON	96 35		93 57	

Net times	min	84	86

* Departure time   † Speed reductions

mph timing up from Chippenham, and was usually worked by a 'King'—very frequently No 6000. With a load of around 400 tons it was normally a fairly easy task, but I have tabulated herewith details of the running on two somewhat exceptional occasions. Both engines concerned were then fitted with double chimneys. On the first run, made in December 1958, we were stopped by signals at Dauntsey, and so took 29¾ min to pass Swindon. Then despite a load of 460 tons to Didcot, and 420 tons beyond, we went like the wind, and averaged 77·5 mph throughout from Swindon to Slough. Down the gentle descent through the Vale of the White Horse we ran at 82-3 mph, and although the pace was not so hot after the marked easing through Reading we nevertheless passed Southall, 78·6 miles from the start at Dauntsey, in 67 min 42 sec. Our actual start-to-stop run from Dauntsey to Paddington, 87·7 miles, was made in 80 min 50 sec inclusive of a final signal check. From Swindon eastwards we were running fully up to the standards required on the pre-war 'Cheltenham Flyer' and 'Bristolian' with double the load. On the second run we had a

heavier load from Chippenham, but a completely clear road to Old Oak Common. On this trip the average speed from Swindon to Southall was 73·3 mph and steam was shut off at the latter station, we having covered 84·9 miles from the dead start in 75 min 8 sec.

Out of a number of runs on the down 'Bristolian' it is perhaps no more than natural that two with the pioneer engine to have the combination of double chimney and four-row superheater should be outstanding. Generally speaking the down train was a harder proposition than the up 'Bristolian', with the long, faintly adverse stretch to Swindon, usually against the prevailing wind, and there were times when the ordinary 'Castles', with the improved draughting, had their work cut out to keep time. In April 1958 engine No 5060 *Earl of Berkeley* gave me a typical run in the single-chimneyed tradition. The start out of London was delayed and it took 22 min 33 sec to pass Slough. Then we averaged 76 mph over the next 58·8 miles on to Swindon, an extremely good piece of uniform running with a maximum of 80·5 mph approaching Reading, and

'Caerphilly Castle', when stationed at Bristol, and working the 9 am Temple Meads to Paddington, in Sonning Cutting

	THE 'BRISTOLIAN'					
	Engine: 4090 *Dorchester Castle* (double chimney)					
	Load: 7 cars, 246 tons tare, 265 tons full					
	Driver (Old Oak)	W. Harris			Jermy		
Dist miles		Actual m s		Speed mph	Actual m s		Speed mph
0·0	PADDINGTON	0	00		0	00	
5·7	Ealing	8	32	62·5	8	22	62
9·1	Southall	11	32	72	11	27	69
13·2	West Drayton	14	53	77	14	52	76·5
18·5	SLOUGH	18	55	79/74	18	51	80·5
24·2	Maidenhead	23	23	78·5	23	08	81
31·0	Twyford	28	26	82	28	12	76·5
		pws		15	pws		15
36·0	READING	33	33		33	38	
41·5	Pangbourne	38	47	75	39	34	71
48·5	Cholsey	44	11	77·5	45	03	80
53·1	DIDCOT	47	20	78	48	28	81
60·4	Wantage Road	53	20	77	53	59	78
66·5	Uffington	58	03	78	58	41	77
71·5	Shrivenham	61	49	79·5	62	36	76·5
					sigs		50
77·3	SWINDON	66	14	78	67	33	
82·9	Wootton Bassett	70	26	81·5	72	15	82
87·7	Dauntsey	73	47	95	75	33	95
91·0	*Milepost 91*	75	52	91	77	40	90
94·0	CHIPPENHAM	78	02	78	79	56	72
98·3	Corsham	81	23	75·5	83	24	76
101·9	Box	84	09	80/72★	86	08	79/76
106·9	BATH	88	34		91	03	
113·8	Keynsham	95	01	72	97	58	74
118·4	BRISTOL (TM)	100	47		103	45	
	Net times min		98¼			99¾	

a minimum of 74·5 mph at Challow. The maximum at Dauntsey was 86 mph and Bristol was reached in 104 min 33 sec. Net time was exactly 100 min. This was an excellent performance in itself, and showed the remarkable consistency of steaming that distinguished the 'Castles' at their best. The two runs with No 4090 *Dorchester Castle*, however, showed a mastery over the schedule that the single-chimneyed engines did not possess.

There was a striking similarity in the work of two different drivers, both of whom I came to know well, and yet were widely differing personalities. In their running as far as Twyford there were no more than seconds in it, and both were sustaining over 80 mph on the 1 in 1,320 rise from Maidenhead. The two runs were made within a week of each other, and both suffered a heavy permanent way check at Reading. Both recovered to make average speeds of 78·3 and 77 mph over the 35·8 miles from Pangbourne to Swindon. The times over this stretch might well have been identical had not the second run experienced a signal check to 50 mph at High-worth Junction. Both trains passed the top of

'Clun Castle', passing Belle Isle, en route from Kings Cross to York, 1967

Dauntsey bank at 85 mph, and then again there was an astonishing correspondence over the next 6 miles between posts 85 and 91: 3 min 53 sec and 3 min 55 sec with maximum speeds of 95 mph on both runs. After that, with clear roads, neither driver had occasion to hurry unduly, and both trains arrived at Bristol comfortably within schedule time. Some

Her last journey and attracting little attention! No 4073 in the streets of Kensington, en route for the Science Museum

Sixtieth anniversary, 1904-1964 : No 4079 'Pendennis Castle' leaving Paddington on high speed run to Plymouth

months later I had a footplate pass to ride one of the double-chimneyed engines on this service, but the occasion was unfortunately marred by very bad weather, dense fog in places, and an exceptional delay due to a road accident having damaged one of the overbridges near Pangbourne.

I used frequently to travel by the 1.15 pm from Paddington, which also required some smart loco-motive work to cover the 106·9 miles to Bath non-stop in a working time of 96½ min. With a slightly slower timing than the 'Bristolian' this train occas-ionally carried an extra coach, but out of many good runs there was not one that stands noticeably above the average of good 'Castle' performance in those last years. I have tabulated one, however, that has something of a sentimental interest in that one of the now-preserved engines, No 4079 *Pendennis Castle*, was involved. It was made just before Christ-mas 1957, and with an entirely clear road we stopped at Bath in 94¼ min from Paddington. There was nothing special about the performance except its complete steadiness of steaming, and an average speed against the slight gradient of 71·4 mph. The engine was in excellent form at that time, and on the various Bristol workings gave a number of sound

runs. Inevitably one thinks of the age of the engine, though of course there would not have been much of the original machine left in 1957. Before she passed into the hands of her present owners

1.15 pm PADDINGTON—BATH
Load : 7 cars, 250 tons tare, 265 tons full
Engine : 4079 *Pendennis Castle*

Dist miles			Sch min	Actual m s	Speed mph
0·0	PADDINGTON	.	0	0 00	
5·7	Ealing	.		8 27	58
9·1	Southall	.	11½	11 41	66
13·2	West Drayton	.		15 20	71
18·5	SLOUGH	.	19	19 40	73·5
24·2	Maidenhead	.		24 19	73·5
31·0	Twyford	.		29 49	74
36·0	READING	.	33	33 48	77
41·5	Pangbourne	.		38 18	70
48·5	Cholsey	.		44 16	70
53·1	DIDCOT	.	49½	48 13	70
60·4	Wantage Road	.		54 28	69
66·5	Uffington	.		59 44	69
77·3	SWINDON	.	72	69 05	68·5
82·9	Wootton Bassett	.		73 42	75·5
87·7	Dauntsey	.		77 23	84
94·0	CHIPPENHAM	.	85	82 05	74
98·3	Corsham	.		85 48	64·5
101·9	Box	.		88 48	79
106·9	BATH	.	97	94 15	

142

Pendennis Castle was to appear still more vividly in the limelight, as will be told later in this chapter.

I now pass to what proved to be the very last years, and there is first a run made in April 1962 on the 60-min evening express from Oxford to Paddington. With a certain amount of encouragement from interested observers the more sporting of the drivers were showing what these engines could do, and the accompanying log illustrates the work of *Llandovery Castle,* when with a clear road the train of six coaches was brought into Paddington 7 min early. The average speed of 71·7 mph was slightly slower than that of the pre-war 'Cheltenham Flyer' over a route that was shorter and which included only 53 miles of uninterrupted fast running. The friend that logged this run told me that on the following day an even faster run was made by engine No 4082 *Windsor Castle.* This, of course, was the changeling (*née* 7013). The time claimed was 51 min though this has not been fully authenticated, other than my friend's testimony that he saw the train pass through Twyford, and the time by his watch was one min faster than on the previous day when he logged the run in detail. These last two experiences are enough to show the spirit that emulated the steam locomotive express drivers in those final years.

There are next two interesting runs logged respectively in 1960 and 1961 on the West to North route, on the Newton Abbot - Shrewsbury double-home turns. They show the work of both sheds concerned, and I have tabulated only the Hereford - Shrewsbury sections of the runs. The double-

Dist miles		Sch min	Actual m s	Speed mph
	5.30 pm OXFORD—PADDINGTON Load: 6 cars, 188 tons tare, 200 tons full Engine: 5001 *Llandovery Castle* (double chimney)			
0·0	OXFORD	0	0 00	
5·1	Radley		6 48	
7·3	Culham		8 37	82
10·6	*Didcot East Jc*	11½	11 35	45*
14·9	Cholsey		15 48	
21·9	Pangbourne		21 01	85
27·4	READING	25½	24 53	87
32·4	Twyford		28 27	82
39·2	Maidenhead	35	33 13	87
44·9	SLOUGH	39½	37 12	85
50·2	West Drayton		40 50	83
54·3	Southall	46½	43 48	82
57·7	Ealing		46 12	87
			sigs	
62·1	Westbourne Park		50 05	
63·4	PADDINGTON	60	53 09	

chimneyed engine *Barbury Castle* was running punctually from Hereford, whereas the veteran No 4037, still with single chimney, was 9¼ min late through a succession of signal and permanent way checks from Bristol. The observer who logged the run of *Barbury Castle* was pardonably astonished by an arrival 14 min early, and spoke to the engine crew on arrival. The driver's only comment was: 'She's on form, so we let her run'. But a further incentive was, of course, that they were Salop men working home after a lodging turn! As a piece of engine performance it was splendid, particularly in the final minimum of 42 mph at Church Stretton, after several miles climbing at 1 in 112. On the

Restored to her former glory : No 4073 outside Paddington before transfer to the Science Museum

Dist miles		Sch min	5095 Barbury Castle 386/410 Actual m s	Speed mph	4037 The South Wales Borderers 386/410 Actual m s	Speed mph
	Engine No		5095		4037	
	Engine Name		Barbury Castle		The South Wales Borderers	
	Load: tons E/F		386/410		386/410	
0·0	HEREFORD	0	0 00		0 00 sigs	s
1·7	Shelwick Jc	5½	3 58		4 50	
4·2	Moreton-on-Lugg		6 50	60	7 46	60
7·5	Dinmore		10 21	55	11 21	53
10·2	Ford Bridge		13 14	61	14 33	64
12·6	LEOMINSTER	17	15 37	62	16 45	62
15·8	Berrington		18 50	57	19 48	60
18·9	Woofferton	24	22 00	72	22 47	71
23·5	LUDLOW	30	26 36	59	27 16	60
25·7	Bromfield		29 05	58	29 30	61
28·1	Onibury			49	32 03	50
31·1	CRAVEN ARMS	40	35 10	56	35 26	60
35·6	Marsh Brook		40 56	47	42 26	sig
					44 01	stop
38·2	CHURCH STRETTON	51½	44 32	42	49 58	35
41·7	Leebotwood		48 18	70	53 40	73 (max)
44·6	Dorrington		50 42	81	56 13	
46·8	Condover		52 33		58 18	
					sigs pws	
51·0	SHREWSBURY	73	58 51		66 58	

companion run my friend rode on the footplate. For those who claim that excellent Great Western performance was only possible with good coal this run provides something of a poser, because the fuel was a mixture of dust and ovoids. Although the fire was getting dirty, after the long run up from Newton, the pricker livened it up quickly. Newton Abbot men were on the job, and engine No 4037 was justifiably a favourite on this arduous double-home turn. The steaming was free, with pressure entirely

North to West express near Kingskerswell : engine No 4037 'The South Wales Borderers'

between 210 and 220 lb per sq in except for some brief lapses quickly remedied with the pricker. Cut-offs were between 15 and 20 per cent with half-open regulator, until the unfortunate signal stop at Marsh Brook. From this recovery had to be made up a continuous gradient of 1 in 112, and with full regulator and 30 per cent cut-off a speed of 35 mph was attained. Despite this stop the recovery margin in the schedule after Church Stretton would have allowed a punctual arrival in Shrewsbury; but a succession of checks after Condover prevented this, and made the train 3¼ min late on arrival.

Early in 1962 proposals were on hand for accelerated service by the Paddington - Birmingham route, and the civil engineer required a high-speed test, with the 'white-wash' car to observe the condition of the track under really high-speed running. For some reasons which I am not concerned with

here the 'special' had to be steam-hauled. One of the double-chimneyed 'Castles', No 7030, was taken out of store at Old Oak, and duly prepared for the job. Very hard work was anticipated, even though the train consisted of no more than five vehicles, and Driver Pimm of Old Oak had two firemen with him, while Inspector Hancock also rode on the footplate. The accompanying logs are important, as embodying what is probably the fastest running ever made over this route, particularly on the return trip. The start of the outward journey was not unduly fast—in fact I have a log of my own on which Gerrards Cross bank was climbed at 64·5 mph by a 'Saint' class engine hauling 320 tons! But after High Wycombe *Cranbrook Castle* was driven to some purpose, and the minimum speed of 76 mph at Ardley was first class. In the circumstances one might have expected faster running between Banbury and Southam Road, and the severe schedule between High Wycombe and Leamington was not maintained.

There was a tremendous start out of Leamington. Warwick was passed at 60 mph and a maximum of 70 attained before entering upon Hatton bank. Then its 3¼ miles at 1 in 110 were climbed with no lower drop in speed than from 70 to 66 mph. After that the delays were too much for timekeeping.

HIGH SPEED TEST TRAIN: 15 MAY 1962
10.25 am PADDINGTON—WOLVERHAMPTON
Load: 5 cars, 176 tons tare, 180 tons full
Engine: 7030 *Cranbrook Castle* (double chimney)

Dist miles		Sch min	Actual m s	Speed mph
0·0	PADDINGTON . .	0	0 00	
3·3	Old Oak West Jc	6½	5 53	
7·8	Greenford . .		10 33	73
10·3	Northolt Jc .	13	12 32	68
14·8	Denham . .		16 30	74
17·4	Gerrards Cross .		18 51	66
21·7	Beaconsfield . .		22 38	78 (max)
26·5	HIGH WYCOMBE	26½	27 39	
5·0	Saunderton . .		6 48	67
8·2	PRINCES RISBOROUGH .	10	9 50	62*
13·6	Haddenham .		13 55	96
17·6	Ashendon Jc . .	16½	16 36	86
20·9	Brill . .		18 58	
23·9	Blackthorn .		21 02	92
26·9	BICESTER .	22½	23 09	83
30·7	Ardley . .	25½	26 05	76
35·9	Aynho Jc . .	30	30 18	85/65*
41·0	BANBURY .	34	34 45	74
44·6	Cropredy .		37 48	72/70
49·6	Fenny Compton .		42 00	75/66*
54·7	Southam Road .		46 04	87 (max)
60·8	LEAMINGTON .	49½	51 45	
2·0	Warwick . . .		3 04	70 (max)
6·2	Hatton . .	7	6 56	66/55*
10·4	Lapworth . .		11 01	75
12·9	Knowle . . .		13 14	
			pws	15
16·3	Solihull . . .		18 56	54
20·1	Tyseley . .	18	22 33	79/60*
23·3	BIRMINGHAM (SNOW HILL) .	22	25 59	
25·9	Handsworth .	28½	30 06	
30·7	Wednesbury .		37 23	
			sigs	
35·9	WOLVERH'PTON	42	46 55	

Net times: High Wycombe - Leamington 50½ min
Leamington - Wolverhampton 38 min
* Speed restrictions

*'Clun Castle' approaching Shap summit,
14 October 1967*

K

There was a turn-round time of 1 hr 55 min at Wolverhampton, and then there commenced the hard run back to Paddington set out in the second table. Once again the schedule proved to be too tight on the central section, despite some most spectacular running. From the start at Leamington there was an acceleration to 68 mph up the 1 in 187 of Southam Road bank, and a maximum of 86 mph preceded a slight easing through Banbury. Even so 1¼ min had been lost to Aynho, and a further ½ min was lost despite the tremendous burst of speed from Bicester to Brill. My friend's claim of a maximum speed of 103 mph at Blackthorn is well authenticated, but one can note the very hampering effect of the Aynho slack, when properly observed, as the average speed from Cropredy to Brill was no more than 80·7 mph. I have seen an average of 75 mph over this same stretch with a 'Star' and 3°0

HIGH SPEED TEST TRAIN: 15 MAY 1962
2.20 pm WOLVERHAMPTON—PADDINGTON
Load: 5 cars, 176 tons tare, 180 tons full
Engine: 7030 *Cranbrook Castle* (double chimney)

Dist miles		Sch min	Actual m s	Speed mph
0·0	WOLVERH'PTON	0	0 00	
5·2	Wednesbury . .		7 52	
10·0	Handsworth . .	15	13 45	69
12·6	BIRMINGHAM (SNOW HILL) .	20	17 08	38*
15·8	Tyseley . . .	24	20 54	70
19·6	Solihull . . .		24 02	80 (max)
			pws	15
23·0	Knowle . . .	29½	27 23	
25·5	Lapworth . . .		31 54	86
29·7	Hatton . . .	34½	35 21	65*
33·9	Warwick . . .		38 38	84
35·9	LEAMINGTON .	40	41 10	
6·1	Southam Road .		7 15	68/78
11·2	Fenny Compton .		11 21	76
16·2	Cropredy . .		15 17	86
19·8	BANBURY . .	17	17 58	78*
24·9	*Aynho Jc* . .	21	22 14	80/65*
30·1	Ardley . . .	25	26 32	76
33·9	BICESTER . .	27½	29 07	98
36·9	Blackthorn . .		30 55	103
39·9	Brill . . .		32 53	85
43·2	*Ashendon Jc* .	34	35 42	61*
47·2	Haddenham . .		39 04	80
52·6	PRINCES RISBOROUGH .	41½	43 31	62*
55·8	Saunderton . .		46 25	68
58·5	West Wycombe .		48 48	81/48*
60·8	HIGH WYCOMBE	50½	51 59	
4·8	Beaconsfield . .		5 15	68
9·1	Gerrards Cross .		8 21	91
11·7	Denham . . .	10½	10 01	103 (max)
16·2	Northolt Jc . .	13½	13 11	
19·7	Greenford . .	15	14 40	
23·2	*Old Oak West Jc* .	18½	18 25	40*
			pws	15
25·2	Westbourne Park .	20½	21 55	
26·5	PADDINGTON .	26	25 15	

* Speed restrictions

tons! But this included an entirely unchecked speed of 75 mph over Aynho Junction. Again the speed restrictions at Ashendon Junction and Princes Risborough were very hampering, and that 1¼ min by which the train was down at Aynho was not recovered by High Wycombe. The final dash for London included a second maximum of 103 mph and as the scheduled stopping times at both Leamington and High Wycombe were cut the latter station was left on time and Paddington reached 1 min early. To all who participated it must have been a very exciting day.

As related in Chapter 10, the year 1962 saw the virtual ending of the Great Western four-cylinder express passenger 4—6—0s in regular passenger service, but there was a number of special runs in farewell. One of the most interesting was the round trip from Paddington to Plymouth and back, organised by Ian Allan to mark the sixtieth anniversary of the ever-famous 'Ocean Mail' record run of 9 May 1904. At that late stage in the superseding of steam it cannot have been easy to find an adequate number of 'Castle' class engines capable of the efforts demanded; because it was to be no sentimental perambulation, but a succession of tremendously hard runs. In actual fact there were, in May 1964, only thirty-nine remaining in traffic. One of these, and an excellent engine too, was No 4079 *Pendennis Castle*, which scored such a triumph for the GWR in the inter-exchange trials of 1925, and she was chosen to make the down journey, non-stop to Plymouth, in the level four hours. On the return journey the route of the 'Ocean Mail' of 1904 was to be followed, via Bristol, and in addition to a very fast run in *City of Truro* style from Plymouth to Bristol the last stage was to be made in the fastest-ever steam schedule from Temple Meads to Paddington, via Badminton, in 100 min start-to-stop. The engines chosen for the return trip were the double-chimneyed 7029 *Clun Castle*, from Plymouth to Bristol, and a standard engine of the '5013' class, No 5054 *Earl of Ducie*, from Bristol to Paddington. It was hoped to reach 100 mph both down Wellington bank, and at Little Somerford. As on the Wolverhampton test runs of 1962 two firemen were to be carried on each engine.

The provision of the two firemen requires a little explanation. On these runs the demands for steam and the associated firing rates were not expected to be more than had been regularly sustained in the hey-day of the 'Castle' class engines, including the working of the 'Bristolian' express. And although the timing proposed for 9 May 1964 was 100 min, the former 105 min steam timing included 8 min

Relief for a diesel : No 5024 'Carew Castle' on the northbound Devonian near Torre, in the autumn of 1960

recovery time, so that an overall time of 97 min was expected to be regularly attainable with any engine put on to the job. In 1964, however, the number of firemen who were regularly working on steam was very small. To fire a big locomotive on a crack duty needs not only physical strength and fitness, but that build-up of physical training so well known to the athlete. Men working as 'second man' on diesels could not fail to be lacking in that physical training, and when long sustained running at 85-90 mph was contemplated the provision of a reserve fireman on the footplate was no more than prudent.

The full story of that exciting day has been told in great detail in *The Railway Magazine;* but brilliant though much of the running was, at that late stage in history, it added nothing to the saga of 'Castle' performance, in that no fact of individual achievement surpassed what had been done previously—if not in precisely the same location then certainly in comparable circumstances. *Pendennis Castle* was going well until part of the grate collapsed and she had to come off the train at Westbury. *Clun Castle* distinguished herself by hauling the 265-ton train from Exeter to Whiteball Box in 17 min 19 sec, and going over the summit at 67 mph, but no *City of Truro* exploit was attempted on the Wellington side. Even so that 75.6 miles from passing Exeter to arrival in Bristol took only

62 min 19 sec against the 64 min 17 sec of the 4—4—0 engine in 1904. A real record was hoped for on the final stage, but a side wind proved troublesome. A brilliant start was made out of Bristol, but although the engine was pressed very hard down the 1 in 300 from Badminton the maximum attained was no more than 94 mph. Many times I have seen the up 'Bristolian' cross the overbridge across the main road near Hullavington aerodrome, and the 'Castles' always seemed to be flying effortlessly on the wings of the wind. While one could hear the beat, it was the beat of an engine working in ideal conditions. On 9 May 1964 at least one very experienced locomotive engineer who was at the lineside thought that the *Earl of Ducie* was being 'slaughtered', to use his own word. The overall time to Paddington was 95 min 33 sec, and the engine suffered no harm in the process; but this time fell a little short of the fastest 'Bristolian' record, when No 7018 *Drysllwyn Castle* in her 4-row superheat days made the run in 93 min 50 sec, including a maximum of 100 mph at Little Somerford.

This year of 1964 saw the virtual end of 'Castle' working so far as official Western Region activities were concerned. By the end of the year only eleven of them remained in traffic; but two of them, both participants in the runs of 9 May 1964, were purchased and preserved under private ownership. These were No 4079 *Pendennis Castle* and 7029 *Clun Castle*. The latter was the last to remain in passenger service, and worked the last steam-hauled train out of Paddington on 11 June 1965. Since then *Clun Castle* has become the most widely-travelled engine of the class. She was in good condition when she was taken out of traffic, and so needed no 'restoration' in the ordinary sense; but her new owners had her repainted in the full Great Western style of the early 1930s, with the company's name in full on the tender, and the coat of arms; with the number on the front buffer beam, and the cast plate removed from the smokebox door. She retained the double chimney with which she was fitted in October 1959. Although this splendid new turnout was stretching a point so far as strict historical accuracy was concerned, in that *Clun Castle*, built in May 1950, was never a Great Western engine, all will rejoice at the enterprise that resulted in her preservation.

Under various auspices *Clun Castle* has made a number of special runs, but one of the most interesting from the performance point of view was on Saturday 14 October 1967, organised by the North Western branch of the Locomotive Club of Great Britain—'Castle to Carlisle'. The outward run was

LOCOMOTIVE CLUB OF GREAT BRITAIN
14 October 1967
SPECIAL TRAIN: GARSTANG—CARLISLE
Load: 7 cars, 215 tons full
Engine: 7029 *Clun Castle* (double chimney)

Dist miles		Sch min	Actual m s	Speed mph
0·0	GARSTANG .	0	0 00	
			pws	10
5·9	Bay Horse .		12 57	52
7·2	Galgate . .		14 30	67·5 (max)
11·5	LANCASTER .	17	18 50	55*
14·6	Hest Bank .		21 30	77·5
17·8	CARNFORTH .	27	24 14	58*
21·0	*Milepost 9½* .		27 47	47
25·1	Milnthorpe .		31 44	67·5
30·6	OXENHOLME .	43	37 57	44/47
37·7	*Grayrigg* .		47 15	42·5
			pws	35
43·7	Tebay . .	65	55 05	56·5
46·7	*Scout Green* .		58 45	38
49·2	*Shap Summit* .	75	62 33	42
			sig stop	
51·2	Shap . .		70 00	
			sig stop	
62·7	PENRITH .	90	90 26	
	Carlisle No 13 Box .	114	109 50	pass slowly

made by the LNWR route and the return by the Midland. By the kindness of one of the participants, Mr J. M. D. Bateman of Todmorden, I am able to include the accompanying logs of the most interest-

'Clun Castle', under private ownership, at Kings Cross, 8 October 1967

'Clun Castle' passing Durran Hill Junction on leaving Carlisle for Hellifield

ing sections of the two runs. The load was a light one compared with that No 5000 *Launceston Castle* had been required to haul on the 10 am from Euston to Glasgow, as between Crewe and Carlisle, in the autumn of 1926; but the circumstances were very different in 1967, when steam-hauled trains were not popular on British Railways. *Clun Castle* did very well from the booked stop at Garstang, and the ascent of Shap, with an acceleration from 38 mph at Scout Green to 42 at the Summit, was

remarkable. The descent to Carlisle was, however, subject to very heavy delay. On the return trip over the Midland line the train had a very easy timing to Appleby, and indeed also on the continuation to Hellifield; but fortunately those responsible were in the mood to 'have a go' over the mountain section, with the excellent results shown in the accompanying table. Speed did not fall below 48 mph on the longest stretches of 1 in 100 ascent, between Smardale viaduct, just south of Crosby Garrett, and the south end of Birkett Tunnel, and again after Mallerstang. On the final stretch there was actually a recovery from 48 to 50 mph on the 1 in 100 before Aisgill summit was reached.

Clun Castle had by that time also become a familiar object on the Eastern Region, having run a 'Castle to Newcastle' trip on 9 September 1967. Between these two outings of the Locomotive Club I myself travelled behind *Clun Castle* on an Eastern Region officers' special from Finsbury Park to Peterborough, on 26 September 1967, an occasion that I am not likely to forget, because on the following morning, travelling by the diesel-hauled 9.45 am from Paddington, I was involved in the high-speed derailment at Foxhall Junction!

Now, *Lode Star* and *Caerphilly Castle* are priceless museum pieces, and with *Pendennis Castle* and *Clun Castle* in retirement, and making occasional appearances at steam 'open days', and *King George V* in the safe and loving care of H. P. Bulmer Ltd at Hereford, the story of the Great Western four-cylinder 4—6—0s seems almost complete. Nevertheless, while such locomotives as 4079, 6000 and

LOCOMOTIVE CLUB OF GREAT BRITAIN
14 October 1967
SPECIAL TRAIN: APPLEBY—HELLIFIELD
Load: 7 cars, 215 tons full
Engine: 7029 *Clun Castle* (double chimney)

Dist miles			Sch min	Actual m s		Speed mph
0·0	APPLEBY	. .	0	0	00	
2·5	Ormside	. .		4	05	61
5·3	*Griseburn Box*	.		7	07	54
7·5	Crosby Garrett	.		9	14	62
10·7	Kirkby Stephen	.		12	41	55/48
14·0	*Mallerstang*	. .		16	41	50/48
17·5	*Aisgill*	. .	28	20	57	50
						65
20·6	Garsdale	. .		24	20	
				pws		20
23·8	Dent	. .		30	30	
25·9	*Dent Head Box*	.		32	35	62·5/60
28·7	*Blea Moor*	.	40	35	25	64
30·0	Ribblehead	.	44	36	30	70
34·8	Horton	. .		40	44	70·5
36·4	*Helwith Bridge*	.		42	05	72/65
40·8	Settle	. .		46	03	72
42·7	*Settle Jc*	.	64	47	47	55*
46·0	HELLIFIELD	.	70	53	29	

* Speed restriction

149

7029 are still in first-class running condition one can never ring down the final curtain. The place in history of the breed as a whole, extending from the construction of the *North Star* in 1906 to the runs of *Clun Castle* in 1967, now extends over a full sixty years, and Smeddle's final development of the 'Kings' placed those engines on a level of efficiency fully equal to that of the Stanier 'Duchesses'. It can only be regretted that the occasion never arose for an all-out trial of the double-chimneyed 'King' in the same way that Nos 6001 and 6013 were tested, and that one of them was not given the chance to reveal her true maximum speed capabili-ties. Nevertheless, on the evidence provided by the test results included in this book, there is material for connoisseurs to analyse, discuss and debate the possibilities for many years to come. The sure-footedness of the Great Western 4—6—0 was pro-verbial. One feels that the logical development would have been a 4—8—0 rather than the sug-gestion of a 'Pacific'. In France, Chapelon demon-strated how it was possible to get a phenomenal power-output from a narrow firebox on his PO Midi rebuilt 4—8—0s. A Swindon 4—8—0, with all the refinements of the Smeddle era, and internally streamlined cylinders, is an intriguing proposition.

ACKNOWLEDGEMENTS

The author and publisher wish to express their thanks to the following for permission to use photographs:

R. L. Blenkinsop Esq, for page 140
P. F. Bowles Esq, for page 124 bottom
E. D. Bruton Esq, for page 43 bottom, 68, 71, 77
H. C. Casserley Esq, for page 72 bottom
C. R. L. Coles Esq, for page 21
Derek Cross Esq, for page 128 top, 149
M. W. Earley Esq, for page 12, 16, 28, 31, 33 top, 54, 60, 63 bottom, 64, 69, 80, 84, 100, 107, 113 bottom, 121, 134 bottom, 136 bottom
R. J. Faux Esq, for 141 top, 148
Peter W. Gray Esq, for 65, 76 bottom right, 128 bottom, 130 top, 136 top, 138, 144, 147
J. G. Hubback Esq, for 73 top
K. H. Leech Esq, for 49 top, 53, 72 top, 74 top, 76 top, 76 bottom left, 78, 82, 83, 85, 86, 87 top, 89, 98, 101 top and bottom, 103, 104 top and bottom, 105, 106, 117 bottom, 127 bottom, 129, 131 bottom, 133 top, 134 top, 137

John K. Morton Esq, for 145
O. S. Nock Esq, for 9, 10, 52 bottom, 56 top, 66
Overend Press Agency, for 57
Ivo Peters Esq, for 95, 117 top, 135 bottom
Real Photographs Ltd, for 36, 55, 79
R. C. Riley Esq, for 74 bottom left and right, 75 top, 87 bottom, 118, 141 bottom, 142, 143
J. F. Russell-Smith Esq, for 70, 102, 135 top
G. H. Soole Esq, for 11, 13 top, 15, 17, 19, 22, 23, 26 bottom, 27, 30, 35, 37, 39 top
Bishop Treacy, for 63 top
G. Wheeler Esq, for 123 top

The frontispiece is reproduced from a painting by Terence Cuneo, by courtesy of H. P. Bulmer & Co, Hereford.

The plate on page 44 is reproduced from a paint-ing by Victor Welch.

For the remainder of the illustrations indebtedness is expressed to British Railways.

CASE HISTORIES

'STAR' CLASS

No	Original Name	Built	Superheated	Outside steampipes Elbow	'Castle'	Withdrawn
4000	North Star (a)	4/06	11/09	R. Castle		11/29
4001	Dog Star	2/07	1/11		10/30	1/34
4002	Evening Star	3/07	8/09	12/29		6/33
4003	Lode Star	2/07	5/11	3/49		7/51 (j)
4004	Morning Star	2/07	1/11	3/46		4/48
4005	Polar Star	2/07	2/11			11/34
4006	Red Star	4/07	4/11			11/32
4007	Rising Star (b)	4/07	5/11	5/47		9/51
4008	Royal Star	5/07	12/11	7/33		6/35
4009	Shooting Star	5/07	10/12	R. Castle		4/25
4010	Western Star	5/07	5/07			11/34
4011	Knight of the Garter	3/08	3/08			11/32
4012	Knight of the Thistle	3/08	1/11			10/49
4013	Knight of St Patrick	3/08	12/10			5/50
4014	Knight of the Bath	3/08	10/10	9/35		6/46
4015	Knight of St John	3/08	9/10	12/48		2/51
4016	Knight of the Golden Fleece	4/08	11/09	R. Castle		10/25
4017	Knight of the Black Eagle (c)	4/08	11/09			11/49
4018	Knight of the Grand Cross	4/08	9/10	5/31		4/51
4019	Knight Templar	5/08	1/10	5/48		10/49
4020	Knight Commander	5/08	11/09	3/49		3/51
4021	King Edward (d)	6/09	6/09	7/48		10/52
4022	King William (d)	6/09	10/10	6/48		2/52
4023	King George (d)	6/09	9/12			7/52
4024	King James (d)	6/09	2/11		2/29	2/35
4025	King Charles (d)	7/09	1/11			8/50
4026	King Richard (d)	9/09	5/13	10/32		2/50
4027	King Henry (d)	9/09	6/12			10/34
4028	King John (d)	9/09	9/11			11/51
4029	King Stephen (d)	10/09	4/11			11/34
4030	King Harold (d)	10/09	1/13			5/50
4031	Queen Mary	10/10	Built	8/48		6/51
4032	Queen Alexandra	10/10	"	R. Castle		4/26
4033	Queen Victoria	11/10	"	4/40		6/51
4034	Queen Adelaide	11/10	"	6/32		9/52
4035	Queen Charlotte	11/10	"		1/31	10/51
4036	Queen Elizabeth	12/10	"	7/43		3/52
4037	Queen Philippa	12/10	"	R. Castle		6/26
4038	Queen Berengaria	1/11	"	8/32		4/52
4039	Queen Matilda	2/11	"	12/48		11/50
4040	Queen Boadicea	3/11	"		2/30	6/51
4041	Prince of Wales	6/13	"	10/47		4/51
4042	Prince Albert	5/13	"	5/48		11/51
4043	Prince Henry	5/13	"		10/31	1/52
4044	Prince George	5/13	"	10/46		2/53
4045	Prince John	6/13	"	1/46		11/50
4046	Princess Mary	5/14	"	1/49		11/51
4047	Princess Louise	5/14	"			7/51
4048	Princess Victoria (e)	5/14	"	8/32	10/38	1/53
4049	Princess Maud	5/14	"		2/35	7/53
4050	Princess Alice	6/14	"	6/46		2/52

No	Original Name	Built	Superheated	Outside steampipes Elbow	'Castle'	Withdrawn
4051	*Princess Helena*	6/14	Built		12/44	10/50
4052	*Princess Beatrice*	6/14	"		4/39	6/53
4053	*Princess Alexandra*	6/14	"		10/33	7/54
4054	*Princess Charlotte*	6/14	"	10/45		2/52
4055	*Princess Sophia*	7/14	"		5/45	2/51
4056	*Princess Margaret*	7/14	"	8/49		10/57
4057	*Princess Elizabeth* (f)	7/14	"		4/30	2/52
4058	*Princess Augusta*	7/14	"	10/44		4/51
4059	*Princess Patricia*	7/14	"			9/52
4060	*Princess Eugenie*	7/14	"	12/30	8/44	10/52
4061	*Glastonbury Abbey*	5/22	"	7/49		3/57
4062	*Malmesbury Abbey*	5/22	"	3/50		11/56
4063	*Bath Abbey*	11/22	"			3/37
4064	*Reading Abbey*	12/22	"			2/37
4065	*Evesham Abbey*	12/22	"			3/39
4066	*Malvern Abbey* (g)	12/22	"			12/37
4067	*Tintern Abbey*	1/23	"			9/40
4068	*Llanthony Abbey*	1/23	"			11/38
4069	*Margam Abbey* (h)	1/23	"			4/39
4070	*Neath Abbey*	2/23	"	3/37		1/39
4071	*Cleeve Abbey*	2/23	"			9/38
4072	*Tresco Abbey*	2/23	"			3/38

Notes:
(a) No 40 (4000) was not added to stock until 6/06 and ran nameless until 9/06.
(b) No 4007 was renamed *Swallowfield Park* in 5/37.
(c) No 4017 was renamed *Knight of Liege* in 8/14.
(d) When the 'King' class was introduced in 1927, Nos 4021-30 were renamed as follows:

4021	*The British Monarch*	6/27
4022	*The Belgian Monarch*	6/27
4023	*The Danish Monarch*	7/27
4024	*The Dutch Monarch*	9/27
4025	*Italian Monarch*	10/27
4026	*The Japanese Monarch*	7/27
4027	*The Norwegian Monarch*	7/27
4028	*The Roumanian Monarch*	7/27
4029	*The Spanish Monarch*	7/27
4030	*The Swedish Monarch*	7/27

Nos 4021-4/6-30 had altered nameplates omitting 'The' fitted in October/November 1927. Names were removed from 4022 (5/40), 4023 (11/40), 4025 (6/40), 4026 (1/41), 4028/30 (11/40), and the words 'Star Class' were painted on the splasher.
(e) No 4048 was temporarily named *Princess Mary* for the Royal Wedding on 28/3/22.
(f) No 4057 was fitted with a small rectangular brass plate above the left-hand number plate in 1951, recording that the engine was driven by HRH Princess Elizabeth from Swindon Works to Swindon station on 15/11/50.
(g) No 4066 was renamed *Sir Robert Horne* in 5/35. The nameplates were removed in 7/37 and new plates *Viscount Horne* fitted in 8/37.
(h) No 4069 was renamed *Westminster Abbey* in 5/23.
(j) Preserved in the Great Western Museum, Swindon.
(k) The following engines carried 'half cone' boilers at various times between 1909 and 1921: 4000-2/4/6/9-16/8/21/3/4/6-9/34/5/40/5.

(l) The engines were allocated Swindon Works numbers and lot numbers as shown below: the works numbers of No 4045 and subsequent engines were not carried on the engine:

Engine Nos	Swindon Works Nos	Lot Nos
40 (4000)	2168	161
4001-10	2229-38	168
4011-20	2300-9	173
4021-30	2365-74	178
4031-40	2380-9	180
4041-50	2536-40	195
4046-60	2572-86	199
4061-72	2915-26	217

'CASTLE' CLASS

No	Original Name	Built	Double Chimney	Withdrawn
111	*Viscount Churchill*	9/24		7/53
4000	*North Star*	11/29		5/57
4009	*Shooting Star* (a)	4/25		3/50
4016	*Knight of the Golden Fleece* (a)	10/25		9/51
4032	*Queen Alexandra*	4/26		9/51
4037	*Queen Philippa* (a)	6/26		9/62
		Built		
4073	*Caerphilly Castle*	8/23		5/60 (o)
4074	*Caldicot Castle* (b)	12/23	4/59	5/63
4075	*Cardiff Castle*	1/24		11/61
4076	*Carmarthen Castle*	2/24		2/63
4077	*Chepstow Castle*	2/24		8/62

No	Original Name	Built	Double Chimney	Withdrawn
40/8	*Pembroke Castle*	2/24		7/62
40/9	*Pendennis Castle*	2/24		5/64 (p)
4080	*Powderham Castle*	3/24	8/58	8/64
4081	*Warwick Castle*	3/24		1/63
4082	*Windsor Castle* (c)	4/24		9/64
4083	*Abbotsbury Castle*	5/25		12/61
4084	*Aberystwyth Castle*	5/25		10/60
4085	*Berkeley Castle*	5/25		5/62
4086	*Builth Castle*	6/25		4/62
4087	*Cardigan Castle*	6/25	2/58	10/63
4088	*Dartmouth Castle*	7/25	5/58	5/64
4089	*Donnington Castle*	7/25		9/64
4090	*Dorchester Castle*	7/25	7/57	6/63
4091	*Dudley Castle*	7/25		1/59
4092	*Dunraven Castle*	8/25		12/61
4093	*Dunster Castle*	5/26	12/57	9/64
4094	*Dynevor Castle*	5/26		3/62
4095	*Harlech Castle*	6/26		12/62
4096	*Highclere Castle*	6/26		1/63
4097	*Kenilworth Castle*	6/26	6/58	5/60
4098	*Kidwelly Castle*	7/26		12/63
4099	*Kilgerran Castle*	8/26		9/62
5000	*Launceston Castle*	9/26		10/64
5001	*Llandovery Castle*	9/26	6/61	2/63
5002	*Ludlow Castle*	9/26		9/64
5003	*Lulworth Castle*	5/27		8/62
5004	*Llanstephan Castle*	6/27		4/62
5005	*Manorbier Castle*	6/27		2/60
5006	*Tregenna Castle*	6/27		4/62
5007	*Rougemont Castle*	6/27		9/62
5008	*Raglan Castle*	6/27	3/61	9/62
5009	*Shrewsbury Castle*	6/27		10/60
5010	*Restormel Castle*	7/27		10/59
5011	*Tintagel Castle*	7/27		9/62
5012	*Berry Pomeroy Castle*	7/27		4/62
5013	*Abergavenny Castle*	6/32		7/62
5014	*Goodrich Castle*	6/32		2/65
5015	*Kingswear Castle*	7/32		4/63
5016	*Montgomery Castle*	7/32	2/60	9/62
5017	*St Donats Castle* (d)	7/32		9/62
5018	*St Mawes Castle*	7/32		3/64
5019	*Treago Castle*	7/32	2/61	9/62
5020	*Trematon Castle*	7/32		11/62
5021	*Whittington Castle*	8/32		9/62
5022	*Wigmore Castle*	8/32	2/59	6/63
5023	*Brecon Castle*	4/34		2/63
5024	*Carew Castle*	4/34		5/62
5025	*Chirk Castle*	4/34		11/63
5026	*Criccieth Castle*	4/34	10/59	11/64
5027	*Farleigh Castle*	4/34	4/61	11/62
5028	*Llantilio Castle*	5/34		5/60
5029	*Nunney Castle*	5/34		12/63
5030	*Shirburn Castle*	5/34		9/62
5031	*Totnes Castle*	5/34	6/59	10/63
5032	*Usk Castle*	5/34	5/59	9/62
5033	*Broughton Castle*	5/35	10/60	9/62
5034	*Corfe Castle*	5/35	2/60	9/62
5035	*Coity Castle*	5/35		5/62
5036	*Lyonshall Castle*	5/35	12/60	9/62
5037	*Monmouth Castle*	5/35		3/64
5038	*Morlais Castle*	6/35		9/63
5039	*Rhuddlan Castle*	6/35		6/64
5040	*Stokesay Castle*	6/35		10/63
5041	*Tiverton Castle*	7/35		12/63
5042	*Winchester Castle*	7/35		6/65
5043	*Barbury Castle* (e)	3/36	10/56	12/63
5044	*Beverston Castle* (e)	3/36		4/62
5045	*Bridgwater Castle* (e)	3/36		9/62
5046	*Clifford Castle* (e)	4/36		9/62
5047	*Compton Castle* (e)	4/36		9/62
5048	*Cranbrook Castle* (e)	4/36		8/62

No	Name	Built	Double Chimney	Withdrawn
5049	Denbigh Castle (e)	4/36	9/59	3/63
5050	Devizes Castle (e)	5/36		8/63
5051	Drysllwyn Castle (e)	5/36		5/63
5052	Eastnor Castle (e)	5/36		9/62
5053	Bishop's Castle (e)	5/36		7/62
5054	Lamphey Castle (e)	6/36		11/64
5055	Lydford Castle (e)	6/36		10/64
5056	Ogmore Castle (e)	6/36	10/60	11/64
5057	Penrice Castle (e)	6/36	7/58	3/64
5058	Newport Castle (e)	5/37		3/63
5059	Powis Castle (e)	5/37		6/62
5060	Sarum Castle (e)	6/37	7/61	4/63
5061	Sudeley Castle (e)	6/37	9/58	9/62
5062	Tenby Castle (e)	6/37		8/62
5063	Thornbury Castle (e)	6/37		2/65
5064	Tretower Castle (e)	6/37	9/58	9/62
5065	Upton Castle (e)	7/37		1/63
5066	Wardour Castle (f)	7/37	4/59	9/62
5067	St Fagans Castle	7/37		7/62
5068	Beverston Castle	6/38	7/59	9/62
5069	Isambard Kingdom Brunel (g)	6/38	11/58	2/62
5070	Sir Daniel Gooch	6/38		3/64
5071	Clifford Castle (h)	6/38	6/59	10/63
5072	Compton Castle (h)	6/38		10/62
5073	Cranbrook Castle (h)	7/38	7/59	3/64
5074	Denbigh Castle (h)	7/38	9/61	5/64
5075	Devizes Castle (h)	8/38		9/62
5076	Drysllwyn Castle (h)	8/38		9/64
5077	Eastnor Castle (h)	8/38		7/62
5078	Lamphey Castle (h)	5/39	12/61	11/62
5079	Lydford Castle (h)	5/39		5/60
5080	Ogmore Castle (h)	5/39		4/63
5081	Penrice Castle (h)	5/39		10/63
5082	Powis Castle (h)	6/39		7/62
5083	Bath Abbey	6/37		1/59
5084	Reading Abbey	4/37	10/58	7/62
5085	Evesham Abbey	7/39		2/64
5086	Viscount Horne	12/37		11/58
5087	Tintern Abbey	11/40		8/63
5088	Llanthony Abbey	2/39	6/58	9/62
5089	Westminster Abbey	10/39		11/64
5090	Neath Abbey	4/39		5/62
5091	Cleeve Abbey	12/38		10/64
5092	Tresco Abbey	4/38	10/61	7/63
5093	Upton Castle	6/39		9/63
5094	Tretower Castle	6/39	6/60	9/62
5095	Barbury Castle	6/39	11/58	8/62
5096	Bridgwater Castle	6/39	1/59	6/64
5097	Sarum Castle	7/39	6/61	3/63
5098	Clifford Castle	5/46	1/59	6/64
5099	Compton Castle	5/46		2/63
7000	Viscount Portal	5/46		12/63
7001	Denbigh Castle (j)	5/46	9/60	9/63
7002	Devizes Castle	6/46	6/61	3/64
7003	Elmley Castle	6/46	6/60	8/64
7004	Eastnor Castle	6/46	2/58	1/64
7005	Lamphey Castle (k)	6/46		9/64
7006	Lydford Castle	6/46	5/60	12/63
7007	Ogmore Castle (l)	7/46	3/61	2/63
7008	Swansea Castle	5/48	6/59	9/64
7009	Athelney Castle	5/48		3/63
7010	Avondale Castle	6/48	10/60	3/64
7011	Banbury Castle	6/48		2/65
7012	Barry Castle	6/48		11/64
7013	Bristol Castle (c)	7/48	5/58	2/65
7014	Caerhays Castle	7/48	2/59	2/65
7015	Carn Brea Castle	7/48	6/59	4/63
7016	Chester Castle	8/48		11/62
7017	G. J. Churchward (m)	8/48		2/63
7018	Drysllwyn Castle	5/49	5/56	9/63

No	Name	Built	Double Chimney	Withdrawn
7019	*Fowey Castle*	5/49	9/58	9/64
7020	*Gloucester Castle*	5/49	2/61	9/63
7021	*Haverfordwest Castle*	6/49	11/61	9/63
7022	*Hereford Castle*	6/49	1/58	6/65
7023	*Penrice Castle*	6/49	5/58	2/65
7024	*Powis Castle*	6/49	3/59	2/65
7025	*Sudeley Castle*	8/49		9/64
7026	*Tenby Castle*	8/49		10/64
7027	*Thornbury Castle*	8/49		12/63
7028	*Cadbury Castle*	5/50	10/61	12/63
7029	*Clun Castle*	5/50	10/59	12/65 (p)
7030	*Cranbrook Castle*	6/50	7/59	2/63
7031	*Cromwell's Castle*	6/50		7/63
7032	*Denbigh Castle*	6/50	9/60	9/64
7033	*Hartlebury Castle*	7/50	7/59	1/63
7034	*Ince Castle*	8/50	12/59	6/65
7035	*Ogmore Castle*	8/50	1/60	8/64
7036	*Taunton Castle*	8/50	8/59	9/63
7037	*Swindon* (n)	8/50		3/63

(a) These engines were renamed as follows:
No 4009 was renumbered and renamed A1 *Lloyds* in 1/36. Additional plates with number 100 were fixed above the 'A1' in 2/36 and the buffer beam bore '100 A1'. For ordinary purposes the engine was known as No 100.
No 4016 was renamed *The Somerset Light Infantry (Prince Albert's)* and fitted with plaques of the Regimental Crest in 1/38.
No 4037 was renamed *The South Wales Borderers* in 3/37; the official naming ceremony took place on 14/4/37.

(b) An early official photograph shows No 4074 with the name spelt **Caldicott** *Castle*.

(c) In 2/52 the number and name 4082 *Windsor Castle* and the commemorative plaques were transferred to No 7013, and the number and name 7013 *Bristol Castle* was transferred to No 4082. The commemorative plaques were later removed from the new 4082.

(d) No 5017 was renamed *The Gloucestershire Regiment 28/61* in 4/54 to commemorate this Regiment's part in the Korean War.

(e) In 1937 it was decided to transfer the 'Earl' names originally allocated to 4—4—0s of the 32XX class to 'Castles' 5043-62. The 'Castles' received their new names as shown:

No	New Name	Date Altered
5043	*Earl of Mount Edgcumbe*	9/37
5044	*Earl of Dunraven*	9/37
5045	*Earl of Dudley*	9/37
5046	*Earl Cawdor*	8/37
5047	*Earl of Dartmouth*	8/37
5048	*Earl of Devon*	8/37
5049	*Earl of Plymouth*	8/37
5050	*Earl of St Germans*	8/37
5051	*Earl Bathurst*	8/37
5052	*Earl of Radnor*	7/37
5053	*Earl Cairns*	8/37
5054	*Earl of Ducie*	9/37
5055	*Earl of Eldon*	8/37
5056	*Earl of Powis*	9/37
5057	*Earl Waldegrave*	10/37
5058	*Earl of Clancarty*	9/37
5059	*Earl St Aldwyn*	10/37
5060	*Earl of Berkeley*	10/37
5061	*Earl of Birkenhead*	10/37
5062	*Earl of Shaftesbury*	11/37
5063	*Earl Baldwin*	7/37

Two of the names displaced by this renaming were transferred to the next two 'Castles' in serial order, as shown below:

5064	*Bishop's Castle*	9/37
5065	*Newport Castle*	9/37

(f) No 5066 was renamed *Sir Felix Pole* in 4/56.

(g) No 5069 was built with nameplates of larger radius, which did not 'fit' the splashers. These were replaced by the standard pattern in 7/38.

(h) After the Battle of Britain in the autumn of 1940 Nos 5071-82 were given the names of famous aircraft of the time, as follows:

No	New Name	Date Altered
5071	*Spitfire*	9/40
5072	*Hurricane*	11/40
5073	*Blenheim*	1/41
5074	*Hampden*	1/41
5075	*Wellington*	10/40
5076	*Gladiator*	1/41
5077	*Fairey Battle*	10/40
5078	*Beaufort*	1/41
5079	*Lysander*	11/40
5080	*Defiant*	1/41
5081	*Lockheed Hudson*	1/41
5082	*Swordfish*	1/41

(j) Nos 7001-7 were renamed in commemoration of the passing of the Great Western Railway. No 7001 was renamed *Sir James Milne* in 2/48, after the last general manager of the company.

(k) No 7005 was renamed *Sir Edward Elgar* in 8/57, at the time of the centenary of the composer's birth.

(l) No 7007 was the last express passenger engine built by the Great Western Railway, and in 1/48 it was given the name *Great Western*. Transfers of the GWR coat of arms were put on the centre splashers soon afterwards.

(m) The nameplates of No 7017 were removed after the engine had been in service for a few days, and were replaced for the naming ceremony of 29/10/48.

(n) No 7037 ran nameless until the naming ceremony of 15/11/50.

(o) Preserved in the Science Museum, South Kensington, London.

(p) Purchased privately for preservation.

'KING' CLASS

No	Original Name	Built	Double Chimney	Withdrawn
6000	*King George V*	6/27	12/56	12/62 (d)
6001	*King Edward VII*	7/27	2/56	9/62
6002	*King William IV*	7/27	3/56	9/62
6003	*King George IV*	7/27	7/58	6/62
6004	*King George III*	7/27	7/58	6/62
6005	*King George II*	7/27	7/56	11/62
6006	*King George I*	2/28	6/56	2/62
6007	*King William III* (a)	3/28	9/56	9/62
6008	*King James II*	3/28	12/58	6/62
6009	*King Charles II*	3/28	5/56	9/62
6010	*King Charles I*	4/28	3/56	6/62
6011	*King James I*	4/28	3/56	12/62
6012	*King Edward VI*	4/28	2/58	9/62
6013	*King Henry VIII*	5/28	6/56	6/62
6014	*King Henry VII*	5/28	9/57	9/62
6015	*King Richard III*	6/28	9/55	9/62
6016	*King Edward V*	6/28	1/58	9/62
6017	*King Edward IV*	6/28	12/55	7/62
6018	*King Henry VI*	6/28	3/58	12/62
6019	*King Henry V*	7/28	4/57	9/62
6020	*King Henry IV*	5/30	2/56	7/62
6021	*King Richard II*	6/30	3/57	9/62
6022	*King Edward III*	6/30	5/56	9/62
6023	*King Edward II*	6/30	6/57	6/62
6024	*King Edward I*	6/30	3/57	6/62
6025	*King Henry III*	7/30	3/57	12/62
6026	*King John*	7/30	3/58	9/62
6027	*King Richard I*	7/30	8/56	9/62
6028	*King Henry II* (b)	7/30	1/57	11/62
6029	*King Stephen* (c)	8/30	12/57	7/62

(a) No 6007 was nominally withdrawn on 5/3/36 and renewed on 24/3/36.
(b) No 6028 was renamed *King George VI* in 1/37.
(c) No 6029 was renamed *King Edward VIII* in 5/36.
(d) Preserved.

APPENDIX 2

NOMINAL VALVE EVENTS

	'Star', 'Castle' 'The Great Bear'	'King'	
Valve diameter, in	8	9	
Valve travel, in	$6\frac{7}{8}$	$7\frac{1}{4}$	
Steam lap, in	$1\frac{5}{8}$	$1\frac{5}{8}$	
Exhaust clearance, in	nil	nil	
Lead, in	3/16	3/16	
Cut-off in full gear, per cent	76·5	76·5	

The lead of the 'Stars' and 'The Great Bear' was originally given as $\frac{1}{8}$ in but later official records showed it as 3/16 in.

The valve travel varied between inside and outside cylinders, the extremes being about $6\frac{3}{4}$ in inside and $7\frac{1}{2}$ in outside. The 'Stars' and 'Castles' had an average travel of about $7\frac{1}{8}$ in and the 'Kings' $7\frac{1}{4}$ in.

APPENDIX 3

BOILER DIMENSIONS

Engine Class	'Star'		'Castle'				'King'		'The Great Bear'		
Barrel:											
length	14 ft 10 in[1]		14 ft 10 in				16 ft 0 in		23 ft 0 in		
outside diameter, maximum and minimum	4 ft 13/16 in & 5 ft 6 in		5 ft 1 15/16 in & 5 ft 9 in				5 ft 6¼ in & 6 ft 0 in		5 ft 6 in & 6 ft 0 in		
Height of centre line	8 ft 6 in		8 ft 8½ in				8 ft 11¼ in		9 ft 0 in		
Firebox casing:											
length	9 ft 0 in		10 ft 0 in						8 ft 0 in		
width	5 ft 9 in		6 ft 0 in				6 ft 3 in		6 ft 6 in at top		
Firebox:											
length	8 ft 1 15/16 in		(a) 9 ft 2 7/16 in	(b) (c) (d) 9 ft 1 15/16 in			10 ft 7⅞ in		7 ft 2⅜ in		
width	4 ft 9 in		5 ft 0¼ in		4 ft 11⅞ in		5 ft 2⅛ in		5 ft 8⅜ in		
height	6 ft 6⅜ in		6 ft 8⅞ in		6 ft 8⅞ in		7 ft 0 3/16 in		6 ft 5 1/16 in		
Superheater: type	None	Swindon No 3	(a) Swindon No 3	(b) Swindon No 3	(c) Three-row	(d) Four-row	Swindon No 3	Four-row	Swindon No 1	Swindon No 3	Swindon No 3
Small tubes:											
number	250[2]	176[3]	201	197	170	138	171	115	141	147	147
outside diameter (in)	2	2	2	2	2	2	2¼	2¼	2½	2½	2½
Flues:											
number		14	14	14	21	28	16	32	21	14	14
outside diameter (in)		5⅛	5⅛	5⅛	5⅛	5⅛	5⅛	5⅛	4¾	5⅛	5⅛
Elements:											
number		84	84	84	84	112	96	128	84	112	84
outside diameter (in)		1	1	1	1¼	1¼	1	1¼	1⅜	⅞	1
Heating surface—ft²:											
tubes	1,989[2]	1,687[3]	1,886	1,858	1,800	1,670	2,008	1,818	2,674	2,597	2,597
firebox	154	155[3]	164	163	164	163	194	195	182[5]	159	159
superheater elements		263[3]	263[4]	263[4]	313[4]	393[4]	313	489	545	506	399
TOTAL	2,143	2,105	2,313	2,284	2,277	2,226	2,515	2,502	3,401	3,262	3,155
Grate area—ft²	27·1	27·1	30·3	29·4	29·4	29·4	34·3	34·3	41·8	41·8	41·8

Notes

1. 4 ft 10¾ in in early boilers.
2. The figures given refer to fifty boilers made between 4/06 and 10/08; in 1908 ten boilers were made with 247 tubes (1,966 ft²), in 1908-9 fourteen boilers were made with 248 tubes (1,973 ft²), and in 1909 four boilers were made with 301 tubes (2,093 ft²). Most of these boilers were later superheated.
3. The figures given refer to 599 boilers made between 1922 and 1944; boilers made in 1909-11 had 166 tubes, except for the original boilers on Nos 4010-11, which had 165 tubes. The Cole superheater of No 4010 had eighteen flues of 4¾ in diameter and seventy-two elements of 1¼ in diameter, giving 269 ft²; the Swindon No 1 superheater in No 4011 was similar, except for having 1⅜ in elements giving 300 ft². In 1914-19 108 boilers were made with Swindon No 3 superheaters with 112 elements in quadruple groups giving 330 ft². There were numerous small changes in the superheating surface of the No 1 boilers resulting from changes in the design or length of elements, for example from 2/52 the elements in the then standard pattern of the boiler were reduced from 263 ft² to 253 ft².
4. Shortening of the elements reduced the superheating surfaces as follows: Swindon No 3 to 253 ft², three-row to 302 and later to 295 ft², and four-row to 381 ft².
5. Including 24 ft² from four arch tubes of 3⅜ in diameter.

INDEX